Praise for *Untamed Hospitality*

"In an extraordinary first book, Elizabeth Newman recovers a theologically rich vision of God's hospitality that is the gift that makes Christian hospitality possible. In beautifully written prose that takes no prisoners, Newman not only challenges safe, domesticated, and comfortable distortions of this central Christian practice, but she also demonstrates step by step how cultural assumptions about religion, politics, economics, and science undercut the faithful practice of the hospitality of God. Equally, she reconstructs the strange, vigilant, and unifying practice of ecclesial hospitality rooted in Christian participation in the divine life—worship. A wonderful book for undergraduate courses and for those concerned about Christian higher education and faithful Christian living, and a powerful contribution to the conversation on theological ethics."

M. Therese Lysaught, University of Dayton

"This is a lovely book, so well researched and eminently readable. Newman draws us in as a gracious host and opens doors that both welcome and astound. The author embodies her message by allowing us into her own life and, in the process, challenges us by unmasking many of the things that we thought made us feel comfortably at home in *our* own lives. Indeed, hospitality is untamed because it is rendered as something other than squishy sentimentality and individual manners, but rather as constitutive of a people called church whose worship is participation in a Triune God's own hospitality. By accepting God's gifts, we become God's guests, and we learn to interact in graced ways befitting that station. This form of hospitality confers a sense of place (yearning for the home of the beckoning kingdom) that, ironically, may make Christians strangers in a land of markets and 'boutique multiculturalism.'"

Joseph M. Incandela, Saint Mary's College

"In this splendid little book, Elizabeth Newman offers a thick theological account of Christian hospitality. Over against our culture's impoverishing reliance on thin notions of tolerance and diversity and inclusiveness, she demonstrates how Christians might yet show the world its true Host by providing it a true home in the household of God."

Ralph C. Wood, Baylor University

"In *Untamed Hospitality: Welcoming God and Other Strangers* Newman provides a much-needed critique of sentimentalized, privatized, economized, and liberalized accounts of hospitality. By arguing that Christian hospitality is graced participation in the triune life of God, this book offers a rich *theological* description that creates the space to rediscover the extraordinariness of this practice for ecclesial and public life. In a world of growing polarization, this first-rate book deserves to be read and discussed widely."

Robert Vosloo, Stellenbosch University, South Africa

Untamed
Hospitality

The Christian Practice of Everyday Life

David S. Cunningham
and William T. Cavanaugh, series editors

This series seeks to present specifically Christian perspectives on some of the most prevalent contemporary practices of everyday life. It is intended for a broad audience—including clergy, interested laypeople, and students. The books in this series are motivated by the conviction that, in the contemporary context, Christians must actively demonstrate that their allegiance to the God of Jesus Christ always takes priority over secular structures that compete for our loyalty—including the state, the market, race, class, gender, and other functional idolatries. The books in this series will examine these competing allegiances as they play themselves out in particular day-to-day practices, and will provide concrete descriptions of how the Christian faith might play a more formative role in our everyday lives.

The Christian Practice of Everyday Life series is an initiative of The Ekklesia Project, an ecumenical gathering of pastors, theologians, and lay leaders committed to helping the church recall its status as the distinctive, real-world community dedicated to the priorities and practices of Jesus Christ and to the inbreaking Kingdom of God. (For more information on The Ekklesia Project, see <www.ekklesiaproject.org>.)

Untamed Hospitality

Welcoming God and Other Strangers

THE CHRISTIAN PRACTICE OF EVERYDAY LIFE Series

Elizabeth Newman

BrazosPress

Grand Rapids, Michigan

Published by Brazos Press
a division of Baker Publishing Group
P.O. Box 6287, Grand Rapids, MI 49516-6287
www.brazospress.com

Printed in the United States of America

Library of Congress Cataloging-in-Publication Data
Newman, Elizabeth, 1960–
     Untamed hospitality : welcoming God and other strangers / Elizabeth Newman.
          p.   cm. — (The Christian practice of everyday life)
     Includes bibliographical references.
     ISBN 10: 1-58743-176-9 (pbk.)
     ISBN 978-1-58743-176-0 (pbk.)
     1. Hospitality—Religious aspects—Christianity. I. Title. II. Series.
BV4647.H67 N49 2007
241'.671—dc22   2006030763

To Jon, Jessica, and Jacob

Contents

Acknowledgments

■ Writing this book was a vivid reminder that mutual dependence is a wonderful way to learn to speak and live more faithfully. I have many friends and colleagues to thank who helped make this book possible. I am particularly grateful to Roger Ward, who volunteered to read some of my earlier essays on hospitality and who first encouraged me to write a book on this topic. I wish to thank two of my BTSR colleagues: Israel Galindo, for offering invaluable support and advice in the early stages of the book, and Richard Vinson, my former dean, for suggesting I take a sabbatical to work on the book. I am deeply grateful for the friendship and support of Therese Lysaught and Murray Jardine, who both read the entire manuscript and offered wonderful suggestions and insights. I would also like to thank the following people for reading all or part of the book and offering helpful feedback: Joe Incandela, Jacob Goodson, the Reverend Vallerie King, Hartley Wootton, and the 2005 Young Baptist Scholars in the Academy (Roger Ward, Andrew Chambers, Doug Henry, Margaret Tate, Paul Fiddes, David Gushee, Barry Harvey, Steve Chapman, Chad Eagleston, Adam English, David Gushee, Thomas Kidd, Michael Lindsay, and Scott Moore). I am thankful to Gordon Cosby, of the Church of the Savior, for allowing me to interview him, and even more, for enjoying a delightful conversation with him over lunch.

I am deeply thankful to have studied with some wonderful scholars and teachers who have influenced my thinking in the writing of this book: William H. Poteat, Geoffrey Wainwright, Stanley Hauerwas, and Ralph Wood.

I would also like to thank Rodney Clapp, editorial director of Brazos Press, and Ruth Goring, both of whom have done an excellent job of suggesting revisions and of editing the manuscript. Bill Cavanaugh and David

11

Cunningham, editors of the Christian Practice of Everyday Life series, and Rebecca Cooper, managing editor of Brazos Press, also provided helpful guidance.

More personally, I wish to thank my parents, Harold and Ernestine Newman, for their immeasurable loving support, their Christian witness, and for raising me in the church: Snyder Memorial Baptist Church, Fayetteville, NC. In addition to Snyder, I am deeply grateful to Maple Lane United Methodist Church (South Bend, IN), where my husband served as pastor for eleven years. Their lives, more than they know, contributed deeply to my understanding of Christian hospitality.

Most of all, I am indebted to my loving and witty husband, Jon Baker. On one memorable occasion, some colleagues and I were *talking* about hospitality (in a panel presentation at Notre Dame) while my husband was at home *making* hospitality possible: preparing a meal for the eight of us, while at the same time trying to care for our then four-year-old daughter and an unhappy one-year-old son. Under these circumstances, he rightly reminded me that it's easy to practice hospitality when you have servants doing all the work. It has been my privilege to have discussed much of this book with Jon, and his wonderful insights have become a part of my own thinking. Even more, Jon's support of me personally has been great. Our children, Jessica and Jacob, now eight and five respectively, have been wonderful gifts in our lives and have, in their own ways, taught us about the surprising twists and turns of hospitality, perhaps most of all how "strangers" can transform your life.

Introduction

■ This book seeks to recover hospitality as a vital practice for Christian living. In what follows, I argue that worship itself is our participation in divine hospitality, a hospitality that cannot be sequestered from our economic, political, and public lives. Such a claim might sound odd to modern ears, since people often assume hospitality simply means welcoming someone into your home or being friendly to others. In fact, when I told one of my family members that I was writing on hospitality, he responded, "Is there really enough on that to fill a book?" Yet, as I intend to show, to equate hospitality with generic friendliness or private service is to domesticate it. Such domestication distorts how extraordinary and strange Christian hospitality really is. Most fundamentally, hospitality names our participation in the life of God, a participation that might well be as terrifying as it is consoling.

For example, if we look at the familiar burning-bush scene from the life of Moses through the lens of hospitality, we see that God's hospitality challenges our typical expectations. God doesn't "invite Moses in" but rather commands him, "Come no closer!" (Exod. 3:5). Even more, he demands that Moses remove his sandals since he is standing on holy ground. Upon hearing God say, "I am the God of your father, the God of Abraham, the God of Isaac, and the God of Jacob," Moses hides his face, for he is "afraid to look at God" (Exod. 3:6). In this instance, hospitality involves not our usual pleasantries but rather command, terror, and, not least of all, a puzzling calling from God, a political calling through which God works to create and sustain the nation of Israel.

The Puritan John Bunyan described this same kind of hospitality when he wrote of the "advantages" gained from his own temptations and struggles. Whereas before he was "tormented by atheism," now, says Bunyan, "the case was otherwise, now was God and Christ continually before my face, though not in a way of comfort, but in a way of exceeding dread and terror. The glory of the holiness of God did at this time break me to pieces."[1] While we might find such language unduly harsh, Bunyan goes on to describe this encounter as "a *strange apprehension* of the grace of God."[2] This strange apprehension not only enables Bunyan to trust God when he was tempted to "sell him, sell him, sell him," but also draws him more fully into the life of the church—the congregation of the "poor people of Bedford."

Only when we envision and receive hospitality before the strange face of God, as did Moses and Bunyan, will we more fully become God's hospitable people. But we need not look far and wide in order to do this. If we locate hospitality fully in the Christian story as embodied in the church and its worship, rather than in other stories and ideologies, we will begin to recover a sense of how extraordinary Christian hospitality really is.

As we seek to recover the place from which we can faithfully engage in the strange practice of Christian hospitality, we must look critically at certain dominant cultural assumptions that are radically at odds with Christianity. These include the following: (1) that Christianity (and religion more broadly) is primarily about personal beliefs, (2) that ethics is primarily about private choices and values, (3) that politics is primarily the work of the government and the nation-state, (4) that economics is only about money and ultimately defined by the market, and (5) that the church is basically a collection of like-minded individuals. Further, these assumptions are sustained by a conviction that the real world of science and facts can be separated from the more symbolic and private sphere of "values" and religion. As long as these kinds of assumptions dominate the ecclesial imagination, it will be nearly impossible for the church to practice faithfully the hospitality of God. Christian hospitality is not a private effort separate from politics and economics. It is rather a practice at once *ecclesial* and *public*, embodying a politics, economics, and ethics at odds with dominant cultural assumptions.

The central conviction that has sustained me in the writing of this book is that "hospitality" names our graced participation in the triune life of God, an extraordinary adventure where together we discover how to live out of an abundance heretofore unimagined. The giving and receiving of God's gracious abundance is not merely "spiritual" but is in fact a material reality embodied in Israel and the church. True, like the ancient Israelites receiving the manna in the wilderness, we are tempted to resist living out of the conviction that our Host will provide. How can we trust God's provision when our lives and our world seem deeply marked by scarcity, when we—like the Israelites—seem to be wandering in a dry and desolate wilderness? Such questions can haunt our lives, leading us to question the very possibility of hospitality. We are tempted rather to hunker down, hoarding for our children, fearing the stranger, and relinquishing the possibility of a good larger than ourselves. And yet to do so is to allow ourselves to be determined by a story that is not our own.

Just as God provided manna for the Israelites in the wilderness, Christians acknowledge that God continues to provide living bread in the body and blood of Christ and living water in the pools of baptism. God provides for us and always will. The question is, are we prepared to receive? This question rightly frightens us, as it did the ancient Israelites. It is much easier and more comfortable to determine and thus control our own idols and images, indeed our own lives. But God's triune hospitality calls us to a different place, a place where we practice living lives determined by God's giving across the grand sweep of time rather than our own limited grasp of the way things are. It is the purpose of this book to consider how we might open our lives more fully to what, in our current context, can only be described as a hospitality at once extraordinary and strange.

Part 1

A "Strange Apprehension" of the Grace of God

■ In this section I explore the theological and liturgical convictions that ought to sustain our practice of hospitality. After discussing various distortions of hospitality in chapter 1, I develop an understanding of hospitality as rooted in the faithful worship of God. In chapter 2, I claim that worship itself *is* hospitality. Rightly understood, worship is not something we have to make happen. Rather, when God gathers us to worship, we are brought by the power of the Holy Spirit into a worship already taking place in the life of God. As Geoffrey Wainwright states, "The classical movement of Christian worship has always meant a participatory entrance into Christ's self-offering to the Father and correlatively being filled with the divine life."[1] To say that worship itself is our participation in divine hospitality is also to say that worship is the primary ritualized place where we learn to be guests and hosts in the kingdom of God. In worship or the liturgy (understood as the work of the people) we receive more fully the truth of whose we are as we offer in return our prayers and thanksgiving, indeed our very lives, to God. Such hospitality is not an individual or even a communal achievement. It is rather a gift to be received, and its faithful reception makes us part of something larger than ourselves: Christ's own body, a body marked by God's triune giving and receiving.

The Distortions of Hospitality

■ In this chapter I seek to say more fully what hospitality is not in order to gain clarity about what Christian hospitality actually is. Such a way of progressing parallels a familiar theological distinction between apophatic or negative theology and kataphatic or positive theology. Negative theology acknowledges that our words can never totally describe or capture who God is. Yet saying what God is not is not the same thing as knowing nothing about God. By eliminating false possibilities, negative theology can provide much-needed correctives to the ways our speech might distort God.[1] In a similar vein, by saying what Christian hospitality is not, we can begin to see what a more faithful hospitality really is.

On Practice and Theory

But first let us briefly examine what it means to call hospitality a "practice." In our culture there is a strong tendency to identify practice with something that an individual does. Thus, one is hospitable when he invites someone over for supper or gives a blanket to a homeless person on the street. While these are admirable actions, it is a mistake to imagine hospitality as an isolated activity done by an individual. To learn a practice is to learn a tradition, one sustained by many people over a long stretch of time. Christian educator Craig Dykstra defines a practice as "participation in a cooperatively formed pattern of activity that emerges out of a complex tradition of interactions among many people sustained over a long period of time."[2] In any given practice, we are participating in something much larger than ourselves.

Does describing a practice as a corporate rather than an individual activity mean that practices can be done only when there are lots of people around? No. Dykstra, in fact, turns to the example of prayer, certainly a practice that can be carried out by a person in solitude. At the same time, the one praying is participating in a complex activity sustained by a long and rich tradition.

To situate a practice within a tradition is also to say that the standards by which we judge a practice are not simply a matter of private judgment. Alasdair MacIntyre argues that we can determine the health of a particular practice by attending to its *internal goods*. When a practice is pursued only for the sake of an external good, such as status, prestige, or money, the practitioner has not truly entered into the good or the *telos* of the practice. Macintyre gives the example of teaching a highly intelligent seven-year-old to play chess by enticing him or her with the reward of candy. So long as the candy itself is the only reward, "the child has no reason not to cheat. . . . But, so we may hope, there will come a time when the child will find in those goods specific to chess" a new set of reasons for excelling in the ways that chess demands.[3] When external goods determine one's participation, the person has not truly entered into the kind of life embodied in the practice, a life that involves standards of excellence and rules of obedience.[4]

For Christians, the internal good of all practices, broadly stated, is communion with the triune God. The broad standard of excellence is holiness, as embodied in the lives of the saints, and the rules of obedience come from the church universal, particularly scripture and tradition. Certainly a practice may shift in the course of history or look rather different in different places and times. But as Jonathan Wilson states, "such modification, even when initiated by an individual, is ultimately judged by the community in relation to its 'living tradition,' its conception of the eschaton and the virtues that it seeks to embody."[5]

Of course, our various practices are flawed, halting, and at times unfaithful. If they were only "ours," this would be a serious setback. But despite our sins and many failings, God's grace makes possible our participation in the life of God and in the communion of saints. This is another way of saying that Christian practices, when engaged faithfully, are God's activity in us, a fact that does not override our free will but rather brings our freedom to fruition.

Dykstra emphasizes that practices enable us to arrive at certain kinds of knowledge we might not otherwise have. "Engagement in certain practices may give rise to new knowledge. . . . Sometimes new *realities* appear on the horizon to be apprehended, thus generating new knowledge."[6] Practices as *ways of knowing* was a theme in the early church. Gregory of Nyssa, for example, criticized his opponent Eunomius "for ignoring Christian practices and relying solely on theological ideas. It is foolish and idle . . . to think that Christian faith consists only in teachings. It also has to do with making the sign of the cross . . . with the 'mystery of regeneration' (immersion in water at Baptism), and the 'mystic oblation' (the offering of consecrated bread and wine in the Eucharist)."[7] In our own day, Stanley Hauerwas has stated that if one wants to learn the practice of prayer, "one had better know how to bend the body. Learning the gesture and posture of prayer is inseparable from *learning* to pray."[8] Practices ought to be understood, then, not only as ways of corporate doing but also as ways of knowing.

Such a claim challenges the sharp distinction often made between theory and practice, or knowing and doing—a distinction that easily traps us in imagining that hospitality has to do only with "doing." Philosopher William H. Poteat objects to the distinction between theory and practice on the following grounds:

> For beings like ourselves whose "practices" and "theories" derive their *telos* and their form, with equal radicality, from the logos implicated in our mindbodies, there can be no ultimately *practice-free theory*, no essentially *theory-neutral practice*. It is therefore impossible to argue to an absolute, context-neutral distinction between theory and practice, since both of these *always* refer back to their ground in which the distinction becomes blurred and then disappears.[9]

Rather than define theory over against practice, Poteat claims that theories are ways of being in space and time, ways that can induce certain disclosures. To illustrate his point, Poteat retells a scene from *The Odyssey*, in which Odysseus washes ashore after a shipwreck, covered with brine and his own blood. He is discovered by Nausicaa, daughter of the king of the Phaeacians. Poteat observes:

> After being bathed and adorned with rich garments he becomes the honored guest at a banquet of the royal court. When the feasting is over, Nausicaa accompanies herself on her lyre as she sings the story of one Odysseus, his deeds and his sufferings. Upon hearing his own story, set before him as a thing in the public space of the banquet, Odysseus *sees* his life for the first time and, as Hannah Arendt comments, "sheds the tears of remembrance." The narrative is a kind of *timescape* for action and passion within which Odysseus can see his life. So regarded, Nausicaa's song is a *theory*.

21

Nausicaa's song, in other words, provides Odysseus with an alternative way of being in space and time, one that induces in him certain disclosures and enables him to shed tears of remembrance. Her song is thus a theory. In this light, Poteat suggests that rituals can be "theories." They disclose what we would otherwise fail to notice. They enable us to experience our quotidian life "as participating in a cosmic drama . . . of seed time and harvest, or sunrise and sunset, of hubris and reconciliation, of sin and atonement."[10]

Surely, too, hospitality is a kind of timescape, a way of being in space and time that induces certain disclosures. In fact, we ought not miss the setting of hospitality that Poteat describes: Odysseus is the guest at a banquet, and Nausicaa's song is offered as a gift for all to hear. Elsewhere in *The Odyssey*, the swineherd Eumaios says, "Stranger [who is actually Odysseus], I have no right to deny the stranger, not even if one came to me who was meaner than you. All vagabonds and strangers are under Zeus, and the gift is a light and a dear one."[11] Such ritualized hospitality enables Eumaios to participate in a "cosmic drama"—Zeus has sent him this stranger. Since hospitality discloses what Eumaios would otherwise fail to notice, it is, in Poteat's sense, a theory.

We ought therefore to see Christian hospitality as both a practice and a theory. As a practice, it is a complex and corporate *activity* done across time that aims for certain goods—communion with God and others. As a theory, it is *way of being* in space and time.

But what actually is *Christian* hospitality? To return to *The Odyssey*: Odysseus recounts the time when he and his men landed in the land of the Cyclops. Trapped in one of their caves, Odysseus tries to beguile the Cyclops with wine in exchange for a gift to the guest, to which the Cyclops, after drinking the delicious wine, responds: "I will eat [you] after [your] friends, and the others I will eat first, and that shall be my guest present to you."[12] This strikes us as funny (and horrifying!) because it clearly violates our expectations for hospitality.

While our distortions of hospitality today might not be as blatant as that of the Cyclops, I argue that we have seriously distorted Christian hospitality. As typically practiced today, hospitality seldom discloses the great truths of the Christian faith. We can certainly acknowledge that hospitality is not a uniform practice that needs to be repeated *identically*. Certainly the Christian drama is, as Barry Harvey states, "an ongoing drama performed by a people who live in a wide variety of times and places." Harvey importantly adds, however, that we must nevertheless attend "with all the critical tools at our disposal to the 'crucial difference . . . between telling a story differently and telling a different story.'"[13]

In what follows, I look at some of the key ways hospitality in our culture has come to tell a different story—how hospitality has been lifted from its theological context and has come to "live in categories quite foreign to Christianity."[14] By focusing on distortions, I hope to begin to tell the story of Christian hospitality so that, like Odysseus, we will be able to shed tears of remembrance and recognition. My aim is to free our imaginations so that we might see alternatives to the distorted hospitalities that dominate our contemporary landscape.

A Sentimental Hospitality

Henri Nouwen notes that hospitality typically brings to mind "tea parties, bland conversation and a general atmosphere of coziness."[15] We could add to this list forced smiles, banal pleasantries, and "nice" manners. Hospitality, like many other Christian practices today, carries with it a kind of sentimental baggage.

Rodney Clapp rightly describes a sentimental capitulation that has come to characterize a dying Christendom. Believing we have nothing distinctive to offer to "our modern (or postmodern), democratic, capitalistic world," the church simply "hangs on" to Christian language but refuses to live out a genuine alternative.[16] A sentimental hospitality lacks substance. As G. K. Chesterton has said, "The sentimentalist is the man who wants to eat his cake and have it. He has no sense of honor about ideas; he will not see that one must pay for an idea as for anything else."[17]

A good illustration of a sentimentalized hospitality can be found in Flannery O'Connor's short story "A Good Man Is Hard to Find."[18] Like all of O'Connor's stories, this one is set in the American South. The central character, a grandmother, humorously embodies a kind of superficial Southern hospitality, focused on appearances and appropriate manners. Eager to go on a vacation with her family, the grandmother dresses up for the occasion—white cotton gloves, lace-trimmed collars and cuffs—so that "in case of an accident . . . anyone seeing her dead on the highway would know at once that she was a lady."[19] Being a "lady" (or gentleman) entails not only dressing appropriately but also "being nice." The grandmother thus bemoans to Red Sammy (the owner of a barbeque joint) that "people are certainly not *nice* like they used to be."[20] While the grandmother will later undergo a kind of conversion, at this point she neatly portrays a social hospitality that focuses above all on proper attire and being pleasant and polite. Such a "surface" style of sentimental hospitality is complexly aware of its appearance to others.

The grandmother's superficial niceness, however, does not prevent her from lying in order to get her way. To convince her son, Bailey, to stop at a plantation that she wants to visit, the grandmother makes up a story. "'There was a secret panel in this house,' she said craftily, not telling the truth but wishing that she were, 'and the story went that all the family silver was hidden in it when Sherman came through but it was never found.'"[21] Further, her superficial niceness does not prevent her from entertaining certain condescending stereotypes. She sees a little black child with no britches standing in a shack and exclaims, "Oh look at the cute little pickaninny! . . . If I could paint, I'd paint that picture."[22] The grandmother is by no means a vicious character. In fact O'Connor noted that the grandmother often reminded her readers, especially Southern ones, of their grandmothers or great-aunts.[23] But she does display how a sentimental, "nice" hospitality easily coincides with a kind of self-blindness and an inability to speak the truth.

Reflecting on misconceptions of hospitality, Reinhard Hütter states that hospitality and honoring the truth seem to be "opposed to one another: to be concerned for truth is to be inhospitable, and to be hospitable means being 'mushy' on matters of truth."[24] Hütter further relates the failure to speak truthfully to self-deception, "a self-protective reaction to our conscience's convicting us when we are forced to face the truth without the gift of forgiveness."[25] To the extent that we lead self-deceived lives, O'Connor's grandmother represents all of us. Yet it is precisely hospitality without truth that causes us to reduce hospitality to a bland niceness.

The sentimental distortion of hospitality often coincides with a distorted picture of God, who becomes "simply a therapeutic nice guy who asks only that we be nice too."[26] As D. Stephen Long notes, "It is as if God has been reduced to a friendly character with open arms who meets us at the entrance to his magic kingdom, inviting us to come in and find our individual fulfillment."[27] This kind of DisneyWorld hospitality might make us feel good, but such feelings will be short lived. A faithful hospitality will not aim for niceness and frozen smiles but rather for truthful communion with God and others. Long rightly concludes, "Jesus is not a personal Savior who only seeks to meet my needs. He is the risen crucified Lord of all creation who seeks to guide me back into the truth of the Triune God."[28]

O'Connor's story, in fact, draws the grandmother into an alternative drama that ultimately transforms her superficial ways. The family has a car accident, and three escaped convicts stop by the road where the family is stranded. The grandmother, having earlier seen pictures of the escapees, recognizes "the Misfit." The outcome of the story is foreshadowed when the Misfit ominously remarks, "It would have been better for all of you, lady, if you hadn't of reckernized me."[29] As the drama unfolds and the grandmother's family is killed, she repeatedly makes a common appeal to "being nice," the basic lens through which she interprets herself and the world: "You don't look a bit like you have common blood. I know you must come from *nice* people!" And later, "I know you wouldn't shoot a lady! I know you come from *nice* people."[30] Not surprisingly, the pleas are pointless. O'Connor indirectly shows how such superficial manners (hospitality) collapse in the face of truly monstrous evil. By implication, too, we can see how they fail to produce true goodness.

The dramatic turn in the story comes at the end, as the grandmother makes a remarkable gesture that stands in radical contrast to her earlier manners. Whereas previously she screamed, pulled away from the Misfit, and pleaded with him, in the final scene she actually touches him.

> His voice seemed about to crack and the grandmother's head cleared for an instant. She saw the man's fact twisted close to her own as if he were going to cry and she murmured, "Why you're one of my babies. You're one of my own children!" She reached out and touched him on the shoulder. The Misfit sprang back as if a snake had bitten him and shot her three times through the chest.[31]

Even though the Misfit violently rejects the grandmother's words and touch, he recognizes that her gesture is a profound one, and he delivers one of O'Connor's best lines: "She would of been a good woman . . . if it had been someone there to shoot her every minute of her life."[32]

It is significant that the Misfit says "good" instead of "nice." In this final scene, the grandmother is finally able to see and speak the truth and thus extend a more truthful hospitality. This hospitality is violently rejected. But she is nonetheless given a kind of vision. She sees the criminal before her not as a misfit but as one of her "babies." O'Connor herself notes that the grandmother's gesture rises to "the *anagogical* level, that is, the level which has to do with *the Divine life and our participation in it*."[33] In this moment of grace, through which the grandmother participates in the divine life, she sees truthfully not only who the Misfit is but also who she herself is: a sinner who is a forgiven child of God. Her gesture of reaching out to touch an escaped convict is not "nice," but it is profoundly good, hospitable, and courageous. Such a hospitality is made possible not by being nice but by recognizing that we can live truthful lives only to the extent that we live out of God's own forgiving grace.

A Privatized Hospitality

Another distortion of Christian hospitality has to do with its relegation to the private sphere of our lives. Hospitality has often been associated with the work of women in the home, especially in an earlier generation when women tended not to work outside the home. Hospitality as a topic in *Ladies' Home Journal*, *Redbook*, and *Southern Living* had (and still has) to do with beautiful homes, delicious dinners, and polite conversation. Such hospitality is really synonymous with entertainment. The home has to be kept "just right." On some occasions, children are an interruption and need to be sequestered. This hospitality is almost always extended to people who are more or less like oneself in terms of status and class.

Most of us recognize some form of this kind of hospitality, and at some level I am hesitant to criticize it, perhaps because it is very much a part of my formation. The main problem, however, with this kind of hospitality is twofold. First, like sentimentalized hospitality, hospitality as "entertaining" can become a subtle form of lying, thus failing genuinely to honor the truth. As Reinhard Hütter describes it, "We present an appearance that is estranged from ourselves, that is, we do not give ourselves as persons. Rather, we use our appearance as a means for other ends and thereby betray both our own personhood and the personhood of those whom we use as instruments."[34] In our day, hospitality as privatized entertainment can easily come to be more about appearances than persons. An external good (approval, social expectation, or something similar) drives the practice rather than the internal good of living into the truth and gift of who and whose we are.

John Thorne, reflecting on Martha Stewart's use of antique pots and her "overwhelming emphasis on things," writes:

> If you take your house and remove from view everything that is quirky, ugly, or difficult, and heap the polished shelves with unthreatening, desirable objects coveted by your neighbors, surface becomes everything: an impenetrable, calculated, and intensely desirable veneer. . . . In most homes, the contents are a mirror of the selves that live there; in this home, the mirror reflects nothing but desire. We don't look into it: we look at it and murmur; "I love it—where can I get one like it for myself?"[35]

This form of "entertaining" hospitality, focused on appearance, becomes a way of holding others at a distance and thus, as Hütter notes, turns into a subtle form of lying.

Second, hospitality as "entertainment" often confines the practice to a single sphere: the private home or our private lives. Once the practice of hospitality gets located in a sphere, it easily legitimates a public space where hospitality itself seems not to belong. Then hospitality is not a way of life (a point I will return to more fully later in the book) but a mode of private entertainment.

This location of a key Christian practice in the private home space parallels and reflects the privatization of religion more broadly. For example, "religion" is avoided as a topic of conversation at the dinner table, especially if guests are present. John Murray Cuddihy explores at length how a modern "religion of civility" has set the topic of religion (as truth) out of bounds. Rather, a "complex code of rites instructs us in the ways of being religiously inoffensive, of giving 'no offense,' of being *religiously* sensitive to religious differences. To be complexly aware of our religious appearance to others is to practice the religion of civility. Thus, civil religion is the social choreography of tolerance."[36] Thus, Cuddihy continues, religion becomes a largely private aspect of public society, such that one tends to say, "I happen to be . . ." Jewish, Catholic, etc. "Religious identities as such must not be pushy, elbowing themselves into contexts where they do not belong."[37]

In a well-known account, Flannery O'Connor tells of eating dinner with some sophisticated intellectuals. One of them, Mary McCarthy (formerly a Catholic), said she now thought of the Host as a symbol and, as O'Connor writes, "implied that it was a pretty good one." O'Connor, who had been sitting quietly for hours, reports her response: "I then said in a very shaky voice, 'Well, if it's a symbol, to hell with it.' That was all the defense I was capable of but I realize now that this is all I will ever be able to say about it, outside of a story, except that it is the center of existence for me; all the rest of life is expendable."[38] O'Connor's no doubt embarrassing response interrupted the civil discourse of the other guests; she was simply unable to play by the rules of polite hospitality.

Jacques Maritain has claimed that, in the face of such polite civility, truth is an uncivil thing. According to Cuddihy, Maritain believed that the church would not survive without a willingness to be uncouth. Maritain identified himself with the rustic faith of a peasant who had no standards of politeness "to keep him from upsetting the applecart." More important, for the peasant, "the faith of the Church is as much *visible* as invisible."[39] Cuddihy and Maritain's point is that civility, by making religion palatable and inoffensive, ends up domesticating it. A civilizing influence inevitably tames and privatizes religion. My point is that hospitality as entertainment *requires* a "religion of civility."

But what is hospitality without some standards of politeness? Can peasants practice hospitality? Peasants would not be able to practice the suave and civil hospitality of cultured individuals. But Christian hospitality is not determined by sophistication or lack of offense; as is well known, Jesus's words offended his listeners time and again. Rather, Christian hospitality is determined by the faithful worship of God. While I will explore this more fully in the next chapter, suffice it to say that Christian hospitality involves not a private set of beliefs (held in check at the dinner table) but rather having "one's body shaped, one's habits determined, in a manner that [makes] the worship of God . . . unavoidable."[40] We could say that hospitality as entertainment, or civilized hospitality, trains one to be, at best, self-conscious about Christianity and, at worst, embarrassed such that Christianity becomes interiorized. Yet we are called to practice a hospitality consistent with our self-confident worship of God, a hospitality that is not *our* achievement (having the home in perfect order, providing entertainment, and the like) but rather is a gift of the Holy Spirit for the sake of the church and the world.

Hospitality as a Mode of Marketing

While hospitality has been privatized in our culture and reduced to a quaint sentimentality, it has also been harnessed in very public ways by the "hospitality industry," to sell things. I recently went on a cruise in Hawaii—a wonderful gift from my parents to our family in honor of their fiftieth wedding anniversary. While we enjoyed the time together and the beautiful surroundings, I could not help but reflect on the cruise "experience" and how the hospitality industry marketed it to us. First of all, their hospitality was expensive. Not only was the cruise itself expensive, but so were the hundreds of excursions offered once the "guests" were on board. This hospitality clearly operated on the model of exchange: service for money.

Second, the crew and the rest of us on the boat pretty much remained strangers to each other. In fact, one of the rules for the crew was that they were not to interact for any length of time with the "guests."[41] At the same time, we were supposed to have become a kind of big family—a sentiment conveyed in the grand finale of one of the evening shows. As all the crew members walked forward, the cruise director sang a sentimental song about our having become family. Her parting words, "And remember, when you've got your health, you've got just about everything"—a phrase familiar from advertising—show how thoroughly a market mentality informed this "hospitality."

Finally, the "cruise hospitality" carried us into a different time, as reflected in some of my family's questions: "Is today Sunday?" "When was Christmas? Was Christmas when we were at the luau?" A marketed hospitality depends upon every day's being just like every other, so that all days are interchangeable. Nicholas Boyle characterizes this market timelessness as follows: "In the unsleeping fluorescent glow of round-the-clock commerce, consumption is as instantaneous as the signature on the contract of sale, the electronic transfer of funds from account to account, the emptying of the supermarket shelf." Time is defined by consumption rather than by history, tradition, or even personal relations. What the market conceals, however, is telling: "behind the market scenes lies a world of people who have 'been there' a long or a short time . . . who have seen changes, who have expectations and worries.

. . . It is they who feel the consequences of the consumer choices out on the exchange-floor."[42] On New Year's Day morning during the cruise, I overheard one of the crew say to another, "I think it should be a rule that adults have to clean up their own barf." A marketed hospitality, focused on consumption, does not know or even care what goes on in time "behind the market scenes."

The timelessness characteristic of market hospitality points to a more general observation: such hospitality is rooted in no story or tradition other than that of the market itself. Exchange value determines worth. When we were in Hawaii I wondered whether the hula—the traditional dance of Hawaiian women—is ever now danced spontaneously during a Hawaiian celebration or gathering. Or do the dancers perform only for the thousands of tourists who visit Hawaii? Is consumerism what keeps the "tradition" alive?

Criticism of consumerism is, of course, hardly original. And most of us like to think we are free at least of the worst aspect of consumerism—being overly materialistic. Perhaps the most common criticism of consumerism is that it constitutes a crassly materialistic way of life, in contrast to the aesthetic approach to life that we find more fulfilling. We should be more focused on the spiritual "side" of life. Or, as Murray Jardine states, we think that "people should stop buying so much junk and instead appreciate great literature, fine art, and classical music."[43]

Such responses, however, as Jardine observes, do not get us out of the web of consumerism, because consumerism itself is based on an aesthetic orientation. It may be a "low" or "high" aestheticism, focused on buying things or having experiences, but it is an aesthetic approach to life. The problem with consumerism, then, is not first of all its materialism. Rather, consumerism underwrites a way of life focused on the subject's satisfying herself through choosing things or experiences. Consumerism is a mode of aestheticism because it promotes the idea that through our choices *we* are creating our identity, our lifestyle, and the image we wish to project to others.

Søren Kierkegaard classically described the aesthetic way of life as the way of immediacy. "When a man deliberates aesthetically . . . one chooses only for the moment, and therefore can choose something different the next moment."[44] Kierkegaard points to Don Juan, a man who seeks to have as many lovers as possible, as the prototypical aesthete. Don Juan is not of course a consumer in our modern sense; he does not live in our capitalist market economy. But Don Juan clearly consumes, noncommittally and thus aesthetically, for the experience. He is—to use a phrase made famous by *Habits of the Heart*—an expressive individualist,[45] and the way he expresses himself aesthetically is through having as many women as possible. For Kierkegaard, aestheticism is a different category from the ethical because the aesthete is always noncommittal. No larger vision of life sustains or guides his choices and pleasure.

Jardine argues that aestheticism is particularly evident today in our frequent use of the word *lifestyle*. *Lifestyle* "implies that how one lives is a matter of style, or fashion. This is turn implies that how one lives is a matter of purely personal choice, or taste, and can be changed as readily as one might change the type of clothes one wears."[46] By contrast, "in premodern societies, people were judged on the basis of moral character, and in early liberal society people were judged on the basis of how productive they were (this standard of judgment itself being a distortion of Protestant conceptions of moral character)." In a consumer culture, however, "people are judged on the basis of the aesthetic image they project."[47] It is small wonder, then, that there is a growing obsession with all kinds of treatments and plastic surgery to "improve" one's looks; these are simply options to improve one's lifestyle.

A marketed or "lifestyle" hospitality feeds off personal choice and taste. If you do not like cruises, then how about this golfing retreat or fine dining at this restaurant? Lifestyle hospitality focuses on the satisfaction of personal desire.

But is the practice of Christian hospitality, then, simply a burden and duty that negates personal desire? We might be tempted to conclude that "lifestyle" hospitality is more fun. Christian hospitality, however, does not negate desire, but it acknowledges that our desires must be rightly formed. It therefore does not feed off personal tastes formed by consumerism; rather it is nourished by the gift of Christ's body. I will return to this point, so suffice it to say here that Christian hospitality is not a "lifestyle" but a way of life in which we allow our desires, tastes, and choices to be formed by the drama of God's grace-filled kingdom in our midst.

Hospitality as Inclusivity

A final distortion of the practice of Christian hospitality is the equation of hospitality with inclusivity and diversity. I once taught at a college that in one of its documents embraced "diversity for diversity's sake." In this view, "hospitality" is used interchangeably with "welcoming diversity," such that calling "diversity" into question is seen as being inhospitable. To be hospitable, this position assumes, is to be inclusive. Indeed, inclusivity is identified with the very heart of the gospel.

Unlike a sentimentalized, privatized, or marketed hospitality, the reader might have more difficulty seeing this kind of hospitality as a distortion. After all, doesn't Jesus welcome the outcasts of his society? He eats with tax collectors and sinners; he welcomes the Samaritan woman at the well;

he permits a sinful woman to pour perfume on his feet, to the chagrin of his host and other bystanders; he allows children to be the center of his attention; he defends the woman caught in adultery from those who would stone her. And Jesus himself seems challenged by the Syrophoenician woman to extend the scope of his ministry: it is not only for the Jews but also for the Gentiles.

We can note at this point, however, that Jesus's inclusivity is not without expectations. This is most obvious in the story of the woman caught in adultery. Jesus accepts her and reminds those who would stone her that they too are sinners: "Let him who is without sin cast the first stone." Yet Jesus also says to her, "Go and sin no more." He loves and accepts her but also calls her to a different way of life. In the story of the anointing with perfume, as recounted in Luke's Gospel, we get a picture of a woman who already has changed or, better stated, who has allowed herself to be transformed. Her tears and perfume are tangible expressions of her gratitude for Jesus's transforming forgiveness.

Hospitality as diversity is really a variation of market hospitality, only more seductive because "diversity" sounds good to contemporary ears— as in "to embrace diversity is to embrace God." But why is hospitality as diversity a distortion? As Christians we can rightly say that a bland homogeneity is undesirable. In 1 Corinthians 12, for example, we read about the multiplicity of gifts God showers upon the church. God gives different people different gifts for the building up of the body of Christ. At this point, however, we have introduced a purpose for hospitality. That purpose is not diversity in and of itself but the building up of Christ's body, the church. To make the "celebration of diversity" the end or the internal good of hospitality is to distort it. The internal good, as defined earlier, is the good of a certain kind of life, a life that reflects and extends the tradition in which the practice is embedded.

So what kind of life aims for embracing difference and celebrating diversity? What kind of life is focused on simply experiencing something different or trying something new? The "good" of hospitality as diversity ends up underwriting a consumeristic and aesthetic way of life. "Diversity" provides us with a vast array of choices, as does the market. Hospitality as diversity, like the market, is essentially aesthetic and noncommittal. No larger commitments enable those who embrace hospitality as diversity to discern which differences are truly good and therefore "gifts" and which are more reflective of our fallen world. Nicholas Boyle states, "The market does not concern itself with whether my choice is rational, whether it is identical or consistent with choices I make yesterday or may make tomorrow, nor does it concern itself with any purposes I may have in making my choice."[48] Such a statement nicely encapsulates a noncommittal embrace of diversity, an embrace that someone like the aesthete Don Juan would have surely understood.

All this is to say that hospitality cannot be reduced to diversity in and of itself. The internal good of Christian hospitality, as displayed beautifully in the life of the woman with perfume, is communion with Christ, a communion that cannot exist separately from communion with Christ's body, the church. A hospitality that is reduced to a generic diversity is usually unable to name an internal good (diversity for what?). But this does not mean there is no overriding "good," a "good" that will inevitably *exclude* other goods. The good life tacitly embraced by "diversity," "pluralism," and "inclusivity" is one in which the self draws its identity from its capacity "to choose autonomously how and where it will work, who it will marry, where it will live, how and where it will seek means of leisure, where it will drive in its car; in short, what it will be. This is a way of life centered on choice, mobility and maximal personal freedom."[49]

We are now in a position to see that this distortion of hospitality is similar to a marketed hospitality. Hospitality as generic inclusivity is deeply formed by what Christopher Lasch calls a culture of consumption. That is, hospitality simply becomes the mechanism through which we experience and therefore consume "difference" and "otherness." As noted earlier, a culture of consumption leads us to see ourselves as individuals whose identity rests in our expressive or aesthetic choices. A hospitality that focuses on a generic "openness" to the other is a kind of aesthetic hospitality, where "otherness" is celebrated, exchanged, and consumed. But to what end? The end is usually not explicitly stated but rather assumed. It is to expand our aesthetic experience of the world.

Stanley Fish has termed this kind of welcoming of diversity "boutique multiculturalism." The boutique multiculturalist, in Fish's definition, is one who embraces difference. "We may dress differently, speak differently . . . worship or not worship differently. . . ."[50] The multiculturalist celebrates all of this. Yet, Fish adds, the multiculturalist does this because he or she believes that our primary identity is really our universal identity as human beings, more fundamental than any particular identity. The boutique multiculturalist therefore cannot really take seriously the particularity of a given culture or tradition but sees these as mere differences. As Fish counters, a "deeply religious person is precisely that, *deeply* religious, and the survival and propagation of his faith is not for him an incidental (a bracketable) matter."[51] Fish notes the irony of "welcoming diversity" as it is currently invoked: in the name of diversity, difference becomes *mere* difference, or, we could say, simply one more lifestyle choice.

As Lasch indicates, this kind of aesthetic hospitality is sustained more deeply by a global market economy that trades on ever-expanding aesthetic appeals in order to market products to the consumer. William Cavanaugh considers how the global market trades on particular images of specific places, though these images turn out to be a sham:

Anyone who has stood at a Taco Bell counter and watched a surly white teenager inject burritos with a sour cream gun knows how absurd these images [the traditional Mexican culture of the *abuelita* before the clay oven, sipping *pulque* and shaping tortillas in the palm of her hand] are, not just because Taco Bell does not conform to the Mexican reality, but because the abuelita herself is a manufactured image. Today's Mexican woman is more likely to wash down her tortillas with a can of Diet Coke, while sitting before dubbed reruns of "Dynasty."[52]

Diversity is "offered" but only when it conforms to the rule of the market; a homogenizing consumption ultimately triumphs. When one actually looks at such diversity, one sees "more and more sameness—of tastes, of clichéd perceptions of the world, of the glum ennui with which one reconciles oneself to the monolithic routines of our world."[53] In Boyle's analysis, "'Pluralism' is these days a popular word, and a comfortable idea, in many more and less theoretical contexts, but it is something of a mystification—an appearance of variety in the adiaphora in order to conceal the unity in what counts, a velvet glove round the hidden hand."[54]

What is concealed by the invocation of pluralism, the conviction that there is not one truth but many, often competing and contradictory, truths? The velvet glove, as it were, is the global market. If we find "pluralism" and the "multiplicity" of the self plausible, it is because, according to Boyle, the game is being played "precisely as the global market wants it played. For the fiction by which the global market commends itself to us and encourages our participation in it is that the human self is purely a consumer."[55] We can conclude that the global market deeply forms a hospitality defined in terms of "pluralism," "inclusivity," and "diversity." In fact, it serves the market for us to think of hospitality in this way. To practice a hospitality of pluralism and diversity is to become a better consumer, rather than a more faithful participant in receiving and giving the love and grace of God.

Homeless Hospitality

Henri Nouwen has said that we can offer hospitality only when we have a place or home from which to extend it. The distortions of hospitality that I have discussed all result from a kind of homelessness. That is, the distorted images of hospitality as a privatized sentiment, a marketed exchange, or mere inclusivity all fail to reflect the *home* or place of Christian hospitality. The loss or distortion of Christian hospitality is therefore at the same time a loss of place, of where we need to dwell in order to participate faithfully in God's hospitality.

The distortions of hospitality that I have explored are all symptomatic of a pervasive feature of late modernity: a gnawing homelessness, a lack of a sense of place. If we are truly to envision and embody a faithful hospitality, we must see how deeply our current understanding and experience of "home" and "place" have up to now prevented us from living a profound Christian hospitality.

A number of authors have written about the growing loss of place in North America. William R. Leach, for instance, in *A Country of Exiles*, argues that over the past fifty or so years Americans have become increasingly placeless.[56] Less and less often do people grow up and continue to live their whole life in one place. Usually people move for economic reasons. More often than not they move into suburbs, often placing their children into childcare, driving twenty-plus miles to work, and leaving their home abandoned for most of the day. Most of us now live in *subdivisions*, a mathematical term, rather than *neighborhoods*, a term that suggests personal connection.

The fact that there even are suburbs is a reflection of the placelessness of society. Increasing numbers of urban planners, in fact, are arguing that the way most North American cities have been built since World War II is destructive of community. Single-use zoning has created urban sprawl by separating different kinds of buildings, such as residential areas from where people work. Such separation makes it necessary to use cars to get from one place to another, which in turn necessitates larger and larger thoroughfares. As Jardine notes, the most important result of urban sprawl is that "it makes it impossible to get *anywhere* except by car."[57] Jardine notes that the outcome of this is especially destructive for people who cannot drive. Children, for example, must be chauffeured everywhere by adults; walking to school or the grocery store on their own is no longer an option.

In addition to changes in the spaces where we live, we can look at differences in how we think about time. More and more people are working longer hours. Most parents, if there even are two parents, now work outside the home. In many instances both parents "need" to work, because in a consumer economy people are encouraged to spend more than they have and thus they must work to pay for what they have bought. One sociologist who studied workers at a large American corporation for a year, Arlie Russell Hochschild, surprisingly discovered that people tended to work longer hours because they preferred being at work to being at home. According to Hochschild's interviews, the home had become an unwelcome place, often lonely or chaotic (because of children).[58] Working long hours can easily turn the home into a stopping-off place where you eat (perhaps), watch TV, and sleep. The use of the term *bedroom community* reflects this sense that home is the place where you happen to sleep while your "real life" is elsewhere.

We could point to more symptoms of a kind of homelessness in contemporary culture: the hours we spend watching TV or playing computer games, which can be done almost anywhere; not knowing our neighbors; the loss of small farms and local businesses in many places. Less and less often do particular places, communities, and traditions provide both limits and expectations that shape our lives. Perhaps we might respond, "That is not necessarily bad. Communities and traditions can be oppressive. It can be a good thing to be free of the narrow convictions associated with some communities." In the eighteenth century, Immanuel Kant classically defined *enlightenment* as freedom from tradition and dogma. As the beginning of his classical treatise "What Is Enlightenment?" Kant tells his readers, "Enlightenment is man's exodus from his self-incurred tutelage. Tutelage is the inability to use one's understanding without the guidance of another person. This tutelage is self-incurred if its cause lies . . . in indecision and lack of courage to use the mind without the guidance of another. Dare to know! Have the courage to use your own understanding; this is the motto of the Enlightenment."[59] Kant's vision exemplifies modernity's bold trust in the individual to achieve freedom, to achieve a truthful place, without the help of another.

In our late modern epoch, however, we can see that a self stripped of context, a "universal self," is at the mercy of global economic and political forces beyond its control. How can the vegetable stand of a farm family compete with Wal-Mart? Abstract market forces rather than communal concern for local farmers determine the economics of our residents, many of whom have moved to our fast-growing Virginia county in the first place for economic reasons. With no concrete place of orientation, hospitality will be subject to the whims of the dominant economic and political forces.

William H. Poteat notes that "we are not the first age in which man has felt that he has lost his place. The disintegration of the polis launched a flood of deracinate men upon the Aegean and Mediterranean world. But we are the first age in which man has felt the radical contingency of every place, felt, indeed, that the very notion of place has lost its meaning."[60] Analyzing this loss, Poteat argues that our modern understanding of *place* has become easily assimilated to that of *space* so that we think of both of these in primarily visual terms. Thinking of place in terms of space might seem harmless enough. Poteat argues, however, that when visual experience dominates, we are inclined to perceive ourselves as spectators, even more as "a mere eye; in fact, a disembodied eye, which is oriented from no body of its own."[61] According to Poteat, this "spectator perception" has profoundly influenced Western culture with its growing sense of placelessness. For example, consider René Descartes' conviction that the thinking mind precedes "that of any corporeal thing, and is more certain." Poteat highlights the difficulty with this conviction: "Since mind is in every particular different from corporeal things, and since our notion of mind *precedes* our notion of body and is indubitable, it follows that our notion of *our* mind as ours has no reference to or dependence upon any *particular* body."[62] The Cartesian notion that mind precedes body, therefore, means that it (we) are not dependent upon any particular body. We easily become spectators rather than inhabitants of a place. Even more, we become deprived of our place, understood not as visual space but as a place of orientation. Poteat helps us see that the elevation of a spectating mind has contributed to a Western placelessness.

In response to these Enlightenment moves, Poteat points us to the thought of a contemporary of Descartes, Blaise Pascal. The Cartesian world terrified Pascal: "The eternal silence of these infinite spaces frightens me. . . . *What is a man in the infinite*?"[63] He was alarmed at living in a world where nothing is finite, that is, where nothing is human, historical, and particular. In infinite space you cannot say, "Once upon a time." Nor can you say, "In the beginning, God created." Pascal could not imagine living in the infinite; for him that meant living without God. We are finite, and only God is infinite.

As is well known, till the day he died, Pascal carried sewn into his coat pocket the following testimony:

> The year of grace 1654. Monday, 23 November, feast of Saint Clement, Pope and Martyr, and of others in the Martyrology.
> Eve of Saint Chrysogonus, Martyr and others.
> From about half past ten in the evening until half past mid-night.
> Fire.
> "God of Abraham, God of Isaac, God of Jacob," not of philosophers and scholars.
> Certainty, certainty, heartfelt joy, peace.
> God of Jesus Christ.
> God of Jesus Christ.
> My God and your God . . .[64]

In our day, we can hardly imagine feeling either the terror or the assurance that Pascal apparently felt. For Pascal, the terror of having no orientation in time or space is countered by a date, one that recalls the feast of a martyr, and the consuming presence of the same God who appeared to Abraham, Isaac, and Jacob. In late modernity, however, we have grown accustomed to not having this kind of orientation in space and time; one shopping mall is like any other, and in the mall we can easily be unaware of whether it's day or night. Furthermore, we only half-believe people who tell us they have such visions. Even those people, if there are any, usually remain silent.

Pascal's terror, however, prophetically points to a feature of the late modern self. This "self" is not so much an autonomous master standing apart from the world, in control of its own destiny. The "self" today is more likely to be fragile and fragmented. The decontextualized self ("man in the infinite") has no story. Isak Dinesen has written that "all sorrows can be borne if you put them into a story or tell a story about them."[65] Dinesen thus implies that an unstoried self cannot bear sorrows. Such a person is not so much a "master" as she is fragile and vulnerable.

Psychologist Philip Cushman suggests in fact that persons today are not so much bounded, masterful selves (a description, Cushman notes, that many psychologists happily embrace) as "empty."

> By this I mean that our terrain has shaped a self that experiences a significant absence of community, tradition, and shared meaning. It experiences these social absences and their consequences "interiorly" as a lack of personal conviction and worth, and embodies the absences as a chronic, undifferentiated emotional hunger. The post–World War II self thus yearns to acquire and consume as an unconscious way of compensating for what has been lost: It is empty.[66]

Cushman points out that economic and political forces create, sustain, and manipulate this self. Consuming individuals buy lifestyles because their lives are unsatisfying, but also, Cushman notes, their lives are unfixable without massive societal change. The self is not only "suffering from feeling unreal . . . as it did at the turn of the century. It is also aggressively, sometimes desperately, acquisitive."[67]

Cushman's analysis highlights a picture of the modern self as empty and fragmented. A well-known scene in J. D. Salinger's *The Catcher in the Rye* has Holden Caulfield walking up Fifth Avenue, hoping he'll not disappear when he steps from the block to cross each street.[68] The most striking feature of this scene is the feeling of instability and unreality, as if he is not real and might in fact simply disappear. While the "empty self" is a type that few embody completely, it is nonetheless a suggestive characterization of the feeling of homelessness in our culture. As Cushman states, "The self embodies what the culture believes is humankind's place in the cosmos."[69]

Given this deep dislocation, it is little wonder that when we try to think about the "place" of hospitality, it becomes very difficult, if not impossible. The very idea of hospitality requires not only a "hospice," a home, but also a particular kind of giving and receiving. An empty self is unable to conceive of the fact that he or she has something to give, something to offer. Such a self is also, oddly enough, unable truly to *receive*. As Cushman indicates, the empty self consumes in order to feed or fix the emptiness. But consuming is different from receiving. Consuming has about it an air of desperation as the consumer seeks to create a persona or satisfy a fabricated need. Genuine reception requires gratitude, the ability to see someone or something not as a product but as a gift. It therefore requires a person, and a culture, that is not interiorly empty or placeless but is capable of giving thanks. And giving thanks is a way of indicating that we are not our own creators. While it has become something of a cliché, Blanche Dubois's "I've always relied on the kindness of strangers" captures a truth about our lives. Truly receiving gifts from others is a way of acknowledging our dependence on others, and so also a way of accepting that we are not our own creation, even if that creation *feels*, for all the reasons Cushman discusses, interiorly empty.

Instead of a fragmented and empty self, then, hospitality draws us into a richer context where we must make sense of ourselves as "guests" and "hosts," acknowledge our dependence on others, and learn to live with gratitude. Dinesen's story "The Roads around Pisa" has a young woman and a count discussing hospitality in this light.

> "Now, tell me, Count" [said the young woman], "what does a guest want?"
>
> "I believe," said Augustus when he had thought for a moment, "that if we do, as I think we ought to here, leave out the crude guest, who comes to be regaled, takes what he wants and goes away, a guest wants first of all to be diverted, to get out of his daily monotony or worry. Secondly the decent guest wants to shine, to expand himself and impress his own personality upon his surroundings. And thirdly, perhaps, he wants to find some justification for his existence altogether. But since you put it so charmingly, Signora, please tell me now: What does a hostess want?"
>
> "The hostess," said the young lady, "wants to be thanked."[70]

I have always liked this brief scene because the young woman's simple response goes straight to the heart of the matter. It can also serve, I think, as a kind of secular parable: God wants to be thanked, not, certainly, because God needs our thanksgiving but rather because God desires our communion. In offering our thanks, we are freed to acknowledge our lives as gifts rather than as our own, often empty or fragmented, creations.

In conclusion, I concur with others who describe our modern homelessness as a mode of gnosticism. A gnostic is not at home in the world but believes that salvation comes in the form of a kind of *gnosis*, or knowledge, given to the interior soul. Salvation thus comes through escape from the world rather than through pilgrimage. In our context, the desire to escape from emptiness and fragmentation is certainly understandable. Gnosticism meets this desire by claiming that a knowing by an "uncreated self, or self-within-the-self," can lead "to freedom, a dangerous and doom-eager freedom: from nature, time, history, community, other selves."[71] In contrast, Christians believe that our salvation and freedom reside in God's acting in history, in the people of Israel, Jesus Christ, and the church, for the sake of the world. To the extent that we allow ourselves to be bound to this history, this story, our fragmentation and modern homelessness are overcome.

In this chapter I have argued that hospitality has been distorted in our contemporary context in a variety of ways. Further, I have suggested that all of these distortions signal a loss of place in our culture. If we are to move beyond the distortions of Christian hospitality, if we are to recover a sense of place from which to extend hospitality, then we must see the church as absolutely *necessary*.

Perhaps such recovery seems obvious to some readers, but to others it will be less so. I can hear numerous questions: "What church are you talking about?" "What about all those churches that have not only failed to practice hospitality but have done terrible things in the name of God?" "How can our 'place' of hospitality be defined by a community in which we spend so little of our lives, maybe three to five hours a week at most?"

In response to the first question, I am talking about the church as the body of Christ into which all Christians are baptized, a body stretching back across time and crossing geographical place. Certainly various embodiments of Christ's body are more or less faithful, more or less accommodated to distortions of Christian hospitality, and more or less attuned to the gift of the Holy Spirit drawing us to be members one of another. But still, both in its sinfulness and in its faithfulness, the church remains Christ's body for the world and thus the place God has given us to be Christ's body for our friends and our enemies. That the church has practiced a distorted hospitality or has failed to practice it at all is a clear sign the church is on pilgrimage. Our place is not fixed or determined by geography or locale, but rather by living as God's people before a faithful God.

The images of "home" and "pilgrimage" may seem contradictory. How can a people be "at home," an image suggesting a fixed place, while also being "on pilgrimage," an image suggesting movement and quest? The language of "home" and "pilgrimage" reminds us that the place from which we both offer and receive God's hospitality is a "movable feast." This term is used today to refer to a holy day whose date is not fixed in the calendar year but moves in response to Easter's date. The image of the "movable feast" also conveys the idea that the place of Christian hospitality is not static but moves in response to the gifts of God, most fully the gift of God in the life, death, and resurrection of the Son. Our place is with the body of Christ, yet this body is on pilgrimage. Contrary to popular imagery, however, the pilgrimage is not our initiative, in which we go out either alone or with a few others to slay the terrible dragon. Rather, as with the Israelites, God gathers us, provides for us, and leads us toward the promised land. As a people, we journey into the time and place of God's kingdom, a kingdom that is both "now" and "not yet." Another name for the journey/home of hospitality is *worship*.

2

The Strange Hospitality of Christian Worship

■ Animal trainer Vicki Hearne tells the story of a horse named Halla that everyone thought was crazy, and so she was treated, until one day along came a trainer who had a different story or vision about the kind of horse Halla was. She wasn't crazy at all, this trainer maintained; rather, Halla was a high strung and extremely gifted horse. Under the supervision of this trainer, Halla went on to excel and become the horse that the new trainer envisioned.[1]

In an analogous sense, I think the distorted stories we have absorbed about hospitality, and about Christianity more generally, have disoriented us, if not made us crazy as we have tried to live out of two competing visions of who we are: the cosmic drama of God's salvific activity in the world, on the one hand, and the various competing ways to define the "real" world, on the other (scientific, political, economic, and so on).

In this chapter I want to put forth a vision of hospitality alternative to the ones described in the previous chapter. I want us to see worship itself as hospitality.[2] Common assumptions regard worship as *motivation* for hospitality or as a place we might garner some useful *information* about hospitality. But such assumptions miss the mark; they make worship a means to an end, and they locate hospitality outside of worship. Even more, worship is itself interiorized, regarded as a motivational force or cognitive act. The alternative vision I wish to set forth sees worship itself as our participation in God's own triune life, a life we can characterize as hospitality. To sing, to pray, to pass the peace, to listen to God's word, to eat at God's table is to share, through the gift and power of the Spirit, in God's own giving and receiving. Such a vision of worship, I hope to show more fully, enables us to practice hospitality more faithfully. Just as Halla became the kind of horse her trainer envisioned, so too can Christians, through participation in God's hospitality, become the hospitable people that God calls and gifts us to be.

At the outset the reader might see at least two difficulties with my approach. First, worship itself is by no means immune to exactly the same kinds of distortions as those that warp hospitality. Second, even if we come to see and practice worship as hospitality, we worship at most only a few hours each week. This hardly seems enough time to transform us into God's hospitable people, especially when we consider the powerful forces that otherwise determine our lives. In the following sections, I will address these so that we can move beyond them to a rich understanding of worship as hospitality.

Distorted Worship

It is certainly the case that worship is often distorted in the same way that hospitality is. For example, worship is often sentimentalized or equated with friendliness and being nice. Most of us probably know people who avoid going to worship simply because they cannot muster the energy to put on a happy face. Or a woman who is pregnant out of wedlock avoids church altogether because she does not fit the expectations of polite society.[3] Recently I heard a reporter on NPR get choked up when a guest band sang "Sweet Hour of Prayer." The hymn generated sentimental feelings: it reminded the reporter of her childhood when she used to go to church, part of her now romanticized past.

Like the distortions of home hospitality examined in the previous chapter, worship is often regarded as a private experience, a place we go to "get our needs met." It has often been assumed "that nothing the church does is more private than its worship. Worship [is] often seen as the gathering of individuals engaged in their own private communion with their God."[4] If worship does not meet one's needs, this view holds, then there is no reason not to change the worship or even to change churches.[5] From this perspective, worship is primarily about the individual and only secondarily "social." In my own tradition, in fact, a well-known early-twentieth-century Baptist theologian, E. Y. Mullins, defined church as "*a group of individuals* sustaining to each other important relations, and organized for a great end and mission."[6] Such a definition, while rightly emphasizing mission, nonetheless imagines our gathering to worship as a collection of individuals.

Worship as a collection of individuals fits a marketed worship quite well. We learn the habit of "getting my needs met" from a market economy, and most of us have probably heard church advertisements that sound like TV commercials (and that in fact are TV commercials). My husband and I recently saw a church marquee announcing, "Worship just got better!" similar to the "new and improved" ads one might hear for laundry detergent or shampoo. Not only does our current economic culture make it tempting to sell worship to the consumer and to go to worship as consumers, but on a deeper level, the world of entertainment turns us into spectators. As Philippe Beneton states about the television, "Thanks to the machine, I seem, in a way, to be above the world. As a spectator, I take on the attitude of an outside observer and have (or seem to have) sovereign freedom."[7] Earlier in the history of the church, it was mistakenly assumed that liturgy or the Mass was something the priest did while the laity simply looked on. The Catholic Church has sought to alter that assumption by stressing the participatory nature of the liturgy, having the priest face the people, and emphasizing the role of the laity. Today, however, the reasons for spectator worship are not so much because we overidentify the church with the hierarchy. If anything, the church is reduced to an assembly of isolated selves. We are rather in danger of spectator worship because we are trained by our culture—through the media, technology, and science—to objectify the world, an objectification that "severs the umbilical cord that ties [us] to what surrounds [us]."[8] So we easily come to worship as detached spectators, waiting to be entertained.

Finally, similar to the reduction of hospitality to inclusivity, some churches have simply transformed the internal good of worship into "inclusivity." From this perspective, the worst possible thing that could happen in worship would be to exclude someone. Recently, the United Church of Christ generated a controversial advertisement whose primary message was "We include everyone." The ad showed two strong-armed men at the doors of a church excluding some (a black girl, a gay couple) and letting others in. The message of the UCC ad appeared to be that more than other churches, it is "inclusive." Yet all too often such inclusivity undermines any meaningful distinction between the church and the world. Jesus did not say, "Be inclusive"; he said, "Follow me." This does not mean the church should close its doors to outsiders. It does, however, mean that worship in the church is about something other than "inclusivity." Christian hospitality disappears when the distinction between church and world is collapsed.

43

Worship (like hospitality) as mere inclusivity is actually the antithesis of hospitality, as it makes us strangers to each other and strangers in the universe. Equality without judgment is not rooted in any particular history or tradition. Beneton has called such purely formal equality an "equality by default." The substantive equality of Christianity says that humans are equal because they are created in God's image and share the same condition, which is sin; "they are heirs of the same history of love and infidelity (Creation, Fall, Redemption)."[9] At the same time, there is a recognition of differences; God, who knows even the number of hairs on our head, creates each of us unique. In equality by default, however, we are alike simply because we are free to be different and "no difference is worth more than another."[10] "The models of excellence that have characterized Western civilization—the wise man, the hero, the saint—are no longer distinct from their contraries."[11] Indeed, *elite* has become a bad word; "elitism" is almost as bad as racism. At the same time, those differences that are extolled are the ones that affirm the radical autonomy of the individual and his or her limitless liberty. Equality by default and the "right to be different" mean basically "the right to live with whom I want and how I want, the right to change 'partners' (as in bridge) when I want, the right to dress eccentrically if I want, in all circumstances."[12]

The language of "inclusivity" and "diversity" underwrites an equality by default and by extension the sovereign Self, cut off from others and liberated from particular norms and traditions. "Default man," Beneton says, "no longer forms part of an order that transcends him. He enjoys a sovereign independence. He is a *stranger* in the universe."[13] Worship informed by such assumptions will be unable to offer Christian hospitality, a practice that relies on a sense of place, a shared tradition, one in which we are not strangers in the universe (or to each other) but part of God's good creation, created so that God might love us and so that we might in return love God, each other, the stranger, and even the enemy.[14]

Is Rehabituation Possible?

If we are so habituated to practicing a distorted hospitality—hospitality as "niceness" or "consumerism" or "inclusivity"—then can worship really make any difference in our truly engaging an alternative? We cannot simply think our way into an alternative way of being hospitable; rather, we must allow our bodies to be rehabituated or repositioned.[15] The typical one-hour worship service, however, seems unlikely really to rehabituate us. One hour of "repositioning" in the face of powerful antagonistic forces that would have us practice a distorted hospitality seems hardly enough.

I do not have an easy answer to this objection.[16] Obviously, our worship of God is not to end when we leave church. The Orthodox refer to the "liturgy after the liturgy" to signal that worship does not end (nor do we cease being church) when we leave the building. The tendency to limit worship to a Sunday-only activity coincides with the assumption that worship has little to do with our political or economic lives, our lives in the "real world." Yet as Hauerwas and Wells remind us, "Worship is, or aspires to be, the manifestation of the best ordering of that body, and is thus the most significantly political—the most 'ethical'—thing that Christians do."[17] The turn to worship, then, is not a merely pious turn away from the real world for a few hours, but is instead a turn to the real world that is the body of Christ.

We still, of course, face what might seem like insurmountable distortions of hospitality and worship such that "rehabituation" seems unlikely. Yet here we do well to remember what a Holy Cross sister once told me in the face of distorted educational practices: "God does not abandon us." Her words rightly remind us that our educational, liturgical, and hospitable efforts are not only a *human* venture. Philosopher Josef Pieper has said, "The decisive result is not to be achieved through action but can only be hoped for."[18] Pieper is not endorsing quietism but rather locating true renewal (or rehabituation) where it ought to be located: in the hands of God. To name worship as hospitality is to claim that neither of these is only a human venture. Stated more positively, God gives us what we need to live lives of faith, hope, and love.[19] The place where we are given most fully the provisions to live and be God's people is worship. Here we can see more fully what we often fail to see: "that everything gained and everything claimed follows upon something given, and comes after something gratuitous and unearned; that in the beginning *there is always a gift*."[20] Our worship of God rests on the fact that in the beginning there is always gift, the overflow of God's eternal triune communion. In worship, as we enter this communion, we learn to be God's guests and hosts. As we gather to worship, we reposition our bodies to receive God's word and body. This liturgical repositioning forms us to be God's hospitable people. Such formation, however, is often tenuous because, as indicated, other forces and habits easily misshape us. In what follows I seek to describe worship as hospitality in a way that makes faithful repositioning more likely.

Worship: "It's Not about You!"

God gives us what we need to live lives of faithfulness. But how is this statement different from defining worship as the place we go to get our spiritual needs met? Ironically, it seems, we have to discover that worship is "not about us" in order to get a sense of how God provides for our needs, including needs we didn't know we had. We might, for example, discover how much we need that person we had earlier thought we could write off. Or we might discover that our weakness is the place where God gives us a holy strength.

James B. Torrance notes that probably the most common view of worship is that it is something "we, religious people, do—mainly in church on Sunday. We go to church, we sing our psalms and hymns to God, we intercede for the world, we listen to the sermon . . . we offer our money, time and talents to God. No doubt we need God's grace to help us do it. We do it because Jesus taught us to do it and left us an example of how to do it. But worship is what *we* do before God."[21] Torrance's questioning of this view might catch us off guard. *Isn't* worship all those things we do together when we gather before God—pray, sing, preach, and so on? If this is not worship, then what is it?

Yet Torrance describes the above view as unitarian rather than trinitarian because the agent of worship is the self. The emphasis falls on our decision, our faith, and our response. When we become the primary agent of worship, it is difficult to resist the belief that worship is primarily about us: our feelings, our experiences, even our gifts and talents. It is then difficult to resist the idea that wherever we feel closest to God is where we ought to worship. If I feel the grandeur of God on a mountaintop, then why do I need to sit in some stuffy church sanctuary? Or why do I really need to gather with other people to worship? This view leads to the idea that the church might be valuable but it is not necessary. It may be an important source of support, but it is secondary to the individual and his or her relation with God. Such an understanding, however, is deeply flawed.

We can begin to get a sense of why from Craig Barnes, a Presbyterian minister, and his appropriately titled sermon "It's Not about You." Barnes writes that when couples come to him for premarital counseling, he tells them, "You know, it's not about you." He goes on to say that worship too is "not about you." Rather, offering praise to God is central to worship "not because God is insecure and needs lots of affirmation, but because the Bible is concerned that we enjoy the freedom in knowing 'it's not about us.' If it is always about God, then we are free from the burden of pretending to be gods (or pretending to be less than God created us to be). Instead, we can return to our mission of witnessing to the grace God is giving us."[22] Barnes's use of the word *freedom* is particularly significant. Worship is about our attending to what God is doing in the church and the world. Concern with "getting my needs met" keeps us bound to ourselves—our deceptions, our distortions, and our autonomy. Barnes rightly sees "it's not about you" as joyful news because it frees us from the burden of focusing on ourselves. It frees us to trust, wait, watch, and participate, through the power of the Spirit, in God's movement in our lives together as church, as those called out by God to be his people for the sake of the world.

Torrance gives an example of such freedom: While he was visiting Fuller Theological Seminary in California, an elderly man approached him on the beach. The man asked him who he was and upon hearing from Torrance that he was a Presbyterian minister said, "How astonishing that I should meet you." He then poured out his story. His wife of forty-five years was dying of cancer, and he didn't know how to face the future without her. His father was a Presbyterian minister, and he had been brought up in a godly home but had drifted away from church. He went on to say that he had been trying to pray but couldn't. Torrance writes,

> Did I tell him how to pray—throw him back on himself? No, I did not. I said, "May I say to you what I am sure your father would have said to you? In Jesus Christ we have someone who knows all about this. He has been through it all—through suffering and death and separation—and he will carry you both through it into resurrection life. . . . You have been walking up and down this beach, wanting to pray, trying to pray, but not knowing how to pray. In Jesus Christ we have someone who is praying for you. He has heard your groans and is interceding for you and with you and in you."[23]

Torrance directs the man away from the notion that prayer or worship is primarily something he does (or fails to do, in this instance). Rather, Torrance directs the man toward Christ who prays with us, in us, and through us such that we are drawn into communion with the triune God. As Torrance says, to pray is "to recognize that none of us knows how to pray as we ought to. But as we bring our desires to God, we find that we have someone who is praying for us, with us, and in us."[24] Jesus takes our prayers—feeble and inarticulate though they are—and "he makes his prayers our prayers and presents us to the Father as his dear children crying: 'Abba Father.'"[25] Worship is not about us, or even about our effort, but about God, who desires through the Spirit to draw us into communion, the communion the Son shares with the Father.

My emphasis on Christ as Mediator who prays for, with, and in us might sound as if I am denying any human effort whatsoever in worship. If so, this would contradict even the meaning of *liturgy*—"the work of the people." Yet it is significant that liturgy is not defined as the experiences or the feelings of the people, an emphasis that in our culture easily locates worship in the individual's interior life. Rather, "work" reminds us that worship is external, an activity people do together. We ought not say, "I didn't really worship this morning," anymore than we would say,

"Because I wasn't 'into it,' I did not really eat my supper." We wouldn't say a couple was not really married because they "didn't feel anything" during their wedding.

True, we might worship is such an anemic way that our worship is diminished. We have all eaten bad meals; we have all been to worship services after which we were tempted to say (or actually said), "I didn't get anything out of that sermon." The sermon may well have been poor, but worship itself is not dependent upon the quality of the sermon. God is no stranger to poverty, including poverty of preaching or "meaning." Worship depends rather on the gift of the Spirit in Christ, through whom we participate in the mutual self-giving of God's triune life. A good preacher knows, after all, that God can use even his or her "bad" sermon to make faithful disciples. The invitation to worship is an invitation to be incorporated into the body of Christ. As such, it is always a gift, in the receiving of which we are called to wait and see what God is doing.

A well-known Russian icon beautifully captures trinitarian worship as gift. Andrei Rublev's *The Holy Trinity* (sometimes called *The Old Testament Trinity*) depicts three divine visitors seated around a table. The setting is Genesis 18, where Abraham receives three mysterious visitors and, with Sarah, prepares a rich meal for these unknown guests. In Rublev's icon, the three guests, seated at an open table, have been transformed into divine hosts. A chalice sits in the middle of the table, and the viewer is invited to join in the triune communion already going on. Rublev's icon suggests that communion or worship is about our participation in something much larger than ourselves, the story of a people stretching back to Abraham who have lived and continue to live before the face of God.

A Whole Greater Than the Sum of Its Parts

This last statement indicates that when we gather together as the church, we are more than simply a collection of individuals, Mullins's definition not withstanding. Or we could say, wherever we are we do not cease to be church, and therefore wherever we are we ought not to think of ourselves as individuals. By "individual" I mean imagining ourselves primarily as an independent, autonomous unit.

I was recently at a conference where members of a Christian community, the Church of the Sojourners from San Francisco, spoke of their life together. They share many of their possessions, live in close proximity to one another, and practice "stability." That is, they commit themselves to stay with this particular church community and encourage only those moves that will build the church. There is a deep sense that they are part of something much larger than themselves as they seek to be faithful disciples before God and one another.

Russian Orthodox theologian Alexander Schmemann emphasizes that worship is not simply a gathering of individuals. The liturgy, Schmemann says, is "an action by which a group of people become something corporately which they *had not been as a mere collection of individuals*—a whole greater than the sum of its parts."[26] Now, I must confess that though I wrote my dissertation on Schmemann, I have had difficulty over the years really absorbing this passage. In the Baptist church that I attended growing up, church was a collection or gathering of some wonderful folks from different places. We came together (Sunday mornings and evenings and Wednesday evenings), went to Sunday school and church training, sang hymns, and listened to sermons, but to my way of thinking we did not become something greater than the sum of the parts. No doubt the "parts," the individuals, became better disciples or more faithful followers of Jesus, but to think of the whole as greater than the sum was alien to my training.

Yet I think Schmemann is right to describe worship as he does. To grasp his meaning, we might consider two types of pastimes: those we can do on our own and those that require the involvement of others. An example of the first sort might be stamp collecting. While it might be fun to belong to a club of collectors, it isn't necessary to the activity. Even the acquisition of new stamps may be conducted on a completely commercial basis. Other persons, as *persons*, are ancillary to the activity.

Contrast this with reenacting groups, such as the Society for Creative Anachronism, which re-creates the societies and cultures of the Middle Ages and Renaissance. Members adopt the role of jester, queen, or knight. They practice the arts and skills of the world they study. To visit one of their fairs is to visit a complete world, recognizable as such. Obviously, a *sine qua non* of such activity is the community. The roles of jester, queen, and knight make sense (come to life) only in the relationships among the players. In other words, the reenactors enter into a world the whole of which is greater than any particular individual. In this world, a queen cannot be a queen without a knight, and vice versa. A part (say a dragon) cannot simply be added under the assumption that the whole *equals* the sum of the parts; such a world would not be whole but an incoherent muddle. Rather, the whole is greater and makes sense because individuals enter into a story, a drama, and a world larger than themselves.

Similarly, when we worship we enter into a whole that is greater than the sum of its parts. This world is greater than anything an individual can generate on his or her own. But what is this world? It is not, says Schmemann, the world of the "cultic" or "sacred" over against the profane. The liturgy is misunderstood, he says, if interpreted as a "spiritual

49

deviation from the real task of the Church." The liturgy is not an imaginary world over against the real one. Rather, Schmemann emphasizes that the liturgy enables us to see our true lives as *eucharistic*, a term Schmemann contrasts with *opaque*. To experience the world as opaque is to divide the spiritual from the material realm, to divide worship from the rest of our lives. It might seem "natural to experience the world as opaque" and as not eucharistic, but this is a result of the fall.[27] In the fall, we "made the world material, whereas [we] were to have transformed it into 'life in God.'"[28] A eucharistic life is truly our natural life, one that involves all of creation, such that even our breathing is as a means of communion with God. To make even breathing communion with God sounds remarkable, perhaps something only the rare saint truly achieves. Certainly for most of us living in the world of raising families, working, paying bills, such a way of life seems unattainable. The world seldom seems shot through with the presence of God. Yet Schmemann characterizes the liturgy as a journey together "into a dimension of the Kingdom . . . [a] sacramental entrance into the risen life of Christ,"[29] a life we do not achieve but are given.

The liturgical whole greater than the sum of its parts can thus be described in a variety of ways: the kingdom of God, the life of Christ, the eucharistic life. This is a whole far greater than ourselves, but in which we nonetheless are given a share. As Geoffrey Wainwright states, "When Christians on earth gather for worship, they too form an assembly, a congregation. What joins them together most profoundly is not a merely human sense of fellowship but rather the divine reality in which they have a common share, namely the 'koinonia' of participation in Christ . . . and in the Holy Spirit."[30] *Koinonia* can be translated "communion," "fellowship," or "participation." As we gather to sing, pray, confess our sins, and hear God's word, we enter more fully into communion with God and each other; we become something more than we are. Water is not just water. Bread and wine are not just bread and wine. The word is not just a word. And the person sitting next to us is not just another autonomous individual.

Church as *Oikos*

And yet this "more" is often difficult to see. As suggested in the last chapter, late modernity has left us with a profound sense of homelessness. By stripping us of particular traditions, locales, and authorities, and by substituting the free and universal self, it has left the actual self bereft, subject to political and economic forces that it is often hopeless to resist. "Nonplaces" easily dominate our lives. Beneton gives us a particularly vivid account:

> Today, to take a long trip involving a number of flights is to find oneself in
> what seems an interminable hallway. Airports as well as shopping centers,
> "international" hotels, modern train stations, university campuses . . . are all
> built on the same pattern: they are made for the satisfaction of the human
> function. . . . They are without substance, places without history, without
> beauty (with a few exceptions), without any symbolic dimension.[31]

In contrast to such homogeneity, "home" relies upon a concrete sense
of place, a location that I can call "mine" because I identify with it in particular ways. It has formed part of my identity and the identity of those
who are from the same place. Home might be the place we grew up, the
place that is so familiar to us as to be part of who we are. The hills and
longleaf pines of my childhood in North Carolina formed part of my home,
in a way I did not realize until I had to live in a place (northern Indiana)
where pine trees were rare and land was flat.

If the practice of Christian hospitality is to flourish, then, the church
needs to recover a more radical sense of home in the face of modern
homelessness. To assist us in this task, let's look at the Greek word found
in the New Testament for home: *oikos*. First, we can observe that in scripture "home" is not so much a geographical location. Rather "home" or
oikos describes a people before God. In the New Testament, *oikos* can
mean "household," but it can also refer to "a whole clan or tribe of people
descended from a common ancestor"[32] and thus descendants or a nation.
In Luke 1:32–33, for example, the angel Gabriel tells Mary she will bear a
son and says that "he will reign over the house (*oikos*) of Jacob for ever."
In this latter usage, *oikos* does not name a building but rather the people
of Israel who are about to receive a Messiah.[33]

Second, and crucial to understanding Christian hospitality, *oikos* is
identified with the church. The writer of Hebrews identifies those gathered together by Christ as God's house: "Now Moses was faithful in all
God's house as a servant. . . . Christ, however, was faithful over God's
house as a son, and *we are his house*, if we hold fast our confidence"
(Heb. 3:5–6). Similarly, 1 Peter 2:4–5 issues this call: "Come to him, a living stone, rejected by mortals yet chosen and precious in God's sight,
and like living stones, let yourselves be built into a spiritual *house*."
Finally, we read in Ephesians that "through [Christ] both of us [Jews
and Gentiles] have access in one Spirit to the Father. So then you are
no longer strangers and aliens, but you are citizens with the saints and
also members of the *household* of God, built upon the foundation of the
apostles and prophets, with Christ Jesus himself as the cornerstone, . . .
in whom you also are built together spiritually into a dwelling place for
God" (2:18–20, 22). The church itself is God's *oikos*, the dwelling place
of God in the Spirit.

51

This imagery of the church as *oikos* is open to a number of misunderstandings. First of all, the use of *home* in our modern context can seem to underwrite the assumption that religion belongs in a private sphere (the home) versus the public sphere of science, economics, and politics. If this were the case, then Christian hospitality would turn into the kind of domesticated practice criticized in the first chapter—a sentimental or "nice" gesture associated with bland manners and tea parties. The *oikos* of God, however, explodes the modern dichotomy between private and public that so readily tames religion by privatizing it. This *oikos* is not the private place from which we seek to be relevant to the public sphere. As Reinhard Hütter observes, such attempts at relevance have followed the path of reason (Gordon Kaufman), mystical experience or "spirituality" (Matthew Fox), and activism (Dorothy Solle). What these attempts have in common is an effort to legitimate faith by appealing to supposedly more public criteria—in other words, abandoning the ecclesial *oikos* for another "home." In so doing, however, they undermine the "public" that is the ecclesial *oikos*.[34]

As Hütter points out, ecclesial *oikos* is itself a public, where *public* is understood as a place constituted by a set of binding teachings and practices. The *oikos* that is the church is thus not a private or apolitical entity. It is not an *oikos* in contrast to a *polis* (political city). The church is also identified as a political entity, "a holy nation, God's own people" (1 Peter 2:9).[35] In fact, Hütter states that the "*ekklesia* explodes the framework of antique politics which is precisely built on the strict dichotomy between *polis* and *oikos*."[36] John Milbank, from whom Hütter draws, discusses how the ancient conceptions of virtue and politics were built on an antimony between *oikos* and *polis*.[37] Thus politics minimized the *oikos* "as a kind of cultural bypass operation to disassociate continuity and succession from wombs and domestic nurture." A virtue that could be possessed by women in the home could not be a true virtue in the political sense. The connection between the *oikos* and *polis* was "external"; it was mediated by the father since neither women, slaves, nor children were citizens.[38] In such a view, hospitality, as discussed in the previous chapter, becomes identified with women's work and private home space.

By contrast, God's *oikonomia* "becomes tangible in a unique 'space,' a public in its own right. Here those who are by definition excluded from ancient *polis* and relegated to *oikos* (namely, women, children and slaves) become through baptism '*sympolitai*' (citizens) of that unique public." Since all members of the *oikos* are citizens, there is now an internal relation between the *oikos* and *polis*. The practice of baptism initiates one into a unique public space that is at the same time identified as the *oikos* of God, God's *oikonomia*. One is a member of this public space, this community centered on a common good (*polis*), not by heroic excellence but because all "are recipients of divine love and grace."[39]

The overcoming of the dichotomy between private home and public political sphere has profound implications for our understanding of Christian hospitality. It is not simply "women's work" or a practice associated only with our private home. It is not apolitical, but neither can it be defined by contemporary economics or politics. Much less can it be reduced to friendliness. If the church is the *oikos* of Christian hospitality, an *oikos* or home that constitutes a unique public, then the way the church embodies hospitality is not by any of the above distortions, nor by heroic excellence, but by treating all as recipients of divine love. This is not a kind of amorphous, feel-good existence but the challenge of living in the unique space of God's baptized people.

It is important to note that this public household is not simply an open space; it is rather built on the foundation of the "apostles and prophets, with Christ Jesus himself as the cornerstone" (Eph. 2:20). The Holy Spirit joins the structure together and enables its growth. As Hütter points out, *contra* the UCC advertisement, "A totally 'open' space . . . is not a human space and cannot create a coming-together for humans to speak, act and cooperate. . . . Openness in all directions actually destroys any public."[40] Analogously, we could say that hospitality reduced to openness destroys the practice. Dwelling in a totally open space is rather like being homeless. Hospitality without a home (a place) is an oxymoron. How could you be a guest or a host? How would you know what it means to give and receive? In ancient Greece, Hütter observes, what made a public possible was laws; in Judaism, it has been the Torah and the tradition of its interpretation. In Christianity, a new public was initiated at Pentecost, "an eschatological *polis* was gathered." "After initial struggles, it became clear that it was not the *torah* anymore, not the life according to the *mizvot*, that constituted this public. Rather it was constituted christologically and pneumatologically by the *kerygma* and peculiar *practices* (especially the breaking of bread)."[41] The kerygma and the practices were most fully realized (made real) when Christians gathered to worship around both word and table. This gathering makes possible the place of hospitality, a place that is at once *oikos* and *polis.*

To imagine what such place might look like, at this point, we can turn to examples from early Christianity. Gerard Lohfink observes that many houses are "known to us by name simply in connection with the apostolic work and journeys of Paul: the house of Lydia the purple-seller in Philippi, the house of Jason in Thessalonica, those of Titius Justus and Gaius in Corinth, the house of the evangelist Philip in Caesarea, and the house of Mnason of Cyprus in Jerusalem."[42] Lohfink reminds us that these ancient houses were not like our modern ones, isolated units for an individual family. Rather, the house was a larger social unit and frequently a place of production. Life and faith, or work and faith, constituted a unity. Given this, it would have been less likely that faith/worship would be placed in one area or sphere while work, family responsibilities, and daily survival tasks were placed in other spheres. Such an example helps us see that home/hospitality as residing in a private sphere is a modern prejudice.

A second misunderstanding of the church as *oikos* is that the Christian "home" has at times been overidentified with life after death. The words of a popular gospel hymn capture this sentiment, "This world in not my home, I'm just a-passin' through." In a sense, this hymn rightly points to a necessary distinction between church and world. At the same time, however, it is important not to undercut the reality of the church in the world as home. God is *now* gathering people into Christ's body; God is now creating the church through water and the word. This will not take place only in the future (the "not yet"); by God's grace it is taking place now. We are now "fellow citizens with the saints and members of the household of God." To think otherwise is to deny the incarnation, God's becoming embodied in a person, the Son, and through the incarnation (death and resurrection) creating a people, now gifted with the Spirit. God's gatherings of both Israel and the church reflect the fact that salvation is now present, even if the fullness is not yet fully actualized.

At this point, the reader may feel some unease with my characterization of the church as *oikos* and *polis*. In contrast to the church as the dwelling place of God in the Spirit, the church is often wounded, if not outright corrupt. Intense infighting within my own denomination has caused some of my students to want to "do ministry" outside the church. How can our hospitality be faithful when our home is in disarray? I do not wish to deny the unfaithfulness of the church. As Lohfink has noted, one of the deepest wounds on the body of Christ is its disunity.[43] And many today, sometimes justifiably, point to the many sins that darken the holiness of the body. Yet as Philip Kenneson reminds us,

> this [probing and criticizing] is as it should be. The *ekklesia*, as an imperfect anticipation of what God desires for all of creation, seeks to conceal neither its faithfulness nor its unfaithfulness. For if the *ekklesia* exists for God's glory and not its own, then its willingness to name its own faithfulness—as well as have its sinfulness named by others—is itself a form of faithful witness to this God and this God's work.[44]

In lifting up the church as *oikos*, I do not wish to portray a perfect home where everything is in its proper place and no dust can be found by Mr. Clean. Rather, as Kenneson indicates, faithfulness involves learning to name our unfaithfulness and our sin. To dwell in God's *oikos* frees us from having to hide behind a shallow perfection or having to put forth an image that "I" have it all together, both of which are forms of modern individualism. Rather, in the *oikos* of God we are free to speak truthfully because we know that the stability of the *oikos* does not depend upon us. God is the one who does the building: "See, I am laying in Zion a stone, a cornerstone chosen and precious" (1 Peter 2:6). As Hütter points out, "It is precisely the Holy Spirit who creates—as *Spiritus Creator*—that which makes the church possible as a public in its own right: dogma and key practices."[45] That God takes up residence in the *oikos* called church is more about who God is than anything else: a God who through Christ makes the church his body and adopts us as his children, in spite of our sins and failures.

Here we come to perhaps the heart of the matter as concerns the *oikos* of Christian hospitality. In contrast to the modern self who seeks to earn and secure his or her own place, the *oikos* of God is pure gift. In the Lukan passage cited above, Gabriel appears to Mary with the surprising (and initially frightening) gift of God's good news: "Greetings, favored one! The Lord is with you" (Luke 1:28). Mary does not "earn" this encounter and calling, though she has apparently lived a life of openness to God that has prepared her to be able to respond as she does. Initially, it is not at all clear that Mary wants to be so "favored," but she trusts God enough to receive the gift that God gives. Mary exemplifies one who learns to receive and live into the gift of God even when deep mystery surrounds it.

We might be tempted to think that Mary and Abraham are extraordinary characters while we are simply ordinary; thus the radical giftedness of our lives and our place as part of God's people does not apply to us in quite the same way. And we might also think of our many failings: our apathy, our indifference, our sin, our lack of faithfulness. If God's *oikos* is pure gift, have we really received it? But this way of thinking would make our sin and unfaithfulness greater than the grace of God. In baptism, we have been made part of the body of Christ, not through our own effort but by the grace of God. Our membership in God's household, *oikos*, is thus rightly described as a pure gift.

As the familiar hymn asserts, "The church's one foundation is Jesus Christ her Lord. / She is His new creation by water and the Word." To call the church God's new creation is not to announce the purity or perfection of the church. Rather, it is to point to God's creating and redeeming activity in Christ, to the pure self-giving of God, who desires to draw us to himself. To call the church God's new creation is not to idealize the church (anyone who has been part of a particular church for any length of time knows that's hard to do!). It is, however, to confirm "that the Church's existence is always a gift and that that gift is always delivered and shaped by the incarnate, crucified, and risen Jesus."[46] In describing the church as God's new creation, we confess that *we* do not create the church, just as we do not create ourselves. Who we are is pure gift. Of course we fail to receive and respond to this in all sorts of ways, but our failure does not negate the fact that God is creating us anew to be the church for the world.

As we reflect on the *oikos* as the home of Christian hospitality, it is also important to acknowledge that at times God's people are made homeless. Abraham leaves Ur of the Chaldeans, the land that had nurtured and sustained him all his life. Moses and the Israelites wander in the desert for forty years. Job, of course, loses his family, his livestock, and even his health. The disciples leave their homes to follow Jesus. A kind of displacement takes place time and again in the biblical stories, indicating that "home" is not a static or fixed place in scripture. It seems more often that the notion of journey or pilgrimage prevails. This displacement and journeying suggest that "home" in scripture is always dynamic. Abraham did lose his home in Ur, but he did so in order to find his home more fully before God and with God's people. That home is so understood means that it is defined by time as much as it is by space. Abraham, in responding to God's promises, enters God's time. He knows he will have descendants as numerous as the stars, but he does not know when. He lives in between the time of the "now" and "not yet" of God's promises. We could say that God calls Abraham to a place where there are no foundations. Abraham's place before God does not allow him to have full knowledge of the end of the journey; he cannot possibly imagine what it means that God will make him a "great and mighty nation, and [that] all the nations of the earth shall be blessed in him" (Gen. 18:18). We could say that Abraham's place is in God's cosmic drama; Abraham responds in faith to what God is doing in the world. So also, to be members of God's *oikos* is to participate in this same drama—creation, covenant, Christ, and church—the consummation of which is yet to come.

Recovery of a sense of our dwelling (*oikos*) and participation in this drama is crucial for Christian hospitality. Beneton notes how our late modern way of seeing and thinking has flattened and debased life. "For the Greeks," Beneton writes, "life was a tragedy and for the Christians, a drama. For the moderns led astray by ideology, life was a melodrama (the happy ending guaranteed). For the moderns of late modernity, life is no more than a trivial TV series."[47] Worship reduced to good feelings or entertainment has clearly succumbed to the TV-series mentality of late modernity. In contrast to mere entertainment, the *oikos* of Christian hospitality draws us into a drama much larger than ourselves: nothing less than God's own drama of creating and redeeming the world in Christ.

56

Liturgical Hospitality as Strange

Liturgy means literally "the work of the people." My use of *liturgy* is meant to indicate not just any worship service but the "recognizable continuation of the historic forms of Word and Table."[48] If *church* names our joining together in the household of God, then *worship* names the way we participate in God's own hospitality. To the extent that worship is our participation in our triune God's mutual giving, worship itself is hospitality. We enter God's home as God's adopted children; we become the home for God, "the fullness of [Christ] who fills all in all" (Eph. 1:23). Certainly Christians practice hospitality at other times, but these other times flow out of the hospitality that is worship. As the title of this chapter suggests, such hospitality is strange, since it is dependent upon our worship of a strange God. I use *strange* here simply to remind us that God is not easily domesticated or reduced to something we can manage or control. The winds of the Spirit blow where they will. Worship ought to train us not to try to control God but to receive from God, no matter how strange or terrifying God might seem. Like Jacob wrestling with God on the banks of the Jabbok, worship in the household of God ought to provide us with the space to encounter and even wrestle with the Divine Stranger.

The liturgy, says Don Saliers, "invites us to a 'home where none of us has ever been.'"[49] On first reading, this statement sounds odd. How can a place be "home" if we haven't been there? Saliers is plumbing the mystery of worship, but *mystery* in this instance does not mean "perplexing" (though it may be that). Wendell Berry notes that modernity thinks of mystery as the "unknown = the to-be-known," and as therefore "attributable entirely to human ignorance."[50] Yet *mystery* can also mean something so rich and so profound that we can never get to the bottom of it; *mystery* applied to God describes the inexhaustible love of God that can never be "used up."

Saliers's description of a home-to-be is enacted in various biblical stories. Abraham is called to a home where he has never been, as are Moses, Mary, the disciples, and many others. They leave a familiar place in order to take up a new place before God. Their journey "home" means they are leaning into the mysterious promises and abundance of God. God's words to Moses drive home this theme: "God will provide." Liturgy too, as discussed earlier, is a journey home; as we worship together, we lean into the mysterious fullness of God, an abundance so profound and deep that it is beyond our grasp. Odo Casel uses the words *mystery* and *liturgy* together:

> When we place the words "mystery" and "liturgy" side by side, and take mystery as mystery of worship, they will mean the same thing considered

from two different points of view. *Mystery* means the heart of the action, that is to say, the redeeming work of the risen Lord, through the sacred actions he has appointed: liturgy, corresponding to its original sense of "people's work," "service," means rather the action of the church in conjunction with this saving action of Christ's.[51]

Mystery acknowledges the fact that God is the primary actor. But even *actor* seems a bit too domesticated here, since when we hear that word we readily think of the folks on TV. God is strange; God is surprising; God is faithful. In worship, we enter this drama with God, as did Abraham, as did Moses, as did Mary. In this liturgical drama, we begin to see what it means to receive the stranger.

Gregory of Nyssa beautifully captures the strangeness and mysterious abundance of God as he compares the contemplation of God with a person looking at a bubbling spring:

> As you came near the spring you would marvel, seeing that the water was endless, as it constantly gushed up and poured forth. Yet you could never say that you had seen all the water. How could you see what was still hidden in the bosom of the earth? Hence no matter how long you might stay at the spring, you would always be beginning to see the water. . . . It is the same with one who fixes his gaze on the infinite beauty of God. It is constantly being discovered anew, and it is always seen as something new and strange in comparison with what the mind has already understood. And as God continues to reveal himself, man continues to wonder; and he never exhausts his desire to see more, since what he is waiting for is always more magnificent, more divine, than all that he has already seen.[52]

This passage powerfully captures the strange abundance of God—the endless supply of water and the continual freshness of the spring. The infinite beauty of God "is always seen as something new and strange in comparison with what the mind has already understood."

To say the liturgy is a home where none of us has been and to refer to God's beauty as always "new" and "strange" reminds us that God cannot be domesticated. As God's *oikos*, we are called to participate in God's abundance and to be ready to receive God, no matter how surprising we might find God's presence. Nothing is stranger than God's presence among us as Christ's body and our incorporation in this body. Nothing is stranger than our own identity as members (citizens) with the saints and the prophets of God's household. Nothing is stranger than the identification of the church with the fullness of Christ (Eph. 1:22). In worship we encounter a strange and extraordinary hospitality, a hospitality we are invited to be a part of both for the church and for the world.

Of course *we* are also the world. It is not as if "church" and "world" existed in isolated, pristine spheres. It is through the church, however, that we learn rightly to see and name the world, both in its goodness as God's creation and in its sin. As Karl Barth has said, "The more seriously and joyfully we believe in Him, the more we shall see such signs in the worldly sphere, and the more we shall be able to receive true words from it."[53] Such a passage points to how our deeper reception of God's hospitality enables us both to see and to receive God in "the world."

A deep reception of God's hospitality also enables us to see how we share the sins of the world. This is why worship can make us strangers to ourselves. God's hospitality can be "inhospitable" by contemporary standards; it can make us feel not "at home." The process of becoming guests and also hosts of God is not necessarily easy or smooth. According to Rowan Williams, Teresa of Ávila "assumes that we are likely to be strangers to ourselves and that we (like her beloved Augustine) need a measure of divine violence to be brought home."[54] Williams's rather startling phrase "divine violence" alerts us to the shock or fear we might experience before the grace of God. Worship trains us to see that God's hospitality may comfort us, but worship also helps us see that God's hospitality has the potential to terrify. Moses before the burning bush comes to mind. At the same time, we can take another cue from Teresa of Ávila when she maintains that God gives us all the grace we need to become both Martha and Mary (both hosts who serve and guests who wait).[55]

Liturgical Hospitality as Joyful

Swiss Reformed theologian Jean-Jacques von Allmen characterizes the liturgy as "an eschatological game." The use of *game* can easily lead to an image of worship as trivial and non-serious, as in "it's just a game." Von Allmen means, however, that like a game worship has rules. Worship's rules are commensurate with our being God's redeemed creatures. Since many generations have played the game, the moves are well tried. At the same time, within such rules there is room for improvisation. And like other games, worship has its own purpose, which is humankind's chief end, "to glorify God and enjoy Him forever."[56]

So *game*, used in this sense, does not trivialize worship but captures the joy and playfulness that ought to mark our gatherings. Worship is not all somber, for it involves a joyful participation in what God is doing in the world, a participation made possible through the Holy Spirit. The language of "game" is not intended to deny the rightful place of lament in worship, nor is it meant to suggest we have to put on a forced happy face. But it is to say that through this gathering and these actions (preaching, praying, baptizing, eating the body and blood) we enter more fully into God's own past, present, and future. The drama of God's work is not finally a tragic one; it is marked by resurrection and new life in Christ—an eschatological game.

Game, playfulness, and joy are closely related to the whole idea of *gift*. Children's birthdays combine all of these elements in a festive celebration. (Having just celebrated both of my children's birthdays, however, I am reminded that they can also quickly become rather raucous, unruly affairs!) Similarly, worship is both a serious, joyful game we play and a gift we receive. Through worship, God invites us to become a people. And not only does God invite us, but God gives us the desire and the means to be what God intends for us to be and do. In her essay "Praying: Poverty," Kelly S. Johnson compares the Prayer of the Faithful in worship to an encore in the live performance of a concert. "Having heard God's deeds, the congregation responds in hope, hungry for more; but it is God who has created that hunger and hope, in something like the way the band moves the crowd to want more. God gives the Church the role of calling for what God intends to give."[57] God gives us the grace to call for his word and body, which God in fact desires to give. God gives us the grace to see our sins and to ask for forgiveness because God desires to give forgiveness.

Yet worship is not only receiving a gift; it is also a gift exchange. In response to God, we give ourselves, our gifts, our needs, our wealth, our poverty. It might seem counterintuitive to treat "needs" and "poverty" as gifts, and I am hesitant to use the word *poverty*. I do not wish to describe involuntary material poverty as a blessing. But *poverty* can also refer to those ways in which we are weak or in deep need, or it can refer simply to the fact that we are "little" and ordinary.[58] In any case, in worship we learn, haltingly and by fits and starts, to give ourselves to God. To call worship "hospitality" is to point to a particular kind of giving and receiving that constitutes our lives with God.

We must not, however, make too much of a distinction *between* giving and receiving, for too sharp a distinction would lead us to misconstrue worship and thus distort hospitality. Our giving is never just "ours," nor for that matter can we claim our "receiving" as solely what we do. Christian hospitality is not primarily about what we do. Rather, hospitality and worship are better thought of as our participation in God's own communion, God's own giving and receiving, made possible in Christ through the Holy Spirit. Hospitality is our participation in what God is doing. It is in this spirit that Milbank emphasizes the unity of faith (as Luther understood it, that is, trust) and charity. "I exist in receiving; because I receive I joyfully give, and one can add to Luther a more Catholic stress that one can only receive God who is charity, by sharing *in* the giving of this charity—faith *is* (against Luther) from the outset a *habitus* and from the outset the work of charity, our work only in so far as it is God's."[59] I quote this passage because it suggests that we cannot draw a clear line between our receiving and our giving. Even our giving is not "ours" but a sharing in what God is doing. Our worship is possible only because God gathers us and gifts us with the capacity to worship. Even more, God does not give to us only as individuals (for our own sakes) but God gives to the church as a whole.[60] Truly to receive from God is to be made part of a people, called to worship, to give and to receive for and on behalf of the world.

This dynamic of giving and receiving can be seen when Jesus teaches his disciples to pray, "Our Father, who art in heaven . . ." Through this prayer, the disciples learn to enter into the communion that Jesus has with the Father. The disciples are adopted into this communion (what Jesus is by nature, as one early theologian said, we are by adoption). In learning to pray in this way and thus receive from Jesus, the disciples participate in the Son's gift (offering) to the Father. In receiving from Jesus, the disciples learn to give. We know of course from scripture that this dynamic of learning to receive and give is a journey; the disciples at times falter and fall, but nonetheless (minus Judas) they continue on until, as the church later realizes, God had made them holy. This emphasis on worship as participation in God's giving and receiving highlights, then, not the disciples' strengths or even their "gifts" but the grace and abundance of God. To refer again to Milbank:

> Without the virtue of worship there can be no other virtue, for worship gives everything back up to God, hangs onto nothing and so *disallows* any finite accumulation which will always engender conflict. Confident worship also knows that in offering it receives back, so here the temporal world is not denied, but its temporality is restored as gift and thereby rendered eternal.[61]

In worship, we learn to "hang onto nothing." Worship enables us to embody the fact that our lives, the church, and the created world are gifts from God; we ourselves are totally dependent on the giving and receiving love of God. This dependence is not bad news, our culture's emphasis on independence to the contrary. Rather, such communion is the way we become more fully the body of Christ. Such liturgical hospitality is marked by joy and gratitude, one might even say celebration, as long as it does not become too raucous and unruly, like my children's birthday parties.

Rehabituation Revisited

In this final section, I would like to draw our attention more fully to how worship can form us in concrete ways to practice God's hospitality.

The use of *rehabituation* is significant, as practicing hospitality or any other Christian practice entails not only thinking differently but also developing alternative habits. Worship itself is a habit. It is not just having thoughts about God; it is learning how to be together bodily in ways that enable us to be faithful. In fact, Fergus Kerr reminds us that "it is *because* people exult and lament, sing for joy, bewail their sins and so on, that they are able, eventually, to have thoughts about God."[62] Often this "body training" is taken for granted, a point that sometimes becomes obvious when we witness "unchurched" people in church. Years ago, my husband was overseeing a wedding rehearsal in our small sanctuary when one of the groom's ushers pulled out a cigarette and lit up. He obviously thought nothing of it and regarded this space as like any other, no different for him from a local bar. Without liturgical training, we will have a difficult time worshiping God, since worship involves an embodied way of being in space and time. Mother Teresa once said, "Teach your children to pray. Parents need to pray with their children. If they don't, it will be difficult for the children to become holy."[63] Being habituated to a life of prayer is part of what it means to become holy. And positioning our bodies in certain ways—open palms, bended knees, head bowed, or prostrate on the floor—is part of praying.

But what, we might ask, are the bodily gestures and habits that sustain the practice of hospitality? What kinds of gestures and manners ought to form the way we welcome another? the way we receive from and give to another? Donald Trump apparently will not shake hands with people for fear of catching germs and getting sick. One of the parishioners in a church I used to attend wanted my husband (pastor at the time) to wear surgical gloves when he presided over the Lord's Table. Theologian Gilbert Bond contrasts the welcoming white gloves in one Baptist congregation with the yellow latex gloves used by members of this same church to search homeless men who want to stay in its shelter; his essay highlights the fact that liturgical gestures may not yet be deeply engrained habits.[64] So we must admit that the gestures and habits of worship might be only superficially formative. If so, this is because other kinds of bodily formation are taking place. Nevertheless, calling attention to liturgy as hospitality and therefore to worship as the primary ritualized place where we learn the manners of God's hospitable kingdom is to enable us to *remember* in our bodies what Christian hospitality is.

"Remembering in our bodies" might strike some as initially an odd phenomenon, as we tend to think that we remember in our mind, or with our head. Yet often our "body" remembers before we remember in our "head." For anyone who has ever played a musical instrument, this experience is commonplace. We may not remember beforehand exactly how a piece of music is supposed to go, but if we sit down and start playing, it comes back to us. Our fingers remember what our mind forgot. One of my favorite examples of this comes from the life of Helen Keller, who as a young twelve-year-old girl wrote a poem entitled "The Frost King" that received much attention and was even published. Later, it was found out that she had plagiarized, much to her bitter astonishment and embarrassment. Yet she denied doing this. After much searching, Helen and her teacher, Annie Sullivan, discovered that the poem had probably been signed to Helen *once*, four years earlier during a brief period when Helen stayed with another woman while Sullivan was on vacation. She later wrote in her autobiography,

> The stories had little or no meaning for me then; but the mere spelling of the strange words was sufficient to amuse a little child who could do almost nothing to amuse herself; and although I do not recall a single circumstance connected with the reading of the stories, yet I cannot help thinking that I made a great effort to remember the words, with the intention of having my teacher explain them when she returned.[65]

Desperate to learn and make contact with the world, Helen Keller's body remembered the poem.

Like playing the piano or writing a poem, worship is an embodied affair. This could go without saying, except for the fact that we often tend to reduce worship to an exchange of ideas or to an experience that ought to generate certain feelings. In worship, however, our bodies learn to remember, through hearing, seeing, touching, and tasting. Schmemann, quoting Ludwig Feuerbach, writes that "man is what he eats."[66] Feuerbach intended this to mean that human beings and the material world are all there is. Schmemann, however, means that through eating and drinking the eucharistic body and blood, we become that body; through Communion, we become communion. Or as Susan White states, "If you 'partake' of the liturgical life of the Church, then you are gradually transformed by its words, images and gestures. In both Eucharist and Baptism, then, our bodies are 're-created' so that they might become vehicles for righteousness, prepared for a lively response to the will of God."[67] To be re-created by God in and through the life of the church involves all of who we are; this means our bodies are transformed such that we become vehicles for God. We learn in and through our bodies how to receive God more fully. St. Paul appeals to his brothers and sisters in Christ "to present your bodies as a living sacrifice, holy and acceptable to God, which is your spiritual worship" (Rom. 12:1).

Worship, then, is ordered so that we are bodily trained to receive from and give to God. Training is required because communion with God is not "natural," in the sense that we know on our own how to receive God's gifts. My young son, for example, is still learning not to grab a fistful of bread from the Communion loaf. Worship, of course, varies widely across different traditions. And some traditions enact this bodily formation differently from (and sometimes better than) others. In what follows, I want to focus on aspects of the liturgy that tend to be common to most traditions. My purpose is to show how the habits of the liturgy can form us in the practice of hospitality.

Passing the Peace, Passing Hospitality

It is interesting that the examples cited above (Trump, surgical gloves, white and latex gloves) all had to do with hands, and further, with not wanting to have to touch people directly. Most of us can identify with this resistance to some extent. Who wants to put themselves at risk by touching another, particularly if the other might be sick? The passing of the peace in worship, however, overcomes this hesitancy to touch another. Here we are asked to welcome the other through touch. Why not just welcome with words instead of touch? In earlier times, passing the peace was actually passing the *kiss* of peace. In Justin Martyr's account, the kiss of peace for the neophyte was exchanged after baptism and before his or her first Communion. Edward Phillips has argued that the kiss of peace was "a ritual enactment of the sharing of the *pneuma* among believers that delineated the boundaries of the community, much in the way that the kiss could delineate family boundaries." In other words, the kiss was a way of enacting one's membership in the family of God, the church. Phillips even states that the Spirit was "communicated through the mouth of one believer to another."[68] Needless to say, most of us today would have a hard time with such a practice. Even so, the kiss was a way of passing the peace and of signaling (and creating) a unity with Christ, "a unity which made brothers and sisters of persons unrelated by blood."[69]

Some traditions today (the Orthodox, for example) still include the kiss, but most are in the habit of extending the hand. Like the kiss, the hand, especially in scripture, is associated with the power of the Spirit and with healing. Jesus, of course, touches people in order to heal them. The well-known story of the hemorrhaging woman who "secretly" touches Jesus shows how central the power of touch is in the Gospel accounts: touching the body of Christ has the power to heal. Thomas touches Jesus not for physical healing but for evidence that he is indeed the risen Christ: touching the body of Christ has the power to convict. Through the touch of baptism, in fact, we are physically linked to the hemorrhaging woman, Thomas and the other disciples, and, of course, Christ himself. If we did not touch each other, our worship would easily become a private

64

affair, a purely spiritual phenomenon, or some mode of disembodied gnosticism.

As we touch each other in the passing of the peace, then, this gesture is not merely a symbol of peace, and thus one remove from real peace. Rather, we are in fact giving and receiving the peace of Christ; the Holy Spirit, as Phillips states, is communicated through touching.

There is a story, originally told by Vincent Donovan and often repeated, about a tribe in East Africa called the Masai who converted to Christianity. The Masai raised cattle, and since both the cattle and the Masai themselves lived off grass, it was a holy sign to them, "a sign of peace and happiness and well-being." Whenever Donovan entered a Masai village, he would pick up a handful of grass and present it to the elders. During stormy arguments that might arise, a tuft of grass from one party presented to another was an assurance that violence would not erupt over their differences. As Donovan writes: "No Masai would violate that sacred sign of peace offered, because it was not only a *sign* of peace; it *was* peace."[70] It did not, in other words, symbolize a hoped-for peace; rather the offering of grass was itself the way that peace was bodily exchanged with the neighbor.[71] Donovan goes on to recount how the passing of grass became for the Masai the passing of peace in the Mass. And if for some reason the grass could not be passed, then the Eucharist was not celebrated.

The passing of peace, then, stands in stark contrast to and judgment of violent, exploitative, or indifferent gestures. We may not even particularly like the person with whom we exchange the peace, but in this case the gesture reminds us that "liking" is not what binds the community together. To pass the peace is to allow ourselves to be bound to others by more than our fickle likes and dislikes. In passing the peace of Christ, we train our bodies to rely on that peace to transform our dislikes, our hatred, and our propensity toward violence.

Such training is, of course, also training in hospitality, a practice sustained and made possible by the gift of Christ, who is himself our peace. Touching another is a way of passing on the love and peace of Christ. Just as hospitality differs from friendliness, so too the passing of peace is more than a friendly handshake. It is rather a way of participating in and making present the peace of Christ. Neither can the passing of peace be reduced to a kind of market exchange, as if one had to earn the peace. It is freely given, freely received. Finally, the passing of the peace is not inclusive in any sort of generic sense. In fact, as Phillips indicates, the earlier kiss of peace (passed only between those who were baptized) delineated boundaries in much the same way a kiss might delineate family boundaries today. While this practice of the kiss of peace is no longer in place (as far as I know), the passing of the peace still delineates boundaries. As the Masai rightly understood, if you cannot become reconciled with your neighbor, then you cannot pass the grass. The boundary in this case excludes those who are unwilling to forgive. How can you exchange the peace of Christ through gesture and touch if you hate your brother or sister? The body itself would register the contradiction. Stated more biblically, you would be bringing judgment upon yourself, passing the peace to your own condemnation (1 Cor. 11:34).

The grandmother in Flannery O'Connor's short story, discussed in a previous chapter, reaches out in the final scene and touches the misfit, a cold-blooded killer. Even though her peace is violently rejected (a boundary), she nonetheless embodies the peace of Christ as more than merely a nice gesture. It is profoundly powerful, casting light in the darkness of our sin and our hatred.

Hymn Singing and Hospitality

While hymn singing is not associated with a particular gesture, as is passing the peace, it is nonetheless a full-bodied act. Within some of our traditions, it is one of the few times during worship when we actually move. "Singing is physical. It is an action of the body. It involves vocal cords, the ears, the mouth. We cannot sing 'lustily and with good courage' from the head up."[72]

Upon first consideration, hymn singing might seem like an odd place to turn to consider habits and gestures germane to a robust sense of hospitality. What do hospitality and hymn singing have to do with each other? To begin to respond to this question, we must consider how gift giving is central to the singing of hymns. Randy Cooper celebrates congregational singing as "a gift of God given to the Church as part of God's plan for bringing all things to Christ."[73] As we sing hymns, we are bodily trained to receive the gift of song and in this very reception return to God—with voice, mouth, and ears—our own gift of gratitude and praise. It is a testimony to the formative power of hymn singing that John Wesley was able, on his deathbed, haltingly to sing,

> I'll praise my Maker while I've breath;
> And when my voice is lost in death,
> Praise shall employ my nobler powers.
> My days of praise shall ne'er be past,
> While life, and thought, and being last,
> Or immortality endures.

The habit of singing hymns enabled Wesley even as he was dying, his body weakened, to sing praises to God. Through hymn singing (though not by itself) Wesley had developed the habit of gratitude. Congregational singing of hymns such as "Amazing Grace," "What Wondrous Love Is This," "And Can It Be That I Should Gain," "Leaning on the Everlasting Arms," and countless others trains us to be a grateful people, relying upon God for sustenance and strength.

Further, congregational singing reminds us that we are not to be passive recipients before God. Congregants usually stand to sing, and such activity reminds us that God desires a *dynamic* response. We are created not as "minds" that happen to have bodies but as whole persons. Thus, singing trains us to see that our response to God involves all of who we are. For example, the Masai felt free to incorporate some of their dances into their worship, as a way to enjoy and give glory to God.[74] Most churches in North American culture tend to be more restrained (with the exception of some communions, such as some African-American churches). In any case, singing can remind us that worship is not a head game. Part of learning to pray is learning to sing hymns, since, as Augustine once said, singing is praying twice. Through hymn singing, we allow ourselves to become praying and praising creatures: bodies of gratitude.

In emphasizing the singing of praises and the habit of gratitude, I do not wish to deny the important place of lament in worship. And there are certainly hymns of lament. "Were You There When They Crucified My Lord?" comes to mind. The hospitality to which we are habituated through hymn singing is not simply the "smiley face" or "rose-colored glasses" variety. Most hymns tell the Christian story, which includes the story of suffering, exile, and crucifixion. To be formed to live in gratitude to God is not to turn a blind eye to suffering, struggle, evil, and death. "Come, O Thou Traveler Unknown," for example, tells the story of Jacob wrestling with the mysterious angel:

> I need not tell thee who I am,
> My misery and sin declare;
> Thyself hast called me by my name,
> Look on thy hands and read it there. . .

Lament and struggle, however, do not negate gratitude but enable us to place ourselves more deeply in the drama between the now and the not yet. We live lives of gratitude not out of some false optimism but because we pray/know/sing that the God we worship has overcome death and suffering. God has, as the Orthodox sing, "trampled down death by death."

Finally, congregational singing means that bodies from different places gather "in one place and time to make music as *one Body*," and thus we are at the same time "learning mutual submission to one another."[75] The unity of residing in God's house (*oikos*) depends upon our learning to be mutually submissive. Inasmuch as hymn singing trains us in this way, it builds up the unity of the body of Christ.

Yet even as I write this, it seems like a tall order. *Submission* is not a popular word these days, particularly for women, since it has been and continues to be used in ways that reinforce a chain of command of man over woman. Even more, in a culture that emphasizes "doing your own thing" and "charting your own path," it is often difficult even to know what mutual submission might look like. We are more familiar (and usually more comfortable) with learning to assert ourselves than learning to be submissive.

Just the same, hymn singing requires submission. We have probably all had the experience of being in a congregation in which people were mistakenly singing different parts of a hymn, resulting in a cacophony of sound. We have also experienced occasions when folks were trying to sing an unfamiliar hymn and everyone was slightly off. Of course, this happens at any gathering where people sing. How is *hymn* singing different? Cooper points us in the right direction: "The home for the practice of mutual subjection is worship, and the habitual practice of mutual subjection is the face to face communication of singing and giving thanks before God and one another."[76] Hymn singing forms us to see that mutual submission is not an end in itself; rather, we practice mutual submission in order to glorify God with one harmonious voice. We listen to each other and seek to harmonize our voices (or get in sync) so that we may praise God. Some are able to sing better than others, and those with weaker voices are sometimes tempted to not sing. But as Dietrich Bonhoeffer reminds us in his significantly titled *Life Together*, to refuse to sing at all is to refuse the gift of praise. On the other hand, to sing out too loudly is also to fail to submit your voice to those around you. At an experiential level, it is always surprising to me how strong a congregation can sound together, even though individually most of the congregants might have weak voices. Mutual submission means that we look to one another in order to receive strength to pray and praise God together.

Training in mutual submission is key for hospitality as well in that it forms us to be faithful guests and hosts. As others who have written on hospitality have pointed out, "guests" and "hosts" are fluid roles that ought to change and shift dynamically.[77] If someone always has to be the host, it quickly becomes oppressive for the other guests; such giving can easily become a way of controlling others. Or if someone is always a guest, the others never receive what this particular person has to give. Stated in more Christian terms: as "guests" and "hosts" in the body of Christ, we acknowledge both our needs and our gifts as contributions to the larger body. In fact, our need may turn out to be a kind of gift, as it allows others an opportunity to give.

My husband once planned to cancel a Good Friday service when I was ill and in the hospital. The members of our congregation were not "liturgically trained," but this fact did not prevent them from deciding that this cancellation was not "right." They gathered anyway, offering prayers for me. I daresay this was the first time any of them had ever planned a Good Friday service. In this instance, they offered a gift they didn't know they had. Even more, they practiced mutual submission as they looked toward one another and toward the needs of Christ's body.

This congregation never was particularly good at hymn singing, and some of our members, contrary to Bonhoeffer's advice, refused to sing (at least for the eleven years we were with them). Every so often my husband would read John Wesley's instructions on singing "lustily," which are printed in the front of the United Methodist Hymnal. For that one Sunday, the singing would sound more robust, but it usually returned to "normal" the following Sunday. This congregation prayed together better than they sang (though singing too is a form of praying), and our prayer-request time on Sundays would sometimes go on for ten or fifteen minutes.

Prayer, whether spoken or sung, trains us to let go of our independence, to speak our needs in public, to confess our dependence on God and one another, and to voice aloud our deep gratitude. In doing so, we become members one of another, more fully capable of practicing the hospitality of God, such that we are able to offer (or receive) gifts that we might not have known we had.

Part 2

Hospitality as a Vigilant Practice

■ Hospitality as liturgical training is not in and of itself sufficient. We live in a culture that daily assaults us with ideologies and powers that fracture and distort our ability to practice the hospitality of God. Discipleship is a lifelong journey, a "process of reconfiguration," and an "ongoing activity, requiring vigilance to resist the atrophy that comes with disuse as well as to resist those powers that would reconfigure us differently."[1] Chapters 3 through 5 can be read as an exercise in such vigilance as I explore how the practice of Christian hospitality enables us to resist the powers and ideologies that would configure and *already have* configured us differently. In what follows, I focus specifically on (1) science and economics, (2) ethics, and (3) politics and education. In each of these chapters, I argue that Christian hospitality, rightly understood and practiced, challenges the way we have come to think about and live in these "domains." These domains, of course, are deeply interrelated; they have to do with our home (*oikos*, from which we get *economics*), our way of life (*ethos*, the root of *ethics*), and our community (*polis*, which gives us *politics*). Christian hospitality gives us a vigilant place to stand to see how easily various cultural assumptions and practices can distort our lives. Free of such distortions, we can begin to see how hospitality is a practice at once liturgical, economic, ethical, and political. In this section, I draw specifically on the theological virtues of faith, hope, and love to show how we might practice a hospitality more faithful to the gospel.

The Challenge of Science and Economics

How the *Faith* of Hospitality Tells a Different Story

■ In this and the following two chapters, I suggest that we think about hospitality as a *vigilant* practice: a practice that helps us keep watch lest our lives degenerate into unfaithfulness. In 1 Peter, the author tells the early Christians that they are now a people, a holy priesthood, living stones who are being built into God's spiritual house. At the same time, the author reminds his readers to "be alert and of sober mind. Your enemy the devil prowls around like a roaring lion looking for someone to devour" (1 Peter 5:8 TNIV). The author perceives that it is not just individuals but the church that is under attack: "your brothers and sisters in all the world" are undergoing similar suffering. Peter identifies the church with God's house, thus indicating that the "home" of hospitality is under threat. Peter's charge to these early Christians is to be vigilant and resist, lest some be devoured. We are called to no less a resistance still today.

For some people, the notion that the church is under threat of attack might seem far removed from their experience of the church today, especially the church in the United States. Yet the fact that hospitality and other Christian practices can become easily domesticated and distorted in our context suggests that the church has unwittingly given itself over to hostile forces, often unnamed and therefore unrecognized. Peter's words apply to our situation as well: be on guard, be watchful, be prepared to resist.

Vigilance, however, does not come naturally, but requires discipline. *Military* vigilance, for example, involves extensive training. In the words of Therese Lysaught: "What is required is a physical and physically grueling program of drills, penalties, uniforms, and communal living designed not only to deconstructively break recruits of any vestiges of individuality but also to constructively produce military bodies."[1] After such intense training, soldiers usually carry themselves differently, showing in their bodies their mental and physical preparedness to fight the enemy. "Bodies so produced often are so for the duration; military bodies are easy to pick out of a crowd—standing, sitting, walking, speaking in a particular way—even if the person left the military long ago."[2] In contrast to military training, however, Peter links the church's resistance not to killing but to steadfastness in the faith and willingness to suffer. "Resist him, steadfast in your faith, for you know that your brothers and sisters in all the world are undergoing the same kinds of suffering" (1 Peter 5:9).

Like military training, then, hospitality requires training, only this training involves learning how to be steadfast in the faith while knowing how to resist that which obstructs the hospitality of God, a resistance that might well call for a willingness to suffer. Now hospitality and resistance *seem* like opposing actions. Certainly if one is equating hospitality with sheer inclusivity, resistance makes little sense. Yet resistance and exclusion are not necessarily opposed to Christian hospitality but can be expressions of it. In John's Gospel, Jesus resists the desecration of the temple. He tells the money changers, "Stop making my Father's house a marketplace!" and his disciples relate this to the psalmist's cry, "Zeal for your house will consume me" (John 2:16–17).[3] From a sentimental perspective, Jesus's harsh action of driving out the buyers and sellers with a whip of cords hardly seems like a hospitable act. He is not being nice; he is not being inclusive. But he is being vigilant. His actions indicate that without a place and people faithful to God, the *oikos* (home) will degenerate into a place that fails to reveal God's glory. If this happens, the practice of Christian hospitality will also quickly decline. In this Johannine passage, it is of course significant that the temple is identified with Christ's resurrected body, a body that not only reveals the glory of God but becomes the place of Christian hospitality, a place that gives us "access in one Spirit to the Father" (Eph. 2:18). The triune reference reminds us yet again that hospitality is nothing other than our learning to receive through the Spirit and the Son the generous overflow of God's own bountiful gifts.

Let us consider more fully, however, the scientific and economic forces that would diminish this place of Christian hospitality.

"A Flight from the Earth"

Years ago, as a student chaplain at a local hospital in Louisville, Kentucky, I sat in the room of an elderly black woman. A group of about ten medical students entered, led by their attending physician. This was obviously a training session: the physician discussed the woman's symptoms with the medical students at some length. They talked about her as if she were not in the room. Several times she asked them questions that were simply ignored. After finishing their medical business, they left.

The students and physician were not being intentionally rude; they actually saw nothing amiss in the way they were acting. They were simply following the rules of medical education, at least the rules at this particular teaching institution. The elderly woman, in this instance, was not a person but rather an object of study. Needless to say, in this *hospital* they were unable to offer her *hospitality*, unable to respond to her as a suffering guest, unable to receive her words and thus respond to her as a person rather than a "mere" patient.[4]

I tell this story not to indict the medical profession. Certainly there are doctors and administrators of medical institutions who would be disturbed by the above scenario. But the story does illustrate how scientism—the elevation of science as the determination of the real—abstracts us from the particular worlds in which we live and move and breathe. The woman in the above story was an object, abstracted from any bond or covenant she might share with the physician and medical students.

In what follows, we shall look more closely at the challenge of science and economics in order to discern more fully the faithful practice of hospitality. While these fields no doubt cover a very wide area, I wish to zero in on one dimension that is common to both: what Hannah Arendt calls the "twofold flight from the earth into the universe and from the world into the self."[5] This flight from the earth, exemplified in the drift toward scientism (the belief that only the world scientifically understood is real), leads to a "faith" that is otherworldly. While this claim sounds counterintuitive, such "scientific" faith alienates and detaches the self from the particular covenantal bonds that sustain it. The physician and medical students in the above story were detached from the patient, yet without her their profession would obviously collapse. One might argue that there will come a day when we can rely completely on medical technology to treat people; it's not too difficult to imagine, for example, that computerized robots might fix certain ailments, with the doctor functioning as a distant technician. Yet this would only exemplify the detachment of scientism. Technologized medicine would be even less likely to respond to the anxious questions of an elderly woman; it would be unable to respond to and empathize with the suffering of the ill and infirm.

Our market economy with its relentless promotion of consumerism also manifests Arendt's "flight from the earth." Similar to scientific objectivism, our modern capitalist economy leads people to detach themselves from the concrete places and communities that constitute their lives. No longer bound by time or place, we easily come to think of ourselves as unlimited. Ragan Sutterfield describes our current economy as "immanent" (in contrast to "transcendent"). Such an economy denies that "nature" has any limits that would shape "our lives as creatures and how we use and care for the gift of creation."[6] An immanent economy is "marked by a denial of cultural, spatial, natural and physical limits." This understanding of the economy owes a debt to science: "Modern science, which has always been an ally of the immanent economy, began with a denial of limits."[7] In science and economics so described, there has been a relentless attempt to free humans (and reason) from tradition, place, and the historical material world. No doubt overcoming some limits, such as various illnesses, is a great good; scientism, however, would have us believe that science will eventually rescue us from all limits.

The key point here is that our scientific/economic culture forms us to live lives of detachment. As David McCarthy puts it, "There is a desire to be free and to detach ourselves from the people and things that bind us in the world."[8] We must be ready to move if the market requires us to do so. We must see patients as problems to cure rather than persons who call for care. Wendell Berry notes that even the language we use to refer to where we are, words like *surroundings* and *environment*, betrays a certain detachment. "Environment," says Berry, "refers to a place that one is *in* but not *of*."[9] In the South where I grew up, it was common for people to ask, "Where are you from?" The inquirer didn't want to know where the house you presently live in is located. He or she wanted to know, rather, what place has formed you and given you roots. People today have a harder time knowing what to make of that question. It's not uncommon to hear "I'm not really from anywhere. I lived here and here and here." Yet the interlocutor is hardly to blame; she is formed by an immanent economy that detaches us from particular places and asks us to move where the market calls.

Those who criticize our dominant economic cultures are sometimes accused of nostalgia for a supposedly simpler and better time. Berry himself could be read in this light, especially when he praises the Amish as people whose concrete practices have enabled the survival of small family farms—particular places not yet erased by a global economy.[10]

Yet Berry is quick to clarify that he is not recommending that all farmers become Amish, nor that the Amish are perfect people. The Amish *have* sustained a strong sense of neighborhood and household. In contrast, Berry argues, the dominant economy has turned the home into a place of consumption, a place to watch TV, eat frozen dinners, and spend time on the Internet. Because of this, the "home" has become primarily a tool for the global economy; Katie Couric's face is more familiar to us than our next-door neighbor's.

Berry posits that homes must once again become places of production if they are to provide alternatives to the global economic forces that form us into consumers. By "production" he means such activities as taking time to cook a meal, providing care for children or elderly, or tending a garden. And indeed according to Christian hospitality, a home needs to produce something if it is going to have anything particular to offer. If not, the "hospitality" it extends easily becomes that of the global economy, a consumer hospitality that continues to underwrite globalization. Our global system is more than willing to move jobs from one place to another around the globe in order to find people who will work for low pay under often harsh conditions because there is no alternative. Berry's comments rightly suggest that concrete productive practices of community and household must be vigorously in place in order to prevent the complete erasure of the household by dominant economic forces. In a similar vein, I want to suggest that the concrete practices of the household (understood as the church) must be vigorously and vigilantly in place in order to live the economy of God rather than the immanent economics of the modern marketplace.

The challenge of Christian hospitality is not simply to return to the past. The challenge is rather to be faithful to the past (scripture, tradition, liturgy, the lives of the saints) even as we live into God's hospitality in the present and await the promised future. It might seem odd to describe the church's hospitality as "productive," but if faithfully practiced, Christian hospitality produces an alternative to the global market.

Of course, as they say, the devil is in the details. What would this economic alternative look like? One response to this question would be to imagine ways to live not consumed by consumerism. There are Christian communities that are doing this well. The Church of the Sojourners in San Francisco, for example, practices economic sharing; twenty-four members own only seven cars. Members are encouraged to practice stability, moving to another place only if it will build the church. Commenting on the "kingdom economics" they seek to practice, Dale Gish cited Jacques Ellul's "dictum": a way to subvert the power of money is to give it away.[11] The practice of tithing is certainly an important step in the direction of "kingdom economics."

For a more commonplace example of such economics, a church I used to attend always provided a home-cooked meal at the church building after a funeral. This is a small gesture, but such a habit displays a hospitality willing to take the time to produce and, in so doing, to help church members resist being identified as only consumers. Of course, the goal is not only to resist consumerism but also to imagine ways more fully to embody the hospitality of God.

One of the first acts of hospitality is naming those powers that would have us be other than God's hospitable people.

The Scientific "Real"

In what ways is science a force against which Christians need to be vigilant? Obviously science has given us many gains in medicine, technology, and understanding the natural world. Here, however, let us consider the belief that science describes the world as it *really* is and that therefore all other ways of understanding the world are merely mythological, symbolic, or personal. Scientism, as it is often called, separates the world into "fact" on the one hand and "values" on the other. From this perspective, facts are thought to be value free and public, while values and faith are personal and private. Certainly this dichotomy has been criticized many times over, yet it still has a grip on the cultural imagination. Nowhere is this more apparent than in the commonsense view, held especially by members of the younger generation today, that "my values" are simply my choices—a point to which I will return in the following chapter.

Science is thus thought to be the discipline that best embodies a free, unfettered quest for truth. Edward O. Wilson claims that the Enlightenment "waved aside everything, every form of religious and civil authority, every imaginable fear, to give precedence to the ethic of *free inquiry*."[12] The implication is that authority and religion are antithetical to freedom and, further, that science exists in a domain free from authority. Marjorie Greene nicely summarizes this way of telling the story of science and religion: "In the Middle Ages everyone relied on authority, and that was arbitrary, non-objective and bad, and then along came Copernicus, Galileo and Newton and everything was scientific, objective and good. Or, in reaction to this: do your own thing."[13] While many philosophers of science,[14] theologians, and others would challenge this summation, it is nonetheless one that continues to form our imaginations. Religion is often described as authoritarian and dogmatic, while science is seen as "unfettered," objective, and thus true.

For example, we still learn in school that water is *really* H_2O. Our educational system, states H. A. Nielsen, still "outfits every generation of young people with a standard, official, thin, and impersonal understanding of water, a lame understanding most briefly expressed in the formula H_2O."[15] Nielsen is reflecting on Ludwig Wittgenstein's earlier statement: "While still at school our children get taught that water consists of hydrogen and oxygen. . . . Anyone who doesn't understand is stupid. The most important questions are concealed."[16] What both of these statements point to and criticize is the equation of reality only with what can be scientifically understood and defined. In the field of medicine, we see the same phenomenon in the tendency to believe that the biological/chemical phenomena of a particular illness sufficiently explain and solve the illness.

Nielsen continues that someone might respond, "But don't you see, in science we try to get at *water itself?*"

"No," says Nielsen, "I don't see. What on earth do you mean by 'water itself'? When is it *not* itself?"[17] Neither illness nor water is simply a puzzle to be defined and solved. The nineteenth-century poet George Macdonald gives us the following account of water, capturing the truth about water in a way that "H_2O" cannot: "Let him who would know the truth of the Maker, become sorely athirst, and drink of the brook by the way—then lift up his heart—not at that moment to the Maker of oxygen and hydrogen, but to the Inventor and Mediator of thirst and water, that man might foresee a little of what his soul might find in God."[18] We could also point to the creative waters of baptism.

Isolating the essence of water to its gaseous components blinds us to all the rich and awesome ways of water in God's created world. Thus can we begin to see how scientism, by identifying the real only with the empirical, underwrites a story at odds with Christianity. It thus undermines the practice of hospitality, since it subverts the story that hospitality embodies and extends. Two examples will flesh out these general observations.

Creation and Evolution

First, let us consider the contested debate between creation and evolution. Scientists who advocate evolution typically defend their position by saying that they are simply doing science and describing the world as they see it. Thus they look at the fossil records, date them, study the subtle differences in the development of animals, and state that the evidence points clearly toward evolution, understood as random natural selection.

As is well known, some Christian opponents resist evolution on the grounds that it seems to contradict the biblical accounts of creation. Some of these opponents who are scientists defend the idea of a young earth to harmonize with the Bible as they read it. They also argue that there is no real evidence for macroevolution (large-scale evolution), though some concede the possibility of microevolution. Those who oppose evolution are typically considered to be "fundamentalists" who read the Bible literally.

In relation to the practice of hospitality, the real problem with evolution is not that it would have creation take longer than the Bible is thought to indicate or that creation evolved across time. Neither of these negates what it means to describe God as Creator. Rather, evolution as a description of how the world *is* and *is intended to be* denies the plenitude of God. Allow me to explain. Darwinian evolution holds that the current state of the world came about through natural selection, also known as survival of the fittest. "Natural selection is the idea that individuals who possess advantageous heritable traits are more likely to survive and reproduce."[19] Advocates of such evolutionary accounts typically hold that supernatural origins are beyond the scope of the scientific method.[20] While this claim does posit a degree of humility, the assumption that science is only describing the way the world is still betrays a kind of scientism, as if one could present "facts" free of any evaluation. To the contrary, description always entails mythic or storied assumptions. Darwinian evolution relies upon an assumption of scarcity. Since there are not enough resources to go around, those that possess "advantageous heritable traits" get to survive. This is simply the way nature works.[21]

But is it? Is scarcity rather than abundance the plotline in God's story with creation, Israel, and the church? Understood correctly, creation is above all a delightfully good and gracious gift that comes to us from God's deep abundance. God did and does not have to create; creation itself is without necessity. God as Trinity rather has "all fellowship, exposition and beauty in perfect sufficiency." So understood, God's freedom is "the perfect and unimpeded fullness with which the divine nature is itself," a nature abundant in "delight, fellowship and love."[22] This abundance and delight can be seen in God's creation not only of the world but also of a people, Israel and the church, for the world so that all may partake of the divine communion and delight. Competition and rivalry are not part of God's creation. Joseph's jealous brothers try to get rid of their competition, only to be told, many years later, that their actions could not defeat the creative purposes of God: "Even though you intended to do harm to me, God intended it for good, in order to preserve a numerous people" (Gen. 50:20).

If rivalry and antagonism are essentially how things are, the practice of hospitality makes little sense. It would be better to look out for oneself and protect one's own family and belongings. It would make sense, as most of Joseph's brothers thought, to kill your competitor. Obviously, we do see rivalry, violence, and lack of resources all around us. These, however, are not a necessary part of God's good creation. Rather, they exist as a negation of what *is* God's good creation. "For what else is called evil," asks Augustine, "but a removal of the good?"[23] Augustine's classic position is not intended to deny evil, scarcity, and sin but to indicate that these are deep derangements and distortions of the created world. As practitioners of God's creative hospitality, we are not called to live merely in the fallen world of rivalry and competition but to live in God's creation, now identified most fully with the church. In confessing sin, we allow God's grace to re-create us, enabling us to live out of God's gracious abundance rather than out of scarcity. John Milbank writes, "It is, of course, quite simply impossible to be a Christian and to suppose that death and suffering belong to God's original plan, or that the struggle of natural selection . . . is how creation *as creation* rather than thwarted creation genuinely comes about. . . . To believe in plenitude is to believe in the already commenced and yet-to-come restoration of Creation as Creation."[24]

Confidence and faith in the plenitude of God enable us to trust that God will provide what we need. "Give us this day our daily bread" is our learning to ask for what God *desires* to give: bread that sustains us in the wilderness, bread that makes us the body of Christ for the world. "Thy kingdom come" is our learning to ask for what again God *desires* to give: the peaceful and hospitable rule of God, where the lion will lie down with the lamb. That a new creation has commenced means we are to act excessively out of God's excess.[25] Such divine excess is the wellspring of Christian hospitality. Inasmuch as scientism as Darwinian evolution denies this and promotes some other vision of the world, we need to be watchful and vigilant in our practice of hospitality, not allowing ourselves to be seduced by a false story of scarcity and want.

Science as "the" Story

Related to the assertion that evolution describes the real world is the conviction that science provides *the* story that can unite us all, the "us" including tribal and national identities around the world. If everyone would reason scientifically, this view holds, then many of the local superstitions and beliefs that separate us could be overcome. On the ground, there is a sense in which this story has taken hold. One reads, for example, about young adults from tribes in Africa who become educated, learn modern medicine, and abandon older tribal ways. Often they move away to the big city. Modern medicine works better than tribal cures, so who can blame them for abandoning their former way of life? In the short term, there may be conflict and disunity as the tribe loses its identity. But, the progressive scientific view holds, this is a small price to pay for modernizing the world and educating people into the same story.

We find a good example of how science ought to provide a unifying story in the thought of Loyal Rue.[26] I look at his argument because Rue nicely illustrates some common assumptions about myth, religion, and science. In his essay "Redefining Myth and Religion: Introduction to a Conversation," Rue sets out to integrate myth and science. He defines myth as "a story of comprehensive scope that concerns . . . the origins, nature and destiny of life" but warns that science, in the face of static myth, "will begin to drift away from myth and religion until it is perceived to be their enemy."[27] Rue wants to present an alternative both to "those who reject the advancement of science" and to "those who desperately engage in the futile activity of reinterpreting the old stories to make them appear compatible with the new knowledge."[28] What then is Rue's alternative? Since religion lacks the universal epistemic authority provided by scientific knowledge, Rue proposes that science, and science alone, provide a new and universal myth that will unify the globe. Rue explains, "So whence comes the story that can unify the globe? Not from Islam, not from Judaism, not from Christianity. . . . These traditions tell *somebody's* story. We are asking, 'whence come the elements for *everybody's* story?'"[29]

Rue assumes that the scientific story unifies by overcoming the particularity of religion and tradition and by positing a common rationalism over against the irrationalism of religious myth. Rue's assumptions, however, are themselves thoroughly drawn from an Enlightenment and modern tradition, a tradition holding that enlightened reason in and of itself could provide unity and peace. From this perspective, the particularity of tradition (a particularity that generates conflict) is something to be overcome. The search is for a story that can be "everybody's" or "anybody's."

Rue, however, does not free himself from historical particularity, from "somebody's" story, but substitutes one particular story for another. It is not as if Rue's proposal had a better standing in some ultimate, context-neutral sense. The scientific story that Rue proposes is no more everybody's than is Judaism, Islam, or Christianity. His faith in scientific rationalism is as particular and mythic as is the belief that God created the world. Neither story is just obvious or "natural"; both require initiation, training, and practice across time.

Rue, of course, acknowledges that the scientific story is a myth, in the sense that it is a "story of comprehensive scope that concerns . . . the origins, nature or destiny of life." We can add to Rue's definition the insight of William H. Poteat: myth is authoritatively embedded in the "actual grain of my life as I live it." He adds, "Wherever memory and hope make their appearance in the temporal structures of my life there are myths, or fragments of myths. And these are not just about the no-longer and the not-yet. They are about *now* in its fullness and depth."[30] Since we are creatures who live in time, we necessarily live in a present given "depth and fecundity by memory and hope," a fact displayed in the various tenses of the language we speak.

The question to ask Rue is, what memories and hopes are embedded in the scientific universal story that he advocates? Rue does not address this question, in part because he is focused on advocating the universality of the scientific story. I think we can say, however, that the memory embedded in the scientific story is not that we were created by God but that we came about through the processes of nature.[31] The hope is that science alone has the power to overcome conflict and to unify everyone around the globe.

One popular response to a position like Rue's has been to embrace a plurality of stories, each manifesting the Real in a different way. The attraction of this plurality is that a single story does not silence all others. But is this option to Rue's position ultimately helpful, particularly in thinking through the practice of hospitality? Lesslie Newbigin responds negatively to this question by rehearsing the popular parable of five blind men who touch different parts of an elephant. Each of the men believes that he alone has the elephant, yet discovers in the end that his colleagues had touched the same elephant, only a different part. The purpose of this story is to suggest that everyone, though different, really lives by the same truth and that none of us can have more than one aspect of this truth. Cantwell Smith has summed this up as follows: "The truth of all of us is part of the truth of each of us." Or, as John Hick concludes, "the great world traditions constitute different conceptions and perceptions of, and responses to, the Real from within the different cultural ways of being human."[32] At various interfaith talks that I have attended, Hick's position has sometimes been endorsed, only instead of the "Real," "peace and justice" are often embraced as the common bond that we all share. Yet as often becomes obvious, it is impossible to say what "peace and justice" look like without inadvertently bringing in some tradition or some story.

Newbigin observes that the real point of the elephant story is constantly overlooked. The story is told from the point of view of a king, and "if the king were also blind there would be no story."[33] The one telling the story (equated with the pluralist) *already* sees the whole elephant; he has a better and fuller truth that the others do not have. He is therefore in a position to tell the others their own stories and truths better than they can themselves. As Newbigin states, this is an "immensely arrogant claim of one who sees the full truth which all the world's religions are only groping after."[34] I once heard a Muslim theologian say, in reaction against such a homogenizing view, to a Christian theologian who was describing how "really alike we are," "Listen, the difference between you and me is that you believe Jesus is the Son of God and I don't." While the Christian theologian *assumed* a "Reality" that he shared with the Muslim, the Muslim clearly did not want to be absorbed into some prior understanding of what they shared.

This kind of pluralism and Rue's scientific story share the conviction that there is a universal story that all people hold in common. Christians too believe there is a commonality or potential commonality, but it has nothing to do with scientific rationality or with an anonymous Real lurking behind all belief systems. It has to do, rather, with the conviction that we are all created and redeemed by God. Some people, of course, do not acknowledge this, but this does not make them any less a creature of God, any less in relation with God. *Creation* itself names not only a beginning in time but also a relation between God and all that is. Our very lives are gifts of God's plenitude. In creating us, God delights in us and desires that we receive the joy and pleasure of God's own communion. Hospitality is grounded in this overflowing communion rather than in a scientific rationality or an understanding of an abstract "Real." Christian hospitality can be easily confused today with reaching for commonalities that are not necessarily there (such as reason or the Real), while ignoring the ones that are—that the "other" is a creation/relation of God and one for whom Christ is present.

We can yet go a step further and note the deep connection between scientism, pluralism, and a global economy. Kenneth Surin, in his essay "A 'Politics of Speech': Religious Pluralism in an Age of McDonald's Hamburgers," argues that religious pluralism is embedded in and formed by the global economy. Pluralism has a "global gaze," notes Surin, such that difference becomes *merely* different, a position that ends up domesticating and assimilating the other. Such pluralism is of a piece with the "global media and information networks, international agencies and multinational corporations . . . [who] declare that nations, cultures, religions and so forth, are simply obsolete if they are maintained in their old forms as fixed and intractable particularities." Surin concludes that "to resist the cultural encroachment represented by the McDonald's hamburger, therefore, is of a piece with resisting the similar depredation constituted by this world ecumenism."[35]

Surin's analysis is supported by Douglas Wilson, who characterizes America as an economic empire, in contrast to an ideological one as the Marxist attempt at empire was. "In many ways, economic empires can be far more benign than the empires built and run by ideologues. The commies wanted to haul us off to the Gulag and take all our stuff. The Americans just want the opportunity to sell us a Windows upgrade. . . . Establishing democracies may be the stated goal, but establishing markets is a close corollary." Wilson goes on to say that the public worship of economic empires "includes an affinity for the pantheon. Many gods are necessary to keep all of the customers happy." He cites as an example the "interfaith deism on display at the National Cathedral after the September 11 attack." The worship, Wilson states, was self-consciously polytheistic, and as a result both Muslims and Christians were compromised. Such polytheism was superficial, however, because "the real god of the worship service was the god called America, the guarantor of economic stability." Wilson compares the unifying principle of economic empires to gigantic yard sales, with every imaginable kind of thing placed before shoppers. "The most apparent thing about the yard sale is the incredible diversity. 'Look!' one might say, getting out of the car, 'Pluralism!' The avid yard sale shopper can buy canning jars, water skis, jigsaw puzzles, tablecloths, and so on. Even here, however, there is a unifying principle—there is only one cash box." The economic empire assigns the church of America the following role: "to neutralize the Faith by making it just one more item in the yard sale."[36]

Both Surin and Wilson help us see that pluralism, by trivializing our particularities, serves a global economy. And precisely this economy, if we allow it, erases Christian hospitality, for Christian hospitality is irreducibly particular, formed by the particular life, death, and resurrection of Christ. Actually, the "global gaze" of pluralism and Rue's "scientific story" are just as particular, only the particularity lies in a different story. The question becomes, then, in our practices of economics and hospitality, who are we serving? Pluralism and McDonald's serve an economy very different from the economy (*oikonomia*) of God.[37]

Economics

We have seen how a kind of scientism (evolution as the way the world is and science as a universal story) distorts the practice of hospitality, ultimately denying God's plenitude in creation and Christ. That certain kinds of economic practice can easily distort hospitality may be more obvious. Numerous passages from scripture warn against hoarding God's blessings. God commands the Hebrews to collect only enough manna for each day. In continuity with this, Christians have long prayed, "Give us this day our daily bread."

Perhaps the most frightening and bizarre (to modern ears, at least) story of hoarding is that of Ananias and Sapphira, struck dead because they held back money and then lied about it (Acts 5). In contrast to hoarding, scripture recounts numerous stories of uncalculating generosity. When Abraham meets three guests, he welcomes them by washing their feet and giving them a tender roasted calf and fine cakes (Gen. 18). The Book of Acts reports that early Christians had all things in common and that "they would sell their possessions and goods and distribute the proceeds to all, as any had need" (2:44–47). While passages such as these do not lay out a full-blown economic "plan," they do suggest that practicing a carefree generosity and not hoarding are marks of the economics made possible by the hospitality of God.

Today, however, we tend to think of economics on a much grander scale, having to do with things like the stock market, the International Monetary Fund, the World Bank, and so on. This grand-scale notion of economics can seem overwhelming, especially when it comes to evaluating its formative power in our lives. It can feel like trying to get your bearings in the middle of the ocean. As Ched Myers reminds us, this is one of the ways our advanced capitalist economy disempowers us.[38] We are led to think that only Harvard MBAs can really understand the science of economics. We imagine that economics is best understood by the experts—"economists, bankers, brokers . . . accountants, attorneys, and other financial advisers."[39] Such a way of thinking, however, is a product of a scientific economic vision that banishes religion to the private realm while dominating the rest of the landscape. From this perspective, too, it is easy to believe that hospitality is something separate from economics, but such a conviction repeats one of the distortions discussed earlier, the reduction of hospitality to a sentimental or private practice. Economics and hospitality are both related to *oikos*. *Hospitality* names the kind of giving and receiving that enables the *oikos* or household to flourish, and economics describes the rules that govern this practice.[40] As we will see, the kind of *oikos* or place we envision makes all the difference in the world for how we understand and practice hospitality.

Criticisms of our capitalist market economy make some of us uneasy. After all, many of us are beneficiaries of a capitalist system. Further, it can be difficult to see any alternatives. A common defense of capitalism is that it is the best system we have, and certainly better than its alternative, Marxism. Yet as Daniel Bell succinctly puts it, "Capitalism is wrong because even if it succeeds in delivering the goods, it nevertheless works against the Good, corrupting (and perpetuating the corruption of) human sociality in competitive and conflictual modalities."[41] As Bell indicates, capitalism forms us to be in competition and conflict with each other. If our churches were managed in a thoroughly capitalistic spirit (and no doubt some are), such conflict and competition would contradict the noncompetitive rule of Christ under the guidance of the Spirit.

When we are trying to think differently about economic matters, it is helpful to consider the distinctions between a market economy—an economy that makes extensive use of markets—and a market society—a society that is completely dominated by market forces. In a *market society*, all human relations are reduced to contract, destroying the longer-term bonds needed to sustain human society. In a *market economy*, the market is not *the* overriding force. Murray Jardine notes that in some cultures various communal bonds or concerns might override market values. In such an economy, people might

> buy from a merchant who charges higher prices out of a sense of personal loyalty. . . . More efficient producers may refrain from putting less efficient producers out of business by limiting their own production. They may do this because they feel it would be uncharitable to destroy the livelihood of others or simply because they feel that they already have enough wealth and don't need any more, preferring instead greater leisure time. This type of behavior was quite common in Europe before liberalism became dominant.[42]

Liberal capitalism, however, takes the market as the model for all of society. Having enough wealth is an alien concept in a *market society*, where the market dominates, producing a ruthlessly fierce competition. Such ruthless competition grows "only in a culture that is both highly individualistic and highly concerned with creating material wealth—that is, the bourgeois culture with its secularized Protestant ethic."[43]

As Jardine notes, in the face of such cultural degradation, some react by advocating a conservative solution that would isolate certain segments of society, such as the family, from market forces. At the same time, these conservatives argue that the market can function properly only if the individuals working in the market are virtuous. Jardine points out, however, that the model of virtue they uphold is essentially a secularized Protestant work ethic, an ethic that is self-destructive because intense focus on creating material wealth also produces a culture of consumerism. Others, in contrast to this conservative solution, support the "reform liberal" position that seeks to control market forces through regulation. But again, Jardine points out, while the (early) reform liberals wanted to control the market and believed that the government has a role in promoting moral virtue, they too wanted to promote the destructive work ethic of both classical liberals and present-day conservatives. Jardine sums up this ethic as follows: "As the single-minded work ethic of early liberalism is applied, a fantastically productive capitalist economy develops, which in turn requires the creation of a consumer culture simply to get rid of its massive overproduction." Jardine calls for a "new kind of culture with a very different attitude toward work."[44] We will return to the idea of a new kind of culture later in this chapter.

For now, I want to turn to what might seem a rather odd analogy, but one that nicely captures how the market dominates our lives, often in ways we barely notice. In an essay on memory and imagination, philosopher William H. Poteat compares writing with a broad felt-tipped Magic Marker with using his delicate Cross porous-point pen.

Not only would what I am able to feel inclined to write be more cryptic, less fluent—cramped—because of the awkwardness of the instrument I use: my thinking, connate as it is with the speaking-writing—and all the activities to which my mindbody is given—will therefore also be cramped, coarse, less cursive. The style, focus, and reach of my thinking is defined by the possibilities that exist for my mindbody *at this moment*.[45]

Indeed our imaginations are constricted or expanded dependent upon the tools we use. Until we have actually written with a Cross pen, we might easily think a broad felt-tipped Magic Marker is great for writing a letter. Our current economics cramps us in similar ways. The fact that many of us are paralyzed when asked, "But isn't capitalism the best system we have thus far?" indicates how constricted our imaginations have become. As Michael Budde states, "So many of us come from churches deeply accommodated to secular power (the so-called Constaninian compromise) that we seem to have lost a sense of how substantial Christian identities and convictions could be formed *without* the support of the dominant culture."[46] The failure to imagine things differently will make it almost inevitable that the dominant global economy will determine our lives.

McDonaldized Hospitality versus Christian Hospitality

Let us now turn more fully to this dominant economic culture. By global economy, I mean a capitalist mode of exchange, production, and consumption that transcends national boundaries, and, increasingly, any boundaries whatsoever, for the sake of the market and for profit. In its preference for abstract market space over particular locale, the global economy is an extension of Cartesian universalism. That is, it prefers economic "reason" over tradition and the "universal" over the particular. As noted earlier, Surin calls our age "the age of McDonald's hamburgers," and McDonald's can serve as a kind of icon for our global economy. George Ritzer, in *The McDonaldization of Society*, in fact, uses McDonald's as an image for how we are formed by our late modern economy. Ritzer does not wish simply to criticize the McDonald's food chain but rather describes how certain elements central to the McDonald's model, and now pervasive throughout our society, have come to dominate our lives. Ritzer uses *McDonaldization* to mean something similar to what Max Weber meant by the "rationalization" of society. According to Weber, a rationalized society, such as that developed by modern capitalism, is more efficient, calculable, predictable, and controlled than more "traditional" societies, though as Weber famously acknowledged, such rationality could become irrational, as when people are dehumanized by modern bureaucracies.

Ritzer applies four of Weber's elements of rationality to McDonaldization. First, he argues, fast-food places are highly efficient; they offer an "optimum method of getting from one point to another . . . from being hungry to being full."[47] Organizational rules and regulations ensure highly efficient work. The second element, calculability, focuses on quantitative aspects: the size of the product and the time it takes to get it. In a McDonaldized society, quantity is more important than quality. Even since Ritzer first published his book in 1993, McDonald's is using an array of robots and computers to lessen delivery time: ninety seconds at rush hour and forty-five at calmer times. As Alan Sica notes, the underlying assumption is "that speed of delivery is more important to consumers than the nature of what is delivered."[48] The third element of Ritzer's schema is predictability: the product will be the same in all locales. Thus people "know that the next Egg McMuffin they eat will not be awful, although it will not be exceptionally delicious, either. The success of the McDonald's model suggests that many people have come to prefer a world in which there are few surprises."[49] Finally, the fourth element of McDonald's success is control through nonhuman technology. The lines, limited menu, and uncomfortable seats all lead people to do what management wants them to do: eat quickly and leave. The workers too are controlled to a high degree, trained to do only a limited number of things in precisely the same way. And technology—such as a soft-drink dispenser or French-fry machine—increases control over workers. Ritzer does not deny that there are certain advantages to McDonaldization: greater availability of goods and service, convenience, more economical alternatives to high-priced goods, and a familiar, stable "environment," among others.[50] Yet part of his thesis is that McDonaldization has spawned its own "irrationalities," not the least of which is a kind of dehumanization and the infiltration of "values" like efficiency into all aspects of our lives.

Philippe Beneton in fact describes the dehumanization of McDonald's as the invention of a "new humanity" in whom

> the pure spirit of the market reigns. . . . Here every person, whoever he or she may be, is exactly like all the others; he or she is a consumer, nothing but a consumer, entirely a consumer, a consumer from head to toe. McDonald's is universalist; its calling is to embrace the whole world without regard to divisions. . . . McDonald's is the missionary of a new humanity, the builder of a new world, in collaboration with all other businesses set to conquer the world market and sharing this great cause with a view to the greatest profit.[51]

It is not surprising that Beneton reaches for religious terminology—"spirit," "missionary," "new world"—in giving an account of the global economy, since it embodies a specific *oikonomia*, a plan of salvation that will unify the globe. Beneton mockingly issues a call to this new humanity: "Consumers of all lands, unite over a Big Mac!"[52] Just as Kant hoped that enlightened reason would bring about world peace, so also the rationalized market imagines it can unify the globe. Ritzer in fact tells of some Dutch students who, when traveling outside their country, always find the first McDonald's they can because it gives them a *feeling of home*.[53] The students, in other words, feel at home in the dominant economic culture, as many of us probably do at least some of the time. I would not therefore cast blame on these students; they have simply been disciplined by the market such that "McDonald's hospitality," with its efficiency, calculability, predictability, and control, seems natural to them. Like Ritzer, I use McDonald's simply as an example of how the global market economy forms us, forms our bodies even, to be one way rather than another.

It is now time to begin to consider an alternative. How does Christian hospitality, when faithfully practiced, discipline us in a way that a "McDonaldized" hospitality does not? Let us take the four elements of a rationalized economy as Ritzer describes them: efficiency, calculability, predictability, and control. At the outset, we can say that Christian hospitality is not particularly concerned with efficiency. For example, Jesus washes *each* of the disciples' feet (John 13). It would have been more efficient to have had them wash their own feet, or even to have had them wash each other's feet. But efficiency, or simply getting the job done, is not the point of the story. Jesus wants to show his disciples that as he is their servant, they too are to be servants. Even more, he wants them to know that, with his time to depart drawing near, he "loved them to the end" (John 13:1). Jesus remains faithful to his disciples to the end, even though they will not be entirely faithful to him. But as we know, the story unfolds, and their lack of faithfulness cannot thwart the faithfulness of God. Christian hospitality aims not for efficiency but for taking time to wash feet and taking time for God to show us that our acts of unfaithfulness cannot negate his loving purpose for our lives.

Jean Vanier, founder of L'Arche communities, where mentally handicapped persons live with others who are not so handicapped, lives a life that could hardly be described as "efficient" in the market economic sense of that term. If anything, his life and ministry could seem like a waste of time: why spend so much time with people who (to most of us) seem to have little chance of improving? We shall return to Vanier in the final chapter; suffice it to say for now that Vanier does not particularly care about efficiency. He cares about taking the time to be with and learn from those who have suffered deeply from the wounds of mental disability. The hospitality of L'Arche is embodied in "being with" rather than "doing for."[54] Yet as Jaques Ellul observes, "One of the results of capitalism . . . is the subservience of *being* to *having*. . . . It is the inevitable consequence of capitalism, for there is no other possibility when making money becomes the purpose of life."[55] In contrast to a McDonaldized efficient hospitality, Christian hospitality allows time to be patient and vulnerable with others. Such hospitality does not fit with the instantaneous demands of the market. Rather, as Vanier rightly sees, it takes time, since such hospitality is, in the final analysis, a way of being.

Another well-known story that exemplifies the inefficiency of hospitality is "Babette's Feast." In this story by Isak Dinesen, Babette, a famous Parisian chef, arrives at the door of some Danish puritans. Her husband and son have been killed, and she is at their mercy for a place to stay. The puritans, two older women, allow her to remain. After fourteen years, Babette comes into some money and decides to prepare a feast for her strict hosts (who have never discovered her background as a famous chef). With her Danish hosts looking on suspiciously, Babette spends weeks planning and preparing the meal. Eventually the day arrives. The Danes decide to attend but promise each other not to show any response to the meal. Despite their intentions, however, the lavish feast, which consists of many courses, "loosens" their reserve and eventually frees them to become warmer and more forgiving toward each other. Long-held animosities melt away, and they discover a shared joy in the pleasures of creation as they eat together. Grace-filled hospitality takes time—time enough for Babette, who has been their guest for fourteen years, to develop bonds of trust so that on this one remarkable evening she can be their host, offering them not only food but also the joy that comes from the giving and receiving of gifts. Whereas the global market aims for efficiency and speed, Christian hospitality is content to wait, to take time, to apparently do nothing if need be, since the aim is to be in God's abundant time of giving and receiving rather than in efficient, productive time.

Calculability, Ritzer's second element of McDonaldization, also inhibits Christian hospitality. Gilbert Bond tells of how the Chicago First Church of the Brethren, where he served as assistant pastor, participated in a government-sponsored program and functioned as a distribution site for surplus agricultural commodities. The government required the church to obtain a "proof of poverty" from every person who came through the door—usually the card issued to those poor enough to participate in the Medicaid program. "The comic absurd part of the requirement became apparent when one reflected upon who else would wait in the Chicago winter outside a church for several hours to receive a five-pound brick of processed cheese if they could afford to buy it or a better grade of cheese in a grocery store."[56] In this situation, counting and quantifying the really poor became terribly dehumanizing. One young man who "failed to prove that he had failed" angrily erupted, "What in the [blankety-blank] do you think all these people come here for? . . . Everybody lining up here is poor. If we weren't poor we wouldn't be here."[57]

The church, after much painful discernment and honest conversation, came to realize that this program, based on calculating who was really poor, was inherently violent and that some institutional structures are incapable of mediating God's peaceable kingdom. Bond goes on to tell how the church developed an alternative ministry of neighborhood fellowship meals that involved eating, singing, and praying together. (The Brethren practice that formed the basis for this alternative ministry was the Anabaptist love feast, which includes a foot-washing ritual and an agape meal.) Fewer people were served, but neighborhood children eventually started coming to church.

As Bond's story illustrates, predictability and control, the other elements of a rationalized economy, can likewise inhibit the faithful practice of Christian hospitality. Some oversight *is* necessary, but the people of First Church of the Brethren rightly saw that they needed to give up control in order to be faithful to who they were. Sitting down at a common meal with the folks in their neighborhood was much more risky (less controlling) than giving food to people in line, yet it also made possible genuine hospitality. While there no doubt are some advantages to simply handing out food, this practice is not rightly called "hospitality," since there is no reciprocity. Rather, hospitality gives up some control by acknowledging that the guest can also be a host, that the one receiving also has gifts to give. One of the deepest theological convictions for this understanding is that the other, as Catholic Worker Dorothy Day has emphasized, *is Christ*. This is difficult for most of us to grasp. Certainly the people we are with and the strangers we meet seldom seem to be like Christ. Day, however, is drawing from Matthew 25:41: "Truly I tell you, just as you did it to one of the least of these who are members of my family, you did it to me." To say another is Christ is to say both that they are in the image of the triune God and that the resurrected Christ is with them.

So understood, hospitality allows space for Christ to come to us on his terms, rather than our own. Day even writes about an experience of kissing a leper. Unlike St. Francis, however, Day describes her encounter with this modern leper as unremarkable, even somewhat disgusting. Christian hospitality gives up predictability and control because it acknowledges that God comes among us in surprising and strange ways that we can never fully predict or domesticate.

Whose Enchantment? Which Economics?

It almost goes without saying that the overriding "good" that drives a rationalized market economy is profit.[58] Consider the beginning of the

McDonald's story in this light. When the McDonald brothers began their fast-food business, using a limited menu and specialized workers, they were content to keep it a single "local sensation" in San Bernardino, California. Ray Kroc, however, described as a man of great ambition, became their franchising agent and eventually bought them out. He combined the McDonald brothers' approach with the principles of other franchises, bureaucracies, scientific management, and assembly lines. Whereas the brothers, we might say, using an earlier distinction, still lived in a market economy (the values of the market did not entirely dominate their lives), Kroc was living in and helped create a market society, where the good was entirely equated with profit and self-interest. The brothers were doing well and did not see the need for further profit, but Kroc saw no reason to stop making as much profit as possible.

The transition from the McDonald brothers to Kroc highlights the fact that economics is not simply an end in itself but always serves some good. Economics always underwrites, even if unwittingly, some conception of what constitutes the good life. It is false to think of economics as only a "scientific" discipline, free from all encumbrances. Rather, as Aristotle saw, "economics is by nature subordinate. . . . It has no other purpose than the *good life* of human beings and . . . consequently the science of economics is a moral and political science."[59] Our own economy easily deceives us on this point, as we are trained to think that all goods, like all preferences, are homogeneous. "Money becomes the universal standard; all is measurable, interchangeable, substitutable—all is homogeneous." Beneton posits the example of a young man "who hesitates between *The Odyssey* and a pornographic video—what is the best choice? There can be no doubt as to the response: the rational choice, the one that allows the maximization of utility, is determined by the law of equalizing marginal utilities adjusted for prices."[60] His point is that contemporary economics knows only the law of consumption, supply and demand, and nothing of what might undo social bonds, isolate human beings, or imprison them in their distorted desires. It knows nothing of the "unbought grace of life,"[61] only the homogenization of all "goods" for the sake of one good: the market.

Weber himself, in discussing the rationalization of economic society, embraced impartiality as a virtue of capitalism because it eliminates "from all official business love, hate, all purely personal and all irrational elements of feeling, elements defying calculation."[62] Whereas earlier, Weber notes, "gentlemen of the old order" were inspired by personal interest, favor, grace, and gratitude, "modern culture requires . . . the less humanly concerned, strictly 'practical expert.'" We might resonate with Weber's approach in that we do not necessarily want people showing partiality to us in the marketplace; we want everyone to be treated the same. At the same time, the coldly calculating expert might frighten us because of his detachment; he knows nothing of grace and gratitude. Weber in fact recognized that rationalization can generate certain irrationalities. His well-known description of the iron cage illuminates the downside of a thoroughly rationalized economy:

> No one knows who will live in this cage in the future, or whether at the end of this tremendous development entirely new prophets will arise, or there will be a great rebirth of old ideas and ideals, or, if neither, mechanized petrification, embellished with a sort of convulsive self-importance. For of the last stage of this cultural development, it might well be truly said: "Specialists without spirit, sensualists without heart; this nullity imagines that is has attained a level of civilization never before achieved."[63]

It is hard not to apply "specialists without spirit" to the attending physician and medical students described earlier who could not hear the voice of their patient. While Weber admitted the potential for "irrationality" and "dehumanization," he equated reason with impartiality and the economics of modern capitalism.

That Weber, brilliant though he surely was, equated modern capitalism with rationality shows us an oversight in his thinking. Rationality is itself always mythic in its assumptions and structure. Thus rationality, as Weber and Ritzer understand it, does not so much disenchant the world as reenchant it with other fantasies, other dreams and myths, some of which have been around for a long time. After reading Rizter's analysis of McDonald's as a place of "disenchantment: where's the magic?"[64] I couldn't help but think of my own children. They love McDonald's and are thoroughly *enchanted* by it. Every month we are subjected to (from my perspective) the terrible "McDonald's Night" when a minuscule part of what we pay for our food goes to support my daughter's school—but only if we remember to tell the cashier the name of her school in the midst of fighting the crowds, ordering our food, and trying to talk amid children's yelling. The enchantment for my children lies mostly in the "free" Happy Meal toy—usually from Disney promoting its latest movie. The McDonald's-Disney alliance doesn't so much disenchant as form my children to be enchanted in other ways, so that they prefer going to McDonald's to eating a home-cooked meal. To the extent that this preference reigns, my children have become "globalized," reenchanted by global industries with cheap plastic stuff, fast food, and self-service.

Often, however, even my children recognize that the promised happiness of this enchantment is tasteless and false: they do not get the toy they thought they would get, the toy breaks, or one child gets a different (better) toy than the other. David McCarthy says about his family's experience at McDonald's, "We have learned to call the Happy Meal the 'Disappointing Meal,' because it doesn't seem to make anyone happy, and it certainly is not a meal."[65]

Yet there is often an enchantment for adults as well. Jake Silverstein recounts the grand opening of a McDonald's in Zacatecas, the only state in Mexico that had been without one. As Silverstein reports, students were let out of school for this festive occasion, and huge crowds of them arrived early, the best students getting to stand at the front. "The governor arrived and the speeches kicked off. . . . 'This day,' he proclaimed, 'this thirtieth of July, is of great importance for all Zacatecans, and for all of us who form the great McDonald's family, nationally and internationally.' Flashbulbs popped. The governor raised his scissors. He opened the blades. 'With Zacatecas, we now have . . . total coverage of the nation."[66] A sense of excitement and magic prevailed among the people of Zacatecas, most of whom believed that the presence of a McDonald's signaled more than the mere opening of a fast-food chain. Zacatecas had now become "modern" and "cultured." Not all Zacatecans agreed, though. One construction worker named Fernando told Silverstein, "The whole world is coming out of one head, and from that head you're getting everything. It's happening all over Mexico with these stores like Wal-Mart and McDonald's, stores that came out of the head of *allá* (over there). Down here, in Mexico, that head is developing all its thoughts."[67] Yet Fernando's views about a far distant head developing the thoughts of the locals are in the minority. Most Zacatecans see McDonald's as a kind of gate into the fairyland of a new economic world; they are reenchanted.

Again, the point is not simply to criticize McDonald's but to examine the colliding myths, stories, and virtues that sustain a capitalist global economy versus an economy that makes possible God's hospitality. One common characteristic of both scientism and global economics is their apparent detachment from particularity and place. Rue believes the story of science is not limiting in the way particular religious stories are. The global economy, exemplified in places like McDonald's, chafes against any limits that inhibit efficiency, calculability, predictability, and control. What is the myth that scientism and a market society reenact? Let us begin with a statement Ray Kroc made in an interview in 1972: "Look, it is ridiculous to call this an industry." He dismissed any sophisticated analysis of the fast-food business. "This is rat eat rat, dog eat dog. I'll kill 'em, and I'm going to kill 'em before they kill me. You're talking about the American way of survival of the fittest."[68] Kroc's statement nicely illustrates how a market capitalist society relies upon a scientific story of survival of the fittest.

At least two mythic elements help sustain such convictions. First, the idea that history, tradition, and place are limiting and need to be transcended is gnostic in impulse. Gnosticism is that set of beliefs that denies the goodness of our creaturely existence; rather, our creaturehood is an evil that needs to be transcended. Thus gnosticism locates our identity not in the material world but rather in the realm of pure spirit. The material world *does not matter*; it can be used up in a spirit of overconsumption and gluttony, or it can be denied as one turns inward with ascetic detachment. The spirit of detachment that dominates both scientism and the global economy sees itself as no part of the created world. To refer back to Hannah Arendt, there is instead a flight from the world, either into the universe (beyond the world) or into the self.

A second mythic element reenacted by both scientism and the global economy can be found within the Christian story itself: the desire to live without limits, as narrated in Genesis 3. In their disobedience of God, Adam and Eve embody the desire to reject one's own nature as a creature in order to be like God and "to be independent from everything."[69] As Gerhard Lohfink notes, the narrative of paradise and fall pictures both what human beings could be from God's perspective and what they became: "They suspect that something is being withheld from them. They want to be everything, in and of themselves. They want to be like God (3:5); that is, they want to be masters of themselves. And precisely that is sin."[70] Just as Adam and Eve refuse to obey God, so also by "embracing a culture of exploitation and consumption, we have come to understand ourselves as the *masters* of creation rather than its *members*, independent of God's grace and life-sustaining gifts."[71] Such mythic elements form us to be enchanted and enticed by a freedom and identity *apparently* unbounded by any limits; in reality, however, we are reenacting gnosticism as well as the story of the fall.

In contrast to the loss of place and detachment that characterize scientism and the economy as described above, Christianity willingly acknowledges certain limits: we are part of creation and not the Creator; we are bound to each other as members of the body of Christ; we will die, a mark of the fallen creation. One limit that is particularly crucial for the faithful practice of hospitality has to do with understanding our existence as gift. Orthodox theologian John Zizioulas rightly points out that the understanding of creation ex nihilo, out of nothing, freed the world from an ontology of necessity. He explains that the church fathers "broke the circle of the closed ontology of the Greeks, and at the same time did something much more important . . . they made being—the existence of the world, existent thing—*a product of freedom*."[72] Because God did not have to create but freely desired to, creation is not a necessity but a gift. In the words of Levio Melina, "The indicative of the gift of being precedes and establishes the imperative of having to be free."[73] Creation is therefore not a trap. We are not bound by a necessary fate, such as survival of the fittest. Rather, creation and our very being are freely given to us so that we may share in God's own communion, a communion made fully possible by the gift of Christ. This means therefore that true freedom does not lie in detachment from our created place and time (gnosticism) nor in mastering creation (Gen. 3). Rather, freedom results from living in communion with God and others. *Hospitality* is but another way of naming this communion.

Our hospitality, then, is not enchanted by mastery and detachment, as is the global market economy. Rather, it is enchanted by the generosity of God, who gifts us with our lives and with the ability to respond freely to others in love. In many ways, then, our challenge today as Christians is to become *reenchanted with* the Christian story. Creation, including our own lives, is to be received as gift; thus gratitude is not to be eliminated but lies at the heart of Christian economics. Blessings said at meals are one small way of reminding us that food is not just food but also a gift and a means of communion. In saying a blessing, we do not enter a different world but recognize that God has transformed the created world. This world, as Orthodox theologian Alexander Schmemann states in writing about the Eucharist, is "*already* perfected in Christ, but not yet in us."[74] Eating matter from the created world thus becomes a means of communion with God. This economics is marked not by autonomy and independence but by dependence, gift, and reception.

The Faith of Hospitality

We can now turn more fully to the faith that sustains Christian hospitality. As indicated above, statements like "The market determines everything" are clearly theological. We are not dealing first of all with rationality (in the market economy or science) versus irrationality (the realm of religion or the dehumanizing results of rationality), but with competing myths, myths that are lived by and through faith.[75]

Modernity has bequeathed to us a sense that faith is what you have or what you turn to when all else fails. Since we do not have scientific certainty or clear and distinct ideas about God, we are necessarily reduced to relying on faith, sometimes called "blind faith." Such a view presupposes that if we only knew more, if we only had more irrefutable evidence about Christ, for example, then we wouldn't need faith, since we have faith in the first place only because of a certain lack of knowledge, evidence, and certainty. As Jean-Luc Marion says, this view leads us to the conclusion that "I believe because, in spite of everything, I want to hold as true that which does not offer . . . data sufficient to impose itself by itself."[76]

Marion rightly calls such an understanding of faith blasphemous. First, it makes the individual a "knight of faith," one "who decides, by himself, on the existence of God and the truth of Christ, like a god deciding on God." And second, God becomes either impotent, incapable of fulfilling the promises of revelation, or a perverse judge, masking himself and exposing "me to unbelief by condemning me to a faith without reason."[77]

As we consider alternatives to this view of faith, it is important to make the fairly common observation that faith—understood as belief and trust—undergirds all that we do. A scientist, for example, would not be able to perform the simplest experiment without faith in the ways she has learned to scientifically proceed, without faith in her colleagues, without faith in the instruments she is using, and, more broadly, without faith in the tradition and discipline of science. More broadly still, there is faith that guides how we understand and look at the world, ourselves, and others. From this perspective, even the atheist has faith, only it is different from that of an explicitly religious person. An atheist has faith in an Enlightenment myth that imagines faith and knowledge reside in separate spheres.

Faith is rightly understood not as an alternative to knowledge but as a means to knowledge. Of course, it makes all the difference in the world what kind of faith one has. In fact, "having faith" is an awkward, if not misleading, use of words. Faith is not so much something we "have" as something we are given. Christian tradition has viewed faith as both a gift and a virtue or habit and therefore more deeply a part of who we are than mere "having" suggests. "Having" implies that, as with money, you sometimes might easily have it and other times easily not; it is external to yourself.[78] But to define faith as both a habit and a gift means that faith is internal and at the same time never ours to possess. As Marion points out, we don't get to decide by ourselves on the existence of God. If we did, faith would not be a gift. Rather, faith names a way of participating in the life of Christ, which is the triune life of gift and reception. Thus we can use the word *habit* to describe faith not because faith is only our work but because through faith we become habituated over time to living in Christ. It is through the gift and habit of faith, for example, that Paul can say, "For to me, living is Christ and dying is gain" (Phil. 1:21). The gift of faith has enabled Paul over time to identify his own life with that of Christ.

Marion's essay "They Recognized Him, and He Became Invisible to Them" provides an interesting analysis of how at the end of the Gospels the disciples of Jesus are not yet habituated in faith and are thus unable to recognize the risen Christ. Discussing Luke 24:13–25, where Jesus walks with two disciples on the road to Emmaus, Marion points out that the disciples are unable to recognize Jesus *not* because there is insufficient evidence—there he is before their eyes. Their inability is rather a failure of the imagination. "They do not recognize him because they cannot even imagine that this is really him. . . . They see nothing—in the sense that one sees nothing in a game of chess if one does not know how to play; they hear nothing—in the sense that one hears nothing (except noise) in a conversation if one does not know the language in which it is being conducted."[79] The disciples lack faith at this point not because they cannot muster the will to believe in the face of deficient evidence but because their eyes have not yet been opened. Marion concludes, "What we lack in order to believe is quite simply one with what we lack in order to see. Faith does not compensate, either here or anywhere else, for a defect of visibility: on the contrary, it allows reception of the intelligence of the phenomenon and *the strength to bear the glare of its brilliance*."[80]

Faith, then, is a way of seeing such that we are able to recognize and receive Christ (habitually) and, even more, to bear the glare of divine brilliance. Faith does not simply compensate for a lack of evidence but enables us to see and live into the evidence of God's abundance and love already present in our lives. Of course, as Lohfink notes, this seeing is "not any kind of superficial consumption with the eyes; it presupposes a believing surrender to the work of God."[81]

Such an account of faith might seem to contradict the well-known passage from Hebrews: "Now faith is the assurance of things hoped for, the conviction of things *not seen*" (11:1). The author goes on to recite a litany of the great faithful figures from the Old Testament. "By faith Abraham obeyed when he was called to set out for a place that he was to receive as an inheritance; and he set out, not knowing where he was going" (v. 9). Faith as a way of seeing and imagining does not negate the fact that much remains that is unseen or not yet fully realized. Yet all the faithful people that the author of Hebrews so vividly describes—Abel, Enoch, Noah, Abraham and Sarah, Isaac, Jacob, Moses, Rahab, and others—see, and therefore trust, that God is faithful and that God's word will not go unfulfilled. They see "from a distance" (v. 13); they look forward to "the city that has foundations, whose architect and builder is God" (v. 10). Even though much remains unseen, their faith still gives them a vision of God and the world that is something radically new and different.

If faith is a way of seeing, as Marion holds, then it is also a way of knowing. Perhaps this seems obvious, but as indicated earlier, often "common sense" separates faith and knowledge. Factual knowledge, such as science gives us, is often separated from faith. Yet early on in the Christian tradition, it was recognized that faith and knowledge are deeply intertwined. According to Robert Wilken, "Christianity did introduce something new to intellectual life, namely, that faith is the portal that leads to the knowledge of God"; he cites, among many examples, "'If you believe you will understand' (in the Greek and Latin versions of Isa. 7:9)."[82] John Milbank states that "faith remains possible, as *another* logos, another knowledge and desire, which we should not hesitate to describe as 'another philosophy' . . . since the Church fathers themselves did not hesitate to do so and Platonic/Neoplatonic philosophy already pressed against any philosophical subordination of *mythos*, *cultus* and community."[83] Stated differently, Christian faith is not an alternative to knowledge but is itself a knowledge and desire different from that which dominates the landscape of late modernity. And as Milbank indicates, this other knowledge (like all knowledges) does not exist above or independently of mythos, cultus, and community. It is in the context of the mythos of the risen Christ, the cultus of the breaking of bread, and the community of gathered disciples that Jesus is recognized and known and thus that the faith of the disciples is realized and strengthened.

Such faith therefore offers another knowledge, another mythos, and another cultus than the one preferred by a market economy, which imagines that "faith" resides in another sphere. Lohfink sees this erroneous division of spheres even back in the Gospels, where the disciples, concerned about the hungry crowd, ask Jesus to stop teaching. "Send them away so that they may go into the surrounding country and villages and buy something for themselves to eat" (Mark 6:36). The disciples' words are sober and realistic. "It's good to preach about the reign of God, but people have to eat, too. For the disciples these are two things that can be clearly separated. Jesus' task is preaching; the people must see to their food themselves."[84] Lohfink argues that the modern separation of faith from life, or of faith from economics, is already anticipated here. Yet Jesus refuses to accept this separation. "He emphatically tells his disciples that everything is part of the reign of God: the entirety of human existence, and eating by no means least."[85] And while the disciples begin to calculate how much money to collect in order to feed the people, Jesus shows that the reign of God is characterized by excess and superfluity. Lohfink in fact asserts that "*feeding* the 5,000" does not capture the true nature of this story. "Feeding" "smacks of sufficiency, school lunches, soup kitchens and not of feasting, banqueting, and festivals." By contrast, Mark tells of a festal banquet; according to Mark 6:39, Jesus tells those present to *recline*. Lohfink points out that in antiquity people ate in two different ways. When eating their normal everyday food, they sat at table. When celebrating a festival or special dinner, they reclined.[86] "Excess, wealth, and profligate luxury are thus the signs of the time of salvation—not economy, meagerness, wretchedness, and neediness. Why is that so?—because God is overflowing Life itself, and because God's whole desire is to share that life. God's love is beyond all measure, and God's gifts to human beings are not measured by their good behavior or deservingness."[87] So understood, faith ought not be confined to a sphere but rests in an abundance that spills over into all aspects of life.

Such faith necessarily has both a subjective and an objective component. It is personal since it is faith in a personal God, who is in relation within God's own self. Yet *personal* ought not be reduced to "private"; rather, faith is personal in the sense that "it involves our whole being."[88] Neither ought *personal* to be equated with subjectivistic; faith is always a gift from outside ourselves, from God, mediated through the body of Christ. To be incorporated into Christ (initiated at baptism) is to be *concorporated* into Christ's body, the church.[89] The "objective" component of faith has to do with who God is and God's own mighty acts in history, manifest through Israel and the church. For my purposes, we can call this objective component the hospitality of God: God's free and generous giving in creation and in new creation so that all the world might be drawn into communion with God. Faith as both gift and virtue leads us to live more fully out of God's abundance.

Hospitality, Economics, and Abundance

The economics that Christian hospitality seeks to embody, then, is marked by abundance, surplus, excess, and surprise. In the Gospel accounts of the feedings of the fish and loaves, there are always baskets left over. An uncalculating generosity characterizes these feasts. At this point, however, some nagging questions persist. Isn't it actually the case that there is *not* abundance? People go hungry and homeless. Increasingly, people are working longer hours just to make ends meet. Don't we need to work and save to secure our livelihood and that of our children? Isn't it more truthful to speak of scarcity rather than abundance? These kinds of questions easily lead us to endorse the spirit of capitalism: to compete and hoard, to have tight fists rather than open hands.

I do not have any easy answers to these questions. They resonate with me and create a deep tension with the conviction that through hospitality we participate in the abundant grace of God. We must see, however, that even though we live in a fallen world of competition and hoarding, this is not the place we are called to dwell. We must therefore see the modern "science of economics" for what it is, something that, as Beneton states, "puts all of its knowledge and power in the service of the new 'values': it gives voice to the social virtues of egoism, and it defines consumption as the ultimate good. Scientistic reason agrees with the materialist commandment: to live is to have."[90] Christian hospitality, in contrast, embodies the conviction that to live fully is to receive and to give God's own plenitude. Such plenitude is eschatologically present; the kingdom of God is at hand. Daniel Bell points in the right direction when he states that the question of alternatives to capitalism "becomes an eschatological one of the appearance of the Kingdom—which is another way of claiming that the alternative to capitalism has already appeared, even if it is not yet present in its fullness."[91] Christians are therefore called to live "as if" the kingdom of God, a reign marked by excess and superfluidity, is now present, because it *is* now present, though not in its fullness.

From this perspective, hospitality marks not so much a better life as an entirely new life.[92] The coming of Christ into the world is unprecedented; something entirely new has begun; and throughout the Gospels, especially in accounts of the resurrection, we are told that this newness is marked by abundance. Lohfink rightly reminds us, however, that "the overflowing grace can only reach people when they allow themselves to be taken into the service of the plan of God. The glory that illuminated Israel through Jesus was not for the purpose of creating a better life for the privileged (contra capitalism!), but was to bring the divine brilliance, through Israel, to the whole world."[93] As we allow ourselves through grace to participate in God's hospitality, we also begin to embody a different economics, one marked by giving and receiving, generosity and abundance, one that displays the "divine brilliance."

Discussing an alternative to capitalism, Bell points to what is classically known in the Christian tradition as the Works of Mercy. These corporeal and spiritual works of mercy constitute God's reordering of "human polity and economy in accord with God's reign." Bell adds that the Works of Mercy ought not be understood as mere individualistic acts of charity or "one-on-one acts of kindness to the exclusion of systemic concerns and communal efforts." Rather, as "they have been practiced across the ages (and continue to be practiced in some quarters), the Works of Mercy are corporate, communal activities. They describe the struggle for justice and liberation of a people, of a public and therefore political body named the Church."[94] For an example, we can look to the Catholic Worker Movement and its founding of the Houses of Hospitality, places where those in need of meals or a place to sleep are welcomed as guests and as "Christ." As Bell indicates, we might be tempted to dismiss these works as Band-Aids that do not really affect the system. But to do so would be shortsighted. Economics is not after all primarily a system or a science but about living in such a way that God's *oikonomia* is manifest. The Houses of Hospitality provide an alternative economics, dominated not by a spirit of competition and stinginess but by a spirit of giving and receiving. The Houses thus serve a good different from acquisition and consumption: communion with and service to Christ. As Dorothy Day firmly believed, the other *is* Christ.

If we find the economical abundance of God unpersuasive, it may be because we see it as unrealistic. But if this is so, perhaps "a picture holds us captive," as Wittgenstein has famously said. It is likely that such economics fails to persuade because of our failure as church to embody an alternative.[95] As Stanley Hauerwas notes, "Only by being initiated into the Christian tradition concerning the economy called 'trinity' does one have a chance of being freed from the necessities called 'economics.' For Christians know that the love displayed in God's life is not a zero-sum game but one of overflowing plenitude."[96]

Finally, we end on what could sound like a more sobering note. The faithful practice of Christian hospitality, of living in and through God's gracious abundance, does not shield Christians from suffering and even persecution. Christian hospitality refuses to gloss over suffering, pain, or injustice as so often happens in the global economy with its spirit of detachment from particular people and places. Rather, since *hospitality* names a way of being, *Christian hospitality* names a way of seeking to be Christ to another and to receive the other as Christ, even when the other is hungry, thirsty, in prison, or naked (Matt. 25). Even more, as Lohfink again points out, the disciples are promised an abundance—a hundred brothers and sisters, a hundred houses and fields, the joy of the reign of God—but only "with persecutions" (Mark 10:30). And Paul develops a whole theology of God's superabundant grace that "appears precisely in the weakness and distress of the faithful in order that it may be clear that the overflowing fullness of glory comes not from human strength, but from God alone."[97] Hospitality is not a hedge against pain and suffering but sees Christ present with us in our suffering, even as we acknowledge that such suffering does not have the last word.

4

Ethics as Choosing My Values?

How the *Hope* of Hospitality Lies Elsewhere

■ Just as the practice of hospitality offers a different economics from that of the global market, so also hospitality gives us a different "ethics" from the one so prevalent in our late modern culture. Of course, economics and ethics (as well as politics, which the following chapter examines) are not separate domains but rather different ways of looking at how we live. In this chapter, I focus on the hope of hospitality and explore the alternative Christian hospitality offers to the illusory hopes that so easily seduce us. As the virtue of the "not yet,"[1] hope reminds us that we live at the intersection of the already and not yet of God's eschaton. We hope because we see that living in this time is a great gift. Thus we can say, as does Karl Barth, that this provisional time is characterized not by "the minus-sign of an anxious 'Not-Yet' which has to be removed, but [by] the Plus-sign of an 'Already.'"[2] The living Christ is already fully present, giving us the gift of new creation. At the same time, however, Christ's presence is often concealed, covered over by our sins, our blindness and tragedy. The renewal of creation—the new heaven and new earth where God shall wipe away every tear from our eyes (Rev. 21:4)—is not yet complete. Hence we journey as disciples between two times, a journey in which we are graciously held by Christ even as we seek to hold on to him in hope.[3] This hope makes possible the extravagant giving and receiving of Christian hospitality and provides an alternative to the false hopes that easily rule our lives.

In what follows, I use the language of "false hopes" to point to the ways we have been trained to think and live such that we refuse to embody the conviction that our lives are gifts from God in time, oriented toward the fullness of God's new age. It might well be the case that such refusal is not so much outright rejection as it is our seduction by false stories and ideologies. Yet as I hope to show, recovering the language and interconnection of gift, hope, and hospitality provides an alternative to certain dominant understandings of ethics that are sustained by a *refusal* to see our lives as gifts from God.

As is well known, modern or Enlightenment approaches to ethics have been dominated by a set of common assumptions: (1) the priority of the subject, (2) the elevation of doubt as the key means to deeper knowledge, and, most notoriously, (3) the search for universal foundations. For example, the individual who "thinks for herself," and thus doubts all received "values," is assumed to be better off than someone who blindly accepts what she has been told. A modern approach assumes that unthinking acceptance of what has been handed down is inevitably naive and immature. Truth must rest on something more stable, more universal, than the merely particular and local. While these modern assumptions have been subjected to criticism many times over, they nonetheless continue to live on in our imaginations, even in our explicit rejection of them. As William H. Poteat notes in discussing these Cartesian or Enlightenment assumptions, "Cartesianism as an explicit philosophical doctrine is virtually without effect in this culture. It functions however at a tacit level like a repetition compulsion; it is ubiquitous and pervades the atmosphere in our life like chronic depression."[4] Still very much shaped by such modern assumptions, our contemporary culture often assumes the individual must appeal to reason rather than tradition to make ethical claims, to gain genuine knowledge, and to obtain peace between differing parties. In the wake of September 11, for example, some identified too strong of an adherence to religion as "fanatical" and as inevitably the source of much violence in the world. Others today wonder, if we have no common rationality, how do we resolve difference?

At the same time various strands of postmodern thought have pointed out that the quest for a common foundation has been illusory. Rather, postmodernism has claimed that all knowing is inevitably a mode of power and domination.[5] This postmodern turn typically maintains that since we have no common foundation, we ought at least tolerate, if not aesthetically embrace, our plurality and so ameliorate the potential for domination.[6] Such a position, however, is itself inherently violent. As we saw in the previous chapter, pluralism relies upon market forces that inevitably and destructively reduce all ways of life to consumer choices. John Milbank is thus exactly right to say that both modern philosophical liberalism and its postmodern aftermath are marked by an "ontology of violence."[7] The violence resides either in rational foundations, which domesticate or even erase the particular (and the stranger), or in the conviction that all truth and interpretation are inherently domination. Furthermore, both a modern foundational approach to ethics and a postmodern emphasis on power (which the subject must resist) share the assumption that ethics, in the final analysis, relies upon individual choice and is thus an individual achievement. Either the individual through reason chooses her ethics, or, in the absence of rational choice, she resists domination by celebrating the diversity of choices and values, what Stanley Fish refers to as "boutique multiculturalism."[8]

In light of Christian hospitality, however, concepts such as "choice" and "value" as currently used make little sense of our lives. In fact, "choice" distorts the hope of Christian hospitality, a hope situated not in us but in a God whose story and life we seek to embody. According to this story we are on pilgrimage, but the journey is not a solitary one.[9] Together with the "communion of saints," we seek to become strangers, guests, and hosts: strangers to that which is opposed to God, guests as we learn to receive from God who comes to us in manifold ways, and hosts as we seek to share what God has given. Such a journey habituates us to be creatures of hope, learning the difference between falsely hoping in ourselves and our personal values and truthfully hoping in the superabundance of God. As Josef Pieper rightly notes, "In the virtue of hope more than in any other, man understands and affirms that he is a creature, that he has been created by God."[10] Not only does God create us out of God's own superabundant love, but God also desires to re-create us so that we might more faithfully display the likeness and glory of God. The "*content* of Israel's fully eschatological hope," writes Robert Jenson, "is, inexorably, hope for the participation in God's own reality," a hope made fully possible by the resurrection.[11] Herein lies the hope of hospitality.

The Contemporary Refusal of Gift

To look more fully at what I am calling the contemporary refusal of gift, let us turn to the work of Alasdair MacIntyre, one of a number of contemporary thinkers who have helped us understand how deeply problematic is the ethos of our modern world.[12] MacIntyre begins his well-known analysis in *After Virtue* with a "disquieting suggestion." Imagine, he says, that the natural sciences have suffered a great catastrophe, so that all we have left are fragments of scientific knowledge but no context that might help us make sense of these fragments. Perhaps we might continue to use certain scientific terms, but such use appears arbitrary since the speakers are ignorant of the larger stories and standards. As MacIntyre himself has acknowledged, he draws this disquieting suggestion from the opening scene in Walter Miller's *A Canticle for Leibowitz*, where a nuclear war has destroyed most of "civilization," especially its scientific and technological knowledge.[13] In Miller's tale, the monks of the Order of St. Leibowitz see it as their calling to preserve these scientific fragments, trusting that some day they will make sense and benefit the world. MacIntyre compares this opening scene to our modern situation. We too are left with fragments in our contemporary context, only the fragments are moral ones: "[the] language and the appearances of morality persist even though the integral substance of morality has to a large degree been fragmented and then in part destroyed."[14] Thus moral judgments or "values" (in contrast to factual judgments) become primarily personal choices and, even worse, mere opinions.[15] Further, as MacIntyre observes, such "choice" is taken to be revelatory not of character but rather of identity, which is entirely self-generated: "I am what my choices have made me." The individual has no alternative but to choose what is to become good or bad for her. To criticize choices is to take a negative view of the individual making the choices, and more often than not the response is a retreat into solidarity with those with whom one agrees.[16] Yet as indicated in the previous chapter, the idea that we are freely choosing our private values easily blinds us to the ideologies and powers (economic and political) that are in fact forming and ruling our lives.

In a well-known passage, William James enthusiastically compares a liberal pluralistic society (especially as manifest in a university) to a kind of hotel:

> Innumerable chambers open out of it. In one you may find a man writing an atheistic volume; in the next someone on his knees praying for faith and strength; in the third a chemist investigating a body's properties. In a fourth a system of idealistic metaphysics is being excogitated; in a fifth the impossibility of metaphysics is being shown. But they all own the corridor, and all must pass through it if they want a practicable way of getting into or out of their respective rooms.[17]

Such a description nicely illustrates our contemporary situation. The individual chooses to do what he or she prefers in his or her own "chamber." We ought not ignore, however, that all are in the same hotel and all must pass through the same corridor, which has been defined as "basic standards of evidence and argument [that] work in separating good arguments from bad."[18] A certain rationality, experienced as suffocating by those who do not share it, governs the hotel space, a rationality that one must accept to get in and out of one's room.[19]

To summarize my all too brief account, our modern/postmodern situation has produced an ethic rooted primarily in the individual and his or her choices. This is problematic at a number of levels. First, while it assumes that it frees the individual from authority and tradition, in reality it binds the individual to one particular tradition, and a narrow one at that, emphasizing the individual as the creator of his or her identity. Second, this tradition of modernity, while advocating pluralism, actually suppresses it; James's image of the supposedly neutral space in the corridor can be entered only by those who share certain foundationalist presuppositions and thus certain assumptions about the good. Since the corridor is a deceptively coercive space, this "modern hotel" cannot offer genuine hospitality.[20] Furthermore, always staying in hotels, which are rootless and temporary places, makes us strangers. Such a modern/postmodern "place," rootless and coercive as it is, is simply unable to see our lives as gifts.

Some Philosophical Observations: Our Lives as Given

Before turning more explicitly to the theology of hospitality and the hope that sustains it, we are helped by considering more fully some key emphases in MacIntyre's analysis, ones he shares with some other significant philosophers. As indicated, MacIntyre points to the necessary givenness of all ethical and philosophical inquiry: "There is no standing ground, no place of inquiry, no way to engage in the practices of advancing, evaluating, accepting and rejecting reasoned argument apart from that which is provided by some particular tradition or other."[21] Thus, following MacIntyre, we could say that we are not "free" simply to choose our morality. We cannot, in other words, abstract ourselves from our context to reach a place where such lucid choice would be available. Nor, we might add, would this make us "free" even if it were a possibility. Some tradition or other always informs "freedom," and thus we deceive ourselves if we imagine freedom lies in abstraction or escape from our particular context.

The chemist and philosopher Michael Polanyi, referred to in the previous chapter, adds to MacIntyre's postcritical approach by analyzing even more fully the ways in which all our knowing is "fiduciary." He means by this that our knowing involves a relying upon or a "faithfulness" to what is given, even as we hope to discover heretofore unknown aspects of reality, a reality that may yet reveal itself to future eyes in an "indeterminate range" of unexpected manifestations.[22] What exactly does Polanyi mean by this description of knowledge? First, like MacIntyre, Polanyi points to the fact that our knowing calls for and in fact requires immersion in a tradition, a particular community where we are able to become apprentices of other persons. Thus, for example, "to be trained as a medical diagnostician, you must go through a long course of experience under the guidance of a master." A doctor comes to recognize certain symptoms "only by repeatedly being given cases for auscultation in which the symptom is authoritatively known to be present, side by side with other cases in which it is authoritatively known to be absent, until he has fully realized the difference between them and can demonstrate his knowledge practically to the satisfaction of an expert."[23] Second, the fiduciary aspect of knowledge reveals itself in the tacit dimension of all knowing. As is well known, Polanyi describes in rich detail how we tacitly rely upon some givens in order to arrive at more explicit knowledge. In a sense, we absorb or know tacitly by indwelling a given "place," whether this is before a telescope, on a bicycle, or while making an esoteric philosophical point. Thus, for Polanyi, knowing is irreducibly personal, where *personal* does not mean subjective but the immersion of our whole persons in that which we are seeking to know. Or, better stated in Polanyian terms, we immerse ourselves in that to which we are called. Faithfulness to our calling yields certain truths; those truths with heuristic depth (those that reveal more to later eyes) show that our antecedent faithfulness was indeed warranted.

So understood, we can claim, as does William H. Poteat, that all our knowing is a bonding and that "our *ultimate* relation therefore to all of our *derived relations* to existence are fiduciary."[24] Poteat can thus make the claim that our "modern derangement" results from a kind of "infidelity." Such language contrasts sharply with the modern emphasis on the choosing self, the self that achieves "freedom" by standing apart from all the "bonds" that constitute its identity. As Poteat notes, "Even though *de facto* we exist amidst a plexus of bonds, *de jure* all the gnostic images of our being in the world can only see these as a *bondage*, a falling into a worldly prison from which we can alone be saved by the *gnosis* of our *in principle* ecumenic doubt. By contrast, only when we remember that nature is our mother can we embrace and affirm these bondings as the very substance of our incarnate existence."[25] Poteat thus interprets our incarnate place not as a kind of bondage and imprisonment from which we must stand apart, as a gnostic would, but as a bonding. From this perspective, the image of the choosing self is inadequate, because it blinds us to all we are that we did not explicitly choose. In other words, it blinds us to the givenness of who we are.

These thinkers are all in different ways making the same logical point: we can come to know, come to hold certain convictions, come to see certain things in a particular way only through our bondedness to the world. For example, it is only through our reliance upon a tradition-formed place that we are able to see and name something as an injustice, or a gift, an act of hospitality, or a gesture of hope. We can describe this as a place of fidelity in that we necessarily rely upon it. As Nicholas Lash notes, "Whether in physics or in politics, in psychology or prayer, to grow in knowledge is to grow through trust: trust given, trust betrayed, trust risked, misplaced, sustained, received, and suffered."[26] An ethic that wishes to move beyond the false assumption that ethics is "choosing our values" must acknowledge that faithfulness, obedience, and hope—that is, a reception to that which is given—precede and necessarily form our ethics. The challenge, of course, is how to turn what is given into gift. For this we must now turn more explicitly to Christian hospitality.

Election and Hospitality

As MacIntyre, Polanyi, and Poteat all in various ways indicate, all approaches to ethics are sustained by some kind of tradition. I would add to this that all ethics are sustained by some kind of theology or *mythos*.[27] Christian hospitality relies upon the conviction that not only are we creatures in time, and thus formed by particular incarnate places in the world (that which is given), but also that ethics has to do with learning to receive our lives as gifts from God, created, redeemed, and sustained through the Word of God.[28]

The language of "election," as well as that of "calling," serves to remind Christians (as well as Jews) that we do not simply choose our own lives. God is the One who elects or chooses us to be a people (Israel and the church), not the other way around. God gives us our identity and even our name (as when, for example, Jacob becomes Israel). Those who are baptized become the church, the *ekklesia* and the body of Christ. They are now "in Christ" and a "new creation," an identity given to them by God that they did not have before. Augustine went so far as to claim that we do not choose our friends; God does. Such a way of putting the matter reminds us that even our friends, who were once strangers, are gifts from God.

Yet, the language of election has been met with numerous objections. Why does God choose some rather than others? Is chosenness simply a category invoked to justify or privilege one's particular self or tradition? Doesn't our response to God involve some choice on our part?

First, it is important to note that chosenness or election is not intended to point to moral superiority. This misinterpretation has no doubt been invoked at times by Christians and Jews, but even so, Jewish theology is

111

careful to deflect this misinterpretation. For example, in one midrash the Jews do not even want to be chosen; in another, God has gone to other people but was turned down.[29] Similar to Jewish self-understanding, the Christian claim that God is the electing God does not rest in a belief that Christians are somehow better than others. The lives of the saints often repeat the midrash insight: the saints do not want to be "chosen," or set aside as saints. Rather election, first and foremost, is a conviction about who God is, a conviction that points to God's deep desire to be embodied and enfleshed in the world. Thus the notion of election radically affirms the goodness of creation and our humble creaturely status. God himself enters history and becomes a body—the body of Israel and the body of Christ—for the sake of drawing the whole world back to God, thus renewing creation.

Jews and Christians, of course, differ in important ways in understanding the embodiedness of God. For Jews, God himself does not become a body but rather, through the covenant with Abraham, calls forth the body of Israel. Jewish theologian Michael Wyschogrod reiterates this conviction when he observes that Nazi anti-Semitism had a theological dimension: "It was the assault by evil on God *through the body of Israel.* This is the only interpretation of the Holocaust that even begins to do justice to that inexplicable mystery."[30] Wyschogrod's claim reflects the Jewish self-understanding that identifies God with the very body of Israel. So also, of course, Christians identify God with the body of Christ—"For in him [the beloved Son] all the fullness of God was pleased to dwell" (Col. 1:19)—an identification later extended to the church as Christ's body.

Election then must first be about who God is, God's goodness to come among us,[31] and God's desire to have a people in the world who will be in covenant with him and serve as a "light to the nations." Second, election is also about human response. Yet such response is misunderstood if it is simply equated with human choice. It is not as if we stand before God as we might stand in a grocery store trying to decide if we should choose apples or oranges. God's electing presence in our lives requires not a one-time "choice" but a response, which might be faithful or unfaithful, on our part. This way of putting the matter emphasizes that hospitality is not so much an isolated choice as a response of faithfulness to God's inviting presence in our lives. Hospitality, as emphasized in chapter 2's discussion of worship, is learning to receive what God offers, and in so doing we become participants in God's own giving and receiving. The initiative always belongs to God; we are first of all guests in God's good creation. Such reception is a lifelong journey, one in which we learn that we do not have to generate our own identity but are free to the extent we receive ourselves from the hands of God. In the church, this reception takes the form of mutual submission. As we respond to other members of Christ's body, we "receive" ourselves as part of that same body, dependent upon others' gifts and needs.

It may well be that the call to receive our lives as gifts leaves us with a certain unease. Surely there are tragedies, illnesses, betrayals—we could name more—that we cannot accept as gift. Yet at this point we must recall the grammar of creation discussed in the previous chapter. Sin, in all its various manifestations, is not part of God's good and generous creation. It is rather a privation, a lack, a feeding off creation by twisting, distorting, and destroying it. Even so, evil has no ultimate power; neither death, nor principalities, nor powers "will be able to separate us from the love of God in Christ Jesus our Lord" (Rom. 8:39). Christ has trampled down death with death, as proclaimed in the Orthodox liturgy. We are given the grace to accept our lives as gifts of Christ because we are also enabled, as Samuel Wells has emphasized, to "overaccept" evil. Wells borrows the term "overacceptance" from dramatic improvisation. In contrast to blocking (refusing) or simply to accepting an offer as is, overaccepting involves placing the offer within a larger framework that helps to keep the story going.[32] Thus Wells writes, "The church does not simply accept the story of evil. It has a story of its own. The church's story begins before evil began and ends after evil has ended. . . . This story does not accept evil—it overaccepts it."[33] The church overaccepts evil by placing it within the cosmic drama of salvation, beginning with creation and moving toward the eschaton, a story that enables us to name, disarm, and confess all that distorts our lives. Through such overacceptance—placing our lives in the wider story of the triune God—we are freed to receive our lives as gifts and enter more fully into communion with God and each other.

Hospitality and "Christian Homelessness"

If it is true that our lives are not our own but are given to us—by our places, by others, ultimately by God—it is also true that we are not entirely at home in the world. Imagery of being strangers in this world, of being pilgrims (as noted in chapter 1), has dominated the Christian imagination. Early Christians, in fact, linked hospitality to a certain kind of homelessness. Early Christian writers refer often to God's command to the Hebrews to welcome strangers because they too were once strangers and aliens in the land of Egypt. Augustine writes: "You take in some stranger, whose companion in the way you yourself also are, for we are all strangers. This person is a Christian who, even in his own house and in his own country, acknowledges himself to be a stranger."[34] Hospitality then appears to rest on a paradox: Christians are called to welcome the stranger even though they have no home, even though they are a diaspora people with no fixed place to call their own.[35] Christians are called even to give up their fixed place in the world—their land, their country, their family (Luke 14:24–33)—for the sake of the kingdom of God.

We seem to be left with an apparent contradiction. Henri Nouwen reminds us that it is inhospitable to welcome others and then leave. He reminds us, rightly, that good hosts need to have a place from which to extend hospitality.[36] How can Christians really practice good hospitality if they themselves are also displaced and homeless? How can strangers and sojourners offer hospitality?

The reality is that Christians (and Jews) are "homeless" or "displaced" only in a sense. We are displaced from locating our identity in our nation, our family, or our position in society, in order to locate it more fully before God. But this place is no timeless abstraction, no Motel 6. Rather, since we understand God as a purposeful actor who acts in and with a particular *people*, for the sake of the world, our place is with a concrete people, a people stretching back in time and now present (also known as the communion of saints). Scripture narrates this understanding of place: God calls Abraham to leave his home in Ur of Chaldees for the sake of the newly established covenant between God and Israel, and Abraham follows, journeying toward the promised land. God calls Moses to lead his people out of Egypt and Moses follows, leading the Israelites to a particular place. God of course comes in the person of Christ in a particular place and time, overcoming the dividing wall of hostility between Gentile and Jew, giving this one body "access in one Spirit to the Father." In this place created by Christ, no longer, Paul writes, are you "strangers and aliens, but you are citizens with the saints and also members of the household of God." Christ is the cornerstone "in whom you also are built together spiritually into a dwelling place for God" (Eph. 2:18–19, 22). The key point here is that those of the church at Ephesus (and so also we) are no longer strangers, not because they have found a comfortable spot to live or because they can feel "at home" with a certain like-minded people. They are no longer strangers because God through Christ dwells with them in the Spirit. God has come to where they are, making them a people, "the Israel of God" (Gal. 6:16), a nation identified not by geographical boundaries nor by bloodline but by the gift of the Spirit.

It might well be the case that we do not feel "at home" in the church today. This disconnect could be caused by any number of reasons. As discussed in chapter 1, it may be that the church itself has bought in to certain economic, ethical, or political assumptions. In light of our discussion of "ethics" as primarily about individual choice, there are no doubt churches today that emphasize the Christian life as simply a lifestyle choice. No doubt we often fall victim to sentimentalized, privatized, or trivial understandings of discipleship that create dissonance. Even more, despite Paul's proclamation that the peace of Christ has overcome divi-sions, we live in a church that is divided in all sorts of ways: economically, racially, nationally, and theologically. We cannot and ought not remain comfortable with a broken body.[37] Finally, it might be that our own sin or brokenness prevents us from seeing the church as Christ's body. Even so, despite these considerable obstacles, Christians are called ultimately not to trust in their own efforts (or failures) but in the promises and gifts of God. Paul reminds the Ephesian church in their renewed household that Christ *is* their peace and that they *are* a dwelling place for the Spirit. This is not an optional reality. The challenge for them is to live into this new reality in a way that shapes how they see both themselves and the world.

How then are Christians to practice hospitality when we are called to follow One who had "no place to lay his head"? As indicated, Christ iden-tified himself with a body, a people, of which he is the cornerstone. This place is not a building but a people, bound together as the communion of saints across time and space. Any particular manifestation of Christ's body (in a local church) is but a drop in the bucket of all the saints and citizens that God has drawn together. Reflecting on this place, Stephen Fowl rightly reminds us that the beauty of Zion, described in Psalm 50 and Isaiah 2, is not a function of its buildings but of "the sort of common life its inhabitants maintain with God and with each other," a life accom-panied by justice, fidelity, and truthful speech. Like the splendor of Zion, the beauty of God's household described in Ephesians 2 is not so much geographical as it is the compelling manifestation of a particular com-mon life, a life that both attracts the nations and reveals God's glory.[38] The place of hospitality therefore does not require a fixed location but a people who share a common life of forgiveness, reconciliation, peace, and, most centrally, worship. Where then do we lay our heads? All of these practices indicate that we "lay our heads" upon Christ and each other and in so doing reveal the beauty of Christ's body to the world.

A particularly significant aspect of the beauty of hospitality is that it is marked by extravagance and abundance. As noted in the previous chapter, God's hospitality does not operate on assumptions of scarcity and saving but rests on the assumption of superabundance where there is no need to hoard and save. Such abundance is reflected in the well-known biblical stories in which God provides daily manna in the wilderness and loaves and fishes for the multitudes. Gerhard Lohfink reminds us, in fact, that the fishes and loaves account, with the ordering of the people in groups, recalls the manna in the wilderness story.[39] The abundance of God's provision in these biblical stories points not only to the continuity of God's hospitality across time but also proleptically to the abundance of life itself, which becomes reality after Easter. *Even death cannot make of life a scarce commodity.* As indicated earlier, the hope of hospitality lies not in our self-creation, our saving for ourselves, nor even in our talents; it rests rather in the overflowing abundant life of God. "I came," says Jesus, in a familiar passage, "that they may have life, and have it abundantly" (John 10:10).

Lohfink adds, however, that the superabundance of God's grace, the purpose of which is to bring the divine brilliance to the whole world, appears precisely in the "weakness and distress of the faithful in order that it may be clear that the overflowing fullness of glory comes not from human strength, but from God alone."[40] Again, the hospitality we both receive and offer is not simply ours but always our reception of a gift.

A final feature of this extravagant hospitality is that it draws people together without obliterating their God-given differences. Indeed the uniqueness of each person is necessary so that there will be a fuller abundance, a genuine giving to another and receiving of what we do not already have. James's image of a hotel with a common corridor through which people merely pass fails to grasp the extravagance and abundance of this hospitality. It is better witnessed by an open and expansive household (*oikos*), the heart of which is a large common table where strangers are welcome and food and wine are generously shared. Lohfink in fact notes that in antiquity "there was a well-known form of the common meal called *eranos* at which the host only provided the space but not the food. Each brought to the meal what she or he had and ate of what all had brought. We have the same practice; it is what Americans call the potluck."[41] As those of us who have been to potlucks know, the particular gifts that each person brings create an abundance, and all are provided for, even those who might not have been able to contribute food. While we will turn more fully to the Lord's Supper in a later chapter, we can note here that this liturgical meal enacts the hope of hospitality as the church gathers to receive the extravagant gift of God in the bread and wine, thus becoming Christ's unique body, marked by a wealth of gifts given so that all may flourish.

The Hope of Hospitality: A Possibility in Our Current Context?

To relate this practice of hospitality more fully to our current context, it would be instructive to revisit MacIntyre in light of the practice of hospitality. As indicated earlier, MacIntyre's profound description of our modern moral dilemma, his disquieting suggestion, was influenced by the beginning of Miller's *A Canticle for Leibowitz*. But what about the ending of Miller's fascinating novel? How does MacIntyre's resolution compare with this? The ending of Miller's tale provides us with important insights into the practice of hospitality, resources that MacIntyre himself does not fully take into consideration.

MacIntyre ends *After Virtue* with a chapter interestingly titled "After Virtue: Nietzsche *or* Aristotle, Trotsky *and* St. Benedict." In this chapter, MacIntyre asks whether we can recover a shared conception of the good and of the narrative unity of a moral tradition or whether we must accept Nietzsche's conclusion that morality is simply a disguise for the will to power. Given the fact that, as MacIntyre argues, advanced capitalism lacks the political and economic structures to sustain an Aristotelian understanding of the moral life, it would seem we have little hope for the recovery of such a tradition. MacIntyre maintains, however, that his solution does not commit him to a "generalized social pessimism." We must now cease to shore up the *imperium*, our current political structure, and instead foster new forms of communities "within which civility and the intellectual and moral life can be sustained through the new dark ages which are already upon us."[42] Since MacIntyre does not elaborate on whether these communities exist or, if not, how one might develop such a community, his solution may sound utopian. Elsewhere, however, MacIntyre defends himself against such a charge. In *Three Rival Versions of Moral Inquiry*, he states that his proposal for a new form of community, a postliberal university of constrained disagreements,[43] is not utopian because, first, something like this has already existed (the University of Paris in the thirteenth century), and second, the charge of utopianism is "sometimes best understood more as a symptom of the condition of those who level it," of their failure to imagine a genuine alternative to the current predicament or even to see this as a predicament.[44]

While MacIntyre defends himself against utopianism as well as pessimism, he does not fully—it seems to me—extricate himself from these charges. At a conference at the University of Notre Dame on the "culture of death," MacIntyre again insightfully diagnosed our modern dilemma, repeating many of the important themes in his published works: moral belief is construed purely in terms of personal choice, the self-created "individual" has replaced character formation as constitutive of identity, and compartmentalization has fragmented our lives such that adaptability is the new virtue and inflexibility the new vice. Further, MacIntyre noted that whereas earlier debates took place in societies that shared standards and attitudes, we now lack these, and for this reason our modern forms of public debate are generally counterproductive. When asked whether the public participation and intervention of someone like Pope John Paul II had been counterproductive, MacIntyre responded that Pope John Paul's service had been to provide "those who were lacking it an idiom," a rhetoric for those who were already in agreement with him. While this has been an important task, MacIntyre noted, it has not significantly altered our impoverished forms of public conversation.[45]

Calling our public efforts to engage another generally counterproductive would seem to make the practice of hospitality[46]—an aspect of which is genuinely giving and receiving from the stranger—unlikely. We need to consider more fully, then, *how* hospitality might be a possibility in our current context. What might it look like?

In part 3 of Miller's *A Canticle for Leibowitz*, "Fiat Voluntas Tua" (Thy Will Be Done), we discover that the scientific fragments have been recovered and placed into a coherent schema so that once again science makes sense. Civilization is no longer "barbaric" (part 1); it has not only passed through a renaissance (part 2) but now "advanced" to the point where atomic destruction has become a real threat once again. The story that clearly dominates the culture in part 3 is the "scientific story": understandings of the good are read in light of scientific-technological solutions. So, for example, local authorities have set up euthanizing centers to extend "mercy" to those suffering from radiation poisoning due to nuclear fallout. In one telling exchange, the euthanizing Dr. Cors confronts Father Zerchi, an abbot:

> "Listen Father. They sit there and they look at you. Some scream. Some cry. Some just sit there. All of them say, 'Doctor, what can I do?' And what am I supposed to answer? Say nothing? Say, 'You can die, that's all.' What would you say?"
>
> "'Pray.'"
>
> "Yes, you would, wouldn't you? Listen, pain is the only evil I know about. It's the only one I can fight."
>
> "Then God help you."
>
> "Antibiotics help me more."[47]

Clearly, the narrative embodied in the person of Dr. Cors—one that sees ethics in terms of choice and one that witnesses to the triumph of death rather than life—appears to have won the day.

But Miller has titled this section "Thy Will Be Done," an indicator that Dr. Cors will not get the final word. As the nuclear war is about to destroy civilization, two significant things happen in the story. First, the church carries forward with its plan to send a spaceship into outer space to preserve a small human colony.

But second, and I think more important, Miller develops the strange character of a certain bicephalous woman, Mrs. Grales, a grotesque reminder of the effects of an earlier nuclear fallout. Throughout the final section of the novel, Mrs. Grales pleads with Father Zerchi to baptize her other, lifeless head, which she has named Rachel. He declines, calling it a matter for "your parish and diocese." In the final scenes of the novel, as

Father Zerchi is hearing Mrs. Grales's confession, a nuclear bomb strikes. As Father Zerchi lies dying, with buzzards circling overhead, he discovers that while Mrs. Grales has died, Rachel has come to life, watching him "with cool green eyes and [smiling] innocently."[48] He makes an effort to baptize her, but she leans "quickly away from him. Her smile froze and vanished. *No!* her whole countenance seemed to shout." Then Rachel offers him, despite his initial refusal, the wafer and wine:

> She used no conventional gestures, but the reverence with which she had handled it convinced him of one thing: *she sensed the Presence under the veils*. She who could not yet use words nor understand them, had done what she had as if by *direct instruction*, in response to his attempt at conditional baptism.
> He tried to refocus his eyes to get another look at the face of this being, who by gestures alone had said to him: I do not need your *first* Sacrament, Man, but I am worthy to convey to you *this* Sacrament of Life.[49]

As he draws his final breath, Father Zerchi weeps in gratitude that "he had seen primal innocence in those eyes, and a promise of resurrection. One glimpse had been a bounty."[50] The passage recalls Simeon's seeing the baby Jesus before his death: "My eyes have seen your salvation, which you have prepared in the presence of all peoples" (Luke 2:25–32).

What are we to make of this mysterious ending? According to theologian Ralph Wood, Rachel "seems thus to be a figure of the remnant church that God raises up even when the world collapses. This Rachel is indeed a dispenser rather than a receiver of grace, as she places the final viaticum in the dying abbot's hand. . . . This new Rachel embodies the hope that can save the world because it is the hope that dissolves all bitterness. . . . It comes whenever the saving words are pronounced . . . Thy will be done."[51] As Wood notes, the hope that presents itself at the end of the novel, in the person of Rachel, lies not simply in human action (we do not know the final outcome of the spaceship) but in God's action with a particular people: Rachel and Father Zerchi. In Rachel, Father Zerchi sees the presence of God: the promise of resurrection and the totally unexpected inbreaking of God's reign in a despairing situation of murder, death, and dying.

How does this ending compare to MacIntyre? MacIntyre of course puts forward a philosophical analysis that in some ways does not lend itself to a neat comparison with a piece of creative fiction. Even so, we can see that the formation of the spaceship community is a possible example of what MacIntyre has in mind when he states we need new forms of community that no longer shore up the *imperium*.[52] At the same time, however, we might note that the spaceship has to *leave* the world, thus lending some credence to those who would call such communities utopian.

Yet what about Miller's bicephalous woman? It is in the story of Rachel that Miller's tale becomes one of hope in the midst of despair, rather than one of utopianism or pessimism. And the hope Miller pictures is rooted in God's own hospitality. Rachel has been *given* the preternatural gifts of Eden, "those gifts which Man had been trying to seize by brute force again from Heaven since first he lost them."[53] It is through Rachel, a fellow creature, that God offers Father Zerchi a promise of resurrection and his presence in the bread and wine, the body and blood of Christ. Zerchi gratefully receives God's abundant hospitality: "one glimpse had been a *bounty*, and he wept with *gratitude*."[54]

In comparing MacIntyre to Miller at this point, it seems as if the narrative whose loss MacIntyre bemoans does not fully appear in MacIntyre's own thinking.[55] As MacIntyre himself acknowledges, even if we are able to "out narrate" our opponents, it often does not seem to matter, for public debate seems counterproductive. Others continue to be postmodern aesthetic Nietzscheans or modern Enlightenment emotivists, and people retreat into solidarity with those who already agree with them. Even Miller's tale registers this dark pessimism, as the priest's attempt to "out narrate" the doctor does not work. Civilization continues on its same destructive path.

At this point, Michael Wyschogrod reminds us of a key point central to both the Jewish and Christian tradition: "The redeemer whom God sends is not a brilliant orator but a stutterer who seems least fit to persuade the tyrant to let the people go. . . . It is God and not the talent of his messenger that deserves praise." In the novel, hope does not rest in the "rational" people but appears in the least likely of places, the bicephalous woman, who stutters and seems irrational. What is the relation between this hope and the practice of hospitality? Wyschogrod continues: "The deepest sign of the presence of God, the fundamental reason for the wonder that is evoked by all contact with the spirit, is the occurrence of the unexpected. Salvation comes from unexpected quarters, at unexpected times, and through unexpected agents."[56] Wyschogrod rightly reminds us that genuine hospitality always involves welcoming the *stranger*, someone who may not be able or inclined to reason as we do. Even more, he indicates that the stranger may well be a messenger of God or a "God-bearer." Such hospitality is sustained not by human ingenuity but by God, who can come to us in unexpected ways and whose presence in the stranger might well be as discomforting as it is comforting.

Such hospitality does not fit on the pessimism/utopianism grid. Certainly in our welcoming of the stranger we seek to engage her in debate, conversation, discussion about the good. But we could well lose the debate, and there's a sense in which it does not matter. Father Zerchi's inability to persuade Dr. Cors does not, in the final analysis, make any difference (a fact that MacIntyre registers, though not in its eschatological light). A new Rachel appears, embodying the hope that saves the world, making more fully present the "not yet" of God's kingdom.

This is by no means to suggest that we ought therefore to withdraw from the world or engage in quietism, a passive form of spirituality that minimizes human activity. It is, however, to ground our hope in the now and not yet of God's kingdom. Such hope frees us to live in and witness truthfully to God's love in Christ, with courage and humility, without having to "win" or control the outcome. In fact, as Reinhard Hütter notes, hospitality and witnessing to or honoring the truth are practices that require each other.[57] Such hospitality is admittedly difficult and may even be painful. Because of self-deception or a need for approval, for example, we ourselves might refuse to receive the truth of how God desires to be in our lives. The guest or host (roles that are fluid when hospitality is rightly practiced) might refuse the truth and even seek to annihilate it, as in the case of martyrdom. Even so, when we live into the conviction that our lives are gifts from God and that our hope is in the now and not yet of God's reign, we have no "choice" but to practice hospitality.

MacIntyre rightly indicates the need for "new forms of community within which the moral life could be sustained." In light of our emphasis on Christian hospitality, we can add that these need to be communities sustained by faithful worship of God, a worship that is our participation in God's own triune hospitality. The church universal has never been without saints and local communities that have witnessed in both extraordinary and ordinary ways to the hospitality of God. Examples of such communities of hospitality include, among others, the Catholic Worker Houses of Hospitality for the poor and homeless (founded by Dorothy Day and Peter Maurin), Brother Roger's ecumenical Taizé community in France, the L'Arche communities for mentally handicapped (founded by Jean Vanier), and the Church of the Saviour in Washington, D.C (founded by Gordon Cosby). We will examine these latter two communities in the final chapter. And, I must add, ordinary churches in places like South Bend, Indiana, can witness and participate in the hospitality of God in truly remarkable ways.

The practice of Christian hospitality enables us to turn from the "choosing subject" that has dominated much of our culture's understanding of ethics, and not only turn but see this subject for what it is: a modern piece of fiction that has blinded us to all of the giving and receiving that constitute our lives. As Christians, we are called to receive the gift of God's forgiving and sustaining grace and allow God to transform who we are, so that, as David Steinmetz says about the eucharistic liturgy, the bread consumes us.[58] In this journey between the now and the not yet, we hope in a God who desires to transform us, such that we have no choice about whether or not to extend God's hospitality to others; it is simply who we have become. Perhaps only the saints reach this point consistently. But we place our hope in a surprising God, who uses ordinary people like us and even complete strangers to manifest his presence in the world.

5

The Politics of Higher Education

How the *Love* of Hospitality Offers an Alternative

■ As I child, I learned bits and pieces of the Presbyterian Westminster catechism from Melinda, my good friend and next-door neighbor. To the familiar first question, "What is the chief end of man?" we learned to respond, "To glorify God and enjoy Him forever." The end or purpose of humanity came first, before questions about creation, sin, redemption, and the rest.

Yet all citizens, as is obvious today, do not share this purpose. Some see this "chief end" as irrational or even crazy. Political philosopher John Rawls, for example, claims that Ignatius of Loyola's conviction (and, of course, the church's conviction) that humanity's chief end is serving God strikes "us as irrational, or more likely as mad."[1] In a defense of liberal democracy, Richard Rorty has written,

> Rather, we heirs of the Enlightenment think of enemies of liberal democracy like Nietzsche or Loyola as ... "mad." We do so not because there is no way to see them as fellow citizens of our constitutional democracy, people whose life plans might, given ingenuity and good will, be fitted in with those

of other citizens. . . . They are crazy because the limits of sanity are set by what *we* can take seriously.[2]

Such statements by leading advocates of liberal democracy highlight the dilemma for Christian disciples not only in the modern academy but also in our broader political context. The Christian conviction that our final end is the love and service of God interrupts rational liberal discourse and therefore seems out of place. In Rorty and Rawls's use of "madness" and "insanity" we see the collision of two worlds or dramas. What the world of Rorty and Rawls cannot allow is that saints like Ignatius of Loyola do not simply choose their final end out of a number of possibilities. They do not choose to be saints. Rather, in the Christian tradition, as emphasized in the previous chapter, it is always the case that God first chooses persons (not the other way around), and it is the church, not the individual, that ultimately recognizes their sainthood. Ignatius did not choose to love and serve God but rather was *given* the grace and power to do so in a way so compelling he could not do otherwise. He thus lived out of a very different political vision from the one embraced by Rorty and Rawls.

From the perspective of Rorty and Rawls, Christian hospitality too will seem like a mad or crazy practice. Since hospitality, like all Christian practices, is grounded in humanity's chief end, it will inevitably interrupt rational liberal discourse and practice. It will be unable to play by the rules of the game, since its understanding of rationality collides with liberal rationality, whether in its encyclopedic (modern) or genealogical (postmodern) form.[3]

My claim in this chapter is that Christian hospitality cannot acquiesce to the kind of positioning that Rorty and Rawls advocate; it cannot try to become less "crazy" by accepting the ground rules they present, rules that have unfortunately come to shape the Christian imagination. Rather, practitioners of Christian hospitality must accept their "madness"; that is, they must accept how radically differently they are called to live, teach, learn, and be from what modern politics, dominant in the academy, allows. In earlier chapters I used the word *vigilant* to characterize a faithful hospitality, and in the politics of our culture, vigilance is especially called for. Faithful political vigilance (like economic and ethical vigilance) can enable Christians to live all aspects of their lives in light of their final end, the love of God.

Politics and Hospitality

For many of us, a kind of nervousness surrounds any talk of "religion and politics." In polite company, one does not discuss "religion" and "politics"; these are too divisive, it is assumed, and therefore best left in separate departments. As noted in chapter 1's discussion of privatized hospitality, John Cuddihy claims that today civility seems to require that religious identities "must not be pushy, elbowing themselves into contexts where they do not belong."[4] Inasmuch as the practice of hospitality has absorbed this understanding of civility, it too has avoided politics. Many therefore regard hospitality as essentially an apolitical practice. If anything, it has often become indistinguishable from the kind of civility that Cuddihy describes. In the educational sphere, such civility is displayed most fully in the dictum "We agree to disagree": each has his or her opinion, and the best way to move on is to allow for this. John Bennett in fact argues that practicing hospitality in the classroom means a "radical openness to the other, attending to him or her in sharing and receiving insights and perspectives about self and world."[5] So understood, hospitality becomes tolerance for a plurality of "perspectives." In the wake of the Los Angeles riots when Rodney King's uniformed assailants were found innocent, King invoked this same understanding of hospitality: "Why can't we all just get along?" In both instances, hospitality has to do with avoiding conflict, tolerating others, and allowing for a plurality of views.

While it might seem that such tolerance and pluralism are equivalent to Christian hospitality, it is my contention that the politics that sustains this understanding inevitably undermines Christian hospitality. This type of politics can be elusive, mostly because we fail to see that an assumption like "we agree to disagree" underwrites a particular kind of politics. Far from being apolitical, the practice of hospitality is always sustained by some political assumptions. A hospitality equated with openness, tolerance, and pluralism is entrenched in a particular kind of politics: the polity of our liberal democratic nation-state. By practicing such hospitality, Christians embrace the politics of liberalism, all the while failing to notice that it is a politics.[6] Liberal democratic politics relegates hospitality, along with "faith" and "religion" more broadly, to an apolitical sphere. Stated differently, our liberal democratic polity has led many Christians to fail to see the church itself as a political body.[7] When we fail to see this, we are easily seduced into serving the nation-state rather than the church.

Pope John Paul II famously described Catholic colleges and universities as coming *ex corde ecclesia*, from the heart of the church. Christian colleges and universities have been birthed from the church, yet are they now serving a different master? I think in many instances the answer is yes. Yet the retrieval of Christian hospitality as a political practice opens the possibility for making our institutions more faithful to the *ecclesia* from whence they came, and thus more faithful in their service to the world.

The Politics of Liberal Democracy

What is the politics of liberalism? And how exactly does the politics of our liberal democracy erase the practice of hospitality? In the popular imagination of the United States, politics refers to "red states" and "blue states."

On the one hand are "conservative" Christians and others who believe that they should get "their people" elected to various offices and assigned to the judicial bench. For them, the nation-state should be "Judeo-Christian," and the way to shore up the United States as a Christian nation is to use the means the government provides.

On the other hand are those who vigorously resist this effort on several grounds. First, they oppose the identification of one party (Republican) with Christian "values." Second, while they believe that one's faith should influence politics, they resent the more direct intrusion into politics that the "conservative" side seems to advocate. Faith should be present in the public political sphere, they say, only *indirectly*. If there is more direct involvement, concern is usually voiced about the separation between church and state. For example, church historian E. Glenn Hinson warns against any kind of partnership between American churches and the U.S. government. "*That kind of partnership is dangerous, especially for the churches!!* Does anyone need to look back on much world history to see how the German churches rallied behind Adolf Hitler . . .?" Hinson rather suggests that, like early Christians and early Baptists in both America and England, "*the churches must train an educated citizenry*. That would include politicians, prepping Abraham Lincolns and Jimmy Carters and Bill Clintons."[8]

Actually the two sides of this great divide share some crucial assumptions. Both assume that the church is being political to the extent that it involves itself in the politics of the nation-state, whether directly (supporting candidates for office) or indirectly (training citizens). Both sides regard the nation-state as the primary bearer of politics. Both accept the tenets of liberal democracy. Democrats can be called "reform liberals," in that historically they have argued for government intervention in the market economy in order to reduce inequalities. Republicans can be described as "classical liberals," in that they typically have retained an allegiance to the free market.[9] These two forms of liberalism have in common some fundamental features, the chief of which is individualism. Correlative to this is the idea that society "is, or should be, a collection of free individuals."[10] These individuals have certain inalienable rights (though there is disagreement about what these rights should be). In any case, it is the duty of the government to protect these free individuals, not only from each other but also from outside threats. John Wright aptly summarizes the "plotline" of liberal political theory that dominates the cultural imagination, both "liberal" and "conservative": "Humanity exists as autonomous, rational individuals who seek to pursue their own self-interests. The ability to engage in this pursuit is called freedom or liberty—a formal category of the will that possesses no specific content, except as it is filled by the individual's choice." Individuals voluntarily submit to the state to protect this freedom, and the state claims sovereignty to maintain liberty, especially against outside threats.[11]

For many Christians, this will sound like political "common sense," sort of like driving on the right side of the road (at least in the United States). And yet as Christians we need to ask, in what ways have we come to see ourselves as autonomous agents pursuing our self-interest, relying upon the state to guarantee freedom? From this perspective, hospitality becomes at best a mere individual effort; at worse, it simply evaporates. Ought we accept such politics as formative of the body of Christ?

Before addressing this question, we need to look more closely at the politics of liberal democracy. First, contemporary politics can be contrasted with earlier understandings of politics. Ancient Aristotelian understandings were concerned with the common good of the *polis*, the city, specifically the city-state. To be a citizen of Athens, for example, was to be a part of a community with a shared history, culture, language, and bloodline. It was not primarily a form of government but a community. Politics was about how that community, that *polis*, was ordered to produce a common good. In contrast, politics today tends to be equated with elections, legislation, and procedural polity, and liberal political theory does not aim for the common good (since there is no way to adjudicate this) but rather imagines the state as a neutral entity that allows individuals to pursue their own goods. Such liberalism is typically characterized as emphasizing procedures, moral rules, or rights over the good. Liberalism therefore is necessarily yoked with pluralism; there are plural understandings of the good. The virtue that provides social cohesion is tolerance. As political philosopher Murray Jardine argues,

> Stated somewhat crudely, the argument made by most present-day advocates of "democracy" is that the central issue of premodern moral reasoning—how people ought to live—can be avoided by taking individual freedom as the basic goal of human societies. All people see the world differently, that is, all people have different "values," so that the best, and indeed the only workable, type of social system is that everyone should be free to act as they please, as long as they do not impose their value on anyone else.

Thus, Jardine continues, "tolerance is the fundamental principle for a modern democratic society, and makes irrelevant the premodern concern about how people should live, since this is left up to each individual."[12]

Some have pointed out, however, that the political "contest" is better characterized not as being between "rights" and "goods" but as competing conceptions of the good society. David Solomon states, for example, "Kantian deontology carries with it a certain picture of the self and its good, as do the various versions of nineteenth-century utilitarianism. These conceptions of the good may appear thin and strained when compared to the rich and comprehensive picture of the human good one finds in classical Thomism, but they are surely conceptions of the human good nevertheless."[13] Even though modern political theory has attempted to move politics to more neutral ground, in reality it has not done so.

For example, John Locke (1632–1704), whose ideas deeply influenced Thomas Jefferson and American political thought more broadly, sought to free "politics from the kinds of traditions and prejudices which naturally bind men together, but which also cause them, in too many instances, to fight."[14] Locke thus proposed a Law of Nature from which could be derived certain basic individual rights: life, liberty, and property. Among many others, however, C. B. Macpherson notes that inherent in Locke's understanding of the individual and his or her rights is already a particular bias (one, he says, that is also in Thomas Hobbes). "The individual with which [they] start had already been created in the image of *market man*." That is, the essence of freedom is freedom from any relations with others beyond those one has entered through contract, with a view to one's own interest.[15] In a similar vein, Jardine observes that Locke's theory of property has a materialistic bias. Locke assumed that "a person who works and produces something *of value* should be rewarded." But Locke tended to think of value in material or economic terms. Thus, for example, he reasoned that European settlers were justified in using the land of the Native Americans, since the Native Americans could live on less land if they just cultivated it.[16] As Jardine points out, however, this argument didn't make sense to the Native Americans, since the land also had spiritual value. From the outset, the conception of the "individual" and of "value" is informed and shaped by certain prior assumptions. Thus attempts to secure neutral limitations on individual freedom inevitably fail. As Jardine rightly concludes, "A strong argument can be made that every version of liberalism does favor certain social groups, does tend to promote a very specific way of life, and does indeed embody a very definite worldview."[17]

In relation to hospitality, it is important to see how liberalism and pluralism underwrite each other. If there is no common good, then the only "good" we share is the "freedom" to choose our own good. We agree to disagree. We "welcome diversity" because . . . diversity in and of itself is the good! As John Rawls has argued, "Variety of conceptions of the good is itself a good thing."[18] A hospitality equated with "welcoming diversity," then, has essentially absorbed the liberal/pluralist polity, a polity that, as I will argue, ultimately makes the faithful practice of Christian hospitality almost impossible.

At this point the reader may feel uneasy. If we had to choose between a politically imposed good and a politics in which individuals had the freedom to choose their good, wouldn't the freedom to choose be much better, risky though it is? Isn't the imposition of a good inherently violent? Yet this way of putting the matter misses the point. If politics has to do with the way we organize and arrange our lives in service to the good, the prior question is, what good are we already serving? We do not start in midair, so to speak; we are always already a part of some story or tradition that we did not explicitly choose. The great illusion of liberal democracy is that freedom to choose is absolute (as long as we don't hurt anyone). Yet in our "culture of choice," such politics is sustained by and underwrites a market economics approach to education, work, family, and so on—a fact we do not explicitly choose. As Stanley Hauerwas notes, such a polity in colleges and universities further inscribes students "into capitalist practices in which they are taught to think that choosing between 'ideas' is like choosing between a Sony or a Panasonic. It never occurs to them that the very idea they should 'choose' is imposed."[19] Now we can see clearly that pluralism is simply an illusion.[20] The prior question to ask of any educational or political endeavor is, which good is it serving?

William Cavanaugh brings this point home when he states that the pluralism of "choice" and "belief" remains a reality only at the private level, a necessary move (according to this view) to avoid conflict and maintain peace. In the public sphere, however, Cavanaugh observes, "the State itself is the ultimate good [and it] is by no means neutral. It defends and imposes a particular set of goods—e.g., the value of the market, scientific progress, the importance of choice itself—which excludes its rivals. Wars are now fought on behalf of this particular way of life by the State."[21] Far from simply allowing for a variety of goods, our dominant politics ends up underwriting the very specific "goods" of late modernity as embraced and coercively defended by the nation-state.

The Academic Politics of Liberalism/Pluralism

This politics of liberalism/pluralism dominates the academy. For one sign of this we can look at how current educational practice typically treats words like *dogma* and *orthodoxy* as entirely negative. *Dogma* is often preceded by the word *narrow* and associated with being close-minded. Education, it is thought, ought to free students from the narrow dogmas and orthodoxies that have heretofore shaped their lives. Education ought

129

to teach them to be open-minded. In the name of education, authority, especially religious authority, is waved aside "to give precedence to the ethic of free inquiry."[22] In contrast to "dogma," concepts like "diversity" and "pluralism" are enthusiastically promoted.

At a 2005 conference at Baylor University on Baptist higher education, this opposition between orthodoxy and pluralism became evident. Baptist historian Bill Leonard paired orthodoxy with fundamentalism, while Kirby Godsey, then president of Mercer University, stated that "the imposition of orthodoxy, however defined, runs counter to the essential character of a college or university."[23] In this view orthodoxy, like dogma, shackles the free search for truth. As another speaker claimed, only fundamentalists believe in indoctrination.[24] True education does not indoctrinate.

Such comments reflect the conventional wisdom about education: students should be free to make up their own minds, indoctrination is antithetical to education, and no kind of "orthodoxy" or even philosophy should be imposed on students. This understanding reflects Immanuel Kant's famous definition of an enlightened individual, one who "dares to know!" without "self-incurred tutelage" and has the courage to use his or her own understanding without guidance from another.[25] Kant, however, did not free education or enlightenment from the shackles of dogma and orthodoxy, but rather substituted one orthodoxy for another.[26] As Hauerwas puts it, "Of course, teaching students to 'make up their own minds' is a form of indoctrination, but since it underwrites the hegemonic character of liberalism, few notice it as such."[27]

In matters of education, the question is not whether or not to "impose" orthodoxy but what kind of orthodoxy we in fact are promoting. Kirby Godsey and Bill Leonard were no doubt responding understandably to a particular kind of conservative Baptist orthodoxy, yet in so doing they were not leaving "orthodoxy" behind but offering (imposing) their own alternative, what we could call the orthodoxy of pluralism.

Godsey, for example, states, "Neither Baptists nor Christians have a corner on truth. We may do well, even in the classroom, to listen to Jews or Muslims or even nonbelievers along the way."[28] He then suggests that a key goal of education is broadening "tolerance for differing ideas and diverse religious perspectives."[29] Leonard embraces "pluralism" as the great good of education because it makes possible freedom of conscience and dissent, values that Baptists hold dear.[30] Pluralism allows for multiple voices. Since the university ought to allow for a free exchange of ideas, it seems as if "pluralism" and "diversity" would be a natural fit. As mentioned earlier, at an institution where I used to teach, one of our documents stated that we believed in "diversity for diversity's sake."

At this point we might acknowledge pluralism as a *reality*; we live in a world where there are a plurality of convictions and ways of life. Pluralism, however, becomes a *superficial* reality in our economic and political context as the market determines our lives and reduces all difference to mere choice. To make pluralism the internal good of the practice of education therefore reinforces the worse aspects of our dominant economic/political culture. This might seem counterintuitive. Doesn't pluralism allow for dialogue, respect, and multiple voices? It does (and this is a *potential* good), but pluralism has absolutely no way to discern between the true, the good, and the beautiful and the false, the bad, and the ugly. In this sense it copies the procedural liberalism of our democratic polity, in which each individual, like a consumer, supposedly has freedom to choose her good(s), a freedom protected (violently) by the nation-state. So understood, politics is not "in the service of the good way of life . . . the fulfillment of a vocation" toward which we are drawn. Rather, the "rules of life give way to the rules of the game designed to allow men, divided amongst themselves, to pursue each his own way, his own interest."[31] From this perspective, appeal to any good is regarded as an imposition, a power move in which one is trying to control or manipulate another. Such pluralism must maintain (self-deceptively) a rigorously agnostic posture toward truth.[32] Further, pluralism generates the idea that truth itself must be chosen through an act of the will. Yet this move displays a "metaphysics in which human will has ontological priority over the created order."[33] In other words, nothing is apparently given—not truth, not goodness, not beauty, not vocation; all is chosen. Such a will is related to no one or no thing, "because it recognizes no one and no thing as prior to its decision."[34]

John Milbank, however, has identified some prior assumptions that form this choosing will. A politics of self-interest, competition, and endless proceduralism relies upon an understanding of reality at the heart of which is chaos and conflict. Such politics is complicit with an "ontology of violence," rather than a politics formed by the peace and reconciliation of the triune God.[35] In other words, the "hidden curriculum" of pluralism/liberalism is a story of the world at odds with the story of biblical creation and Christianity.

To those deeply formed by the liberal polity of the modern academy, and of our political culture more broadly, it may seem difficult to imagine an alternative. Am I suggesting that we impose one viewpoint on students? If so, this hardly seems conducive to genuine learning. To the contrary, I am saying that the pluralism imposed on many students in fact shuts down true learning. By imposing a "culture of choice," pluralism underwrites a market approach to education, fueled by self-interest and competition. Such an approach makes desiring and loving the good unlikely.

A common defense of a liberal/pluralist politics in the academy is "The university is not the church." Unlike the church, which catechizes its young, the university seeks free and open exchange and debate. Yet such an opposition—catechesis versus debate—obscures the issue. In biology or politics or any other discipline, there must be some catechesis before there can be genuine debate. And for catechesis to be fruitful, whether in the church or in the university, there must be the ability eventually to engage in discussion and debate. That "the university is not the church" does have a point: the university is not necessarily the place where we baptize or preach or celebrate the Lord's Supper, though some Christian colleges and universities do celebrate Mass or provide regular worship services on campus.

Discussion about how to relate the church and the university is well-traveled ground. Often in contemporary discussions, the interlocutors (usually academics) worry about how to relate the university, where they locate themselves (at least in these discussions), to the church, which is imagined as being elsewhere. At the outset, there are two different spaces that then need to be "integrated," "interrogated," or "delineated" and "confined."[36] Some of these approaches provide helpful insights, but the way the problem is posed can easily obscure the domestication of the church by our liberal polity. Do Christians cease being church simply because they move into a different space? True, we are not gathered around the Word and the Table when we are in the classroom, but this does not mean we cease being Christ's body. The oddness of constructing different spaces and then trying to relate them becomes clearer when we consider why there is so little hand wringing about how the university ought to relate to the nation-state. That we typically assume there is little conflict shows how deeply we have absorbed a politics other than the politics of the body of Christ. As John Wright states, "American universities, church-related or otherwise, have always understood their fundamental mission as embedded within the larger polity of the contemporary liberal democratic nation-state."[37] The university remains liberally based and "church related." In it "Christian convictions are abstracted from the polity of the church so that students may serve as *individual private citizens* within the liberal society."[38] Another way of saying this is that in a liberally based college or university students are educated *out of* the church. They might leave the church altogether, or it might remain a part of their private lives for emotional or family support. But such a way of understanding the church perpetuates the liberal project of domesticating it.

Wright argues that we ought to think instead of the Christian university or college as ecclesially based and liberally or state related. This way of putting the matter prevents our assuming a smooth continuity between the nation-state and the academy. It thus frees our imaginations from seeing the nation-state as the keeper of the common good. While the state may be useful for certain very limited services, the purpose of the Christian college or university is to serve not the limited and geographically defined nation-state but the universal church that directs us to our true end.

The Invention of Religion

A political commentator captures how many Americans today think about religion:

> All in all, religion among religious Americans is more like something you can *add* to your life, possibly to make it more livable for you or others, as you would add some spice to your meal to make it tastier, more digestible, perhaps even more profitable. And, since everyone naturally has his own tastes (some prefer sweets; others, salt), in the same way, there is a sect, if not for every, at least for a great variety of tastes. Religion in America does not forbid materialism; it just makes it more palatable.[39]

If we are to offer an alternative political vision, it is important to see how modernity "invented" what we typically think of as religion. We can begin by looking at Locke's understanding of religion and religious liberty. Locke defines the church as a voluntary association of individuals. The true mark of the church is tolerance, as Locke states in the opening of his "Letter concerning Toleration": "I esteem that toleration to be the chief characteristic mark of the true Church."[40] Thus does Locke replace the classic four marks of the church (one, holy, catholic, and apostolic) with an Enlightenment virtue aimed at avoiding conflict. As Kenneth Craycraft notes, however, not only is Locke's church antisacramental, but orthodoxy becomes located in the individual, and thus religion devolves into a taste or sentiment.[41] Craycraft argues that while Locke is widely credited with a philosophy that separated church and state, he in fact unites them.[42] That is, by "taming" the church and reducing it to a collection of self-interested individuals, he ends up legitimating the liberal democratic state by making the church look just like it: a collection of individuals. In Locke, the church is not so much separated from the state as it is enmeshed in the same "enlightened" politics.

In a similar vein, Philip E. Thompson argues that postrevolutionary Baptists in America, fearing an encroachment upon human freedom, developed an anthropocentric version of religious liberty and "rejected the sacraments that earlier served a critical function vis-à-vis the state." They have thus "fallen prey to what they fear the least. Unsuspectingly legitimating the liberal democratic state in the name of religious liberty, they have effected a union of sorts between the earthly and heavenly cities."[43]

According to William Cavanaugh and Talal Asad, in fact, modern religion, as understood by Locke and others, was "invented" in order to shore up the powers of the nation-state. Such a claim flies in the face of much conventional wisdom that maintains the nation-state became the peacemaker in the midst of numerous religious wars. The idea is commonly held that "since religious wars (the ultimate outcome of the dissolution of medieval Christianity) had shown the faith to be a source of particularism and division, the intellectuals of Europe turned confidently to reason as the means to establish a truly universal ethics for human society."[44] In other words, the state as "rational" and "nonparticular" was necessary to tame potential religious conflict and violence. Kant famously defended the state as the great peacemaker.[45] The idea that we need the nation-state to protect us against religious conflict and violence continues today.[46]

Yet according to Cavanaugh and Asad, this way of telling the story—the state as peacekeeper in the midst of religious wars—is false. In fact, "to call these conflicts 'Wars of Religion' is an anachronism, for what was at issue in these wars was the very creation of religion as a set of privately held beliefs without direct political relevance."[47] Rather, according to Cavanaugh, the so-called religious wars are better understood as the birth pangs of the nation-state. Catholics and Protestants at times fought on the same side, and doctrinal issues were secondary to the defeat or rise of a strong centralized state. Yet, as Cavanaugh stresses, at issue is not the sincerity of religious convictions themselves but the creation of religion "as a set of beliefs which is defined as personal conviction and which can exist separately from one's public loyalty to the state."[48] Asad summarizes this understanding:

> Historians of seventeenth- and eighteenth-century Europe have begun to recount how the constitution of the modern state required the forcible redefinition of religion as *belief*, and of religious belief, sentiment and identity as personal matters that belong to the newly emerging space of *private* (as opposed to *public*) life. . . . Scholars are now more aware that religious toleration was a political means to the formation of the strong state power that emerged from the sectarian wars of the sixteenth and seventeenth centuries rather than the benign intention to defend pluralism.[49]

In contrast to religion as a private affair, the root of *religion* is usually associated with *religare*, to bind, and early on, *religion* referred to a whole way of life bound by monastic vows, or to a virtue shared by all Christians. Cavanaugh observes that Thomas Aquinas understood *religio* (to which he devotes only one question in the *Summa*) as a virtue (understood as piety or sanctity) that directs a person to God. In discussing this virtue or habit, Aquinas presupposes a context of ecclesial practices such that *religio* cannot be separated from the communal worship of God. It includes bodily acts of devotion, not simply private mental or "spiritual" thoughts. In other words, "*religio* is not an individual thing" but names the virtue of engaging the communal liturgical practices of the church.[50]

At the dawn of modernity (around the late fifteenth century), however, religion became identified as various manifestations of a common impulse. As this happened, religion was "interiorized and removed from its particular ecclesial context."[51] A second major shift occurred through the late sixteenth and seventeenth centuries as religion became identified with an abstract set of beliefs. No longer a habit rooted in the practices of the church, religion became instead a set of propositions. Most crucial, religion so defined can now "exist separately from one's public loyalty to the State."[52]

As religion gets redefined, so too does the church. The church is not itself a political body but an apolitical association. The church is no longer primarily a body apart from which its members cease to have life in Christ, but primarily a collection of individuals. In the words of Locke, the church is "a voluntary society of men, joining themselves together of their own accord in order to the public worshipping of God in such manner as they judge acceptable to Him, and effectual to the salvation of their souls."[53] As noted earlier, Locke conceives of the church in the same way he conceives of the politics of the state: people are individuals who come together because of shared interests. To our modern ears, especially modern Protestant ears, such a view of the church might seem unproblematic. Individuals, after all, should not be coerced into the life of the church; therefore the right of the individuals to choose seems to make perfect sense. Such thinking, though, ignores Tertullian's insightful dictum that Christians are made, not born. The church is not a place where individuals with common interests gather but the body of Christ through which we are transformed to be not "individuals" but members one of another (1 Cor. 12). A key part of such transformation is that we learn to acknowledge that we did not choose God but God chooses us, enabling us to become a people capable of offering hospitality, even to strangers.

In order to see how the "invention" of religion in modernity supports the nation-state as the bearer of politics, it is instructive to look at the theology and life of Friedrich Schleiermacher (1768–1834), the great father of modern Protestant theology. He famously defined religion as a "taste for the infinite" and as a "feeling" or "intuition" of absolute dependence. As such, "piety cannot be an instinct craving for a mess of metaphysical and ethical crumbs."[54] True religious piety is something entirely different, an "immediate consciousness of the universal existence of all finite things, in and through the Infinite."[55] While Schleiermacher affirmed the social dimension of religion, his basic premise about the nature of religion as a universal impulse leads him inevitably to give priority to the individual subject. He speculates, "Might the time come, which as ancient prophecy describes, when no one should need to be taught of man, for they should all be taught of God?"[56] Thus does Schleiermacher entertain the idea that the church as the mediator of salvation might one day be unnecessary. He suggests in fact that at the end of a future culture, "we expect a time when no other society preparatory for religion except the pious family life will be required."[57] For the present, however, "according to the principles of the true church, the mission of a priest in the world is a private business, and the temple should also be a private chamber where he lifts up his voice to give utterance to religion." Such a priest, Schleiermacher happily notes, will be a speaker for all but not a "shepherd for a definite flock."[58]

Schleiermacher's understanding of religion leads him to describe the social aspect of the church primarily in terms of "fellowship," a fellowship that occurs because the pious individual will naturally wish to share his thoughts and feelings with others. "If there is religion at all, it must be social, for that is the nature of man, and it is quite peculiarly the nature of religion. You must confess that when an individual has produced and wrought out something in his own mind, it is morbid and in the highest degree unnatural to wish to reserve it to himself."[59] At the same time, Schleiermacher notes, some few individuals might not find themselves "at home" in any existing religion, in which case they are bound to produce a new one.

I review aspects of Schleiermacher's theology not simply to emphasize his turn to the subject but to look at what happens politically in Schleiermacher's thought when this understanding of "religion" determines his project. Later in his life, Schleiermacher did become "politically active," eventually resisting a liturgical uniformity in the Prussian churches (Reformed and Lutheran) imposed by Friedrich Wilhelm III. The dispute lasted from 1822 to 1829, and Schleiermacher's side eventually lost. After his death in 1834, a conservative political movement continued unabated, putting down an 1848 revolutionary movement under the cry "Throne and altar." As James Brandt notes, "Schleiermacher's political career was marked by a profound irony: the neo-Pietists continued the political activism of the church, which he had championed, but steered in a direction very different from his." When we consider how Schleiermacher defined religion, however, that his fellow neo-Pietists steered in a different political direction from his is not ironic at all. Both shared the conviction that religion is primarily an interior impulse; both located politics in the German nation. Robert Biglar even claims that "the inability of German Protestantism to side with the people during and after the Revolution of 1848 had the baneful consequences of alienating the German masses from the church and eventually driving them to embrace the secular religions of Marxism and National Socialism." Commenting on this sobering observation, Brandt notes that Schleiermacher succeeded in inspiring the church to political activisim. "He was a significant political player, but the long term results were not what he had hoped for. Also evident is the enormous power of the nation-state—its ability to sweep away everything in its path and co-opt the church to serve its interests."[60] If Cavanaugh and Asad are right, however, Schleiermacher's theology shored up the nation-state, contributing to its enormous power, even though such a contribution was clearly unintentional.

The lesson here, when applied to institutions of higher education, is compelling. Inasmuch as our Christian colleges and universities are embracing the politics of liberalism/pluralism with its "invention" of religion, they are at once shoring up the power of the nation-state and contributing to the ongoing domestication of the church.

Politics in the Academy and the Recovery of Hospitality

That Christians have contributed to the "dying of the light" or secularization of their own institutions is an indication, I think, of how deep the problem is. This secularization thesis has, of course, been contested as critics have offered more hopeful analyses of our contemporary situation. Yet often these approaches end up underwriting current political assumptions, thus continuing the legacy described and criticized by Cavanaugh and Asad.[61]

To think differently about "politics" can be difficult because most of us are immersed in a particular usage and understanding of the term. Thus "the naturalness of the liberal society seems to form an unquestionable good that the church-related university must presuppose."[62] In contemporary culture and going back to the sixteenth and seventeenth centuries, *politics* has referred to the "science dealing with the form, organization and administration of a state, or part of one, and with the regulation of its relations with other states."[63] In earlier usages, however, as noted in my mention of Aristotelian politics, *polis* had to do not with the administration of the state but with the collective life of the whole community. Inherent in the idea of *polis* was the conviction that no one can prosper unless the *polis* prospers. As this more ancient meaning receded, however, "the epic and tragic [became] increasingly hard to realize; an art that had emerged from the social organization of the Greek *polis* no longer applied to the mysterious forces of capitalism."[64] Whereas *polis* was associated with a lived story (the epic and the tragic) and with the art of living together, the forces of capitalism have undermined this usage.

137

Contemporary author Eugene Peterson relies on the earlier definition, however, when he writes that politics is "everything people do as they live with some intention in community, as they work toward some common purpose."[65] Theologian Barry Harvey gives us an even fuller definition: politics is the "art and science not simply of statecraft, but of everything that has to do with both the actuality and the possibility of human life, which according to the Christian tradition is realized only through participation in the divine life of the triune God."[66] Harvey importantly adds that a retrieval of this premodern understanding of politics is crucial for the church today.

As is well known, the early Christians were perceived as a political threat to the Roman Empire. If these early followers of Christ had understood religion as private and politics as the machinations of government in the public sphere, there would have been no conflict. The early church, however, refused to avail itself of the protection of *cultus privatus* (private cult) that it could have had under Roman law. They saw, rather, that Christianity entails a whole way of life, one that involves both the so-called private and public spheres. Thus they described their identity in political terms: "a holy nation"(1 Peter 2:9), citizenship (Eph. 2:19), and the "Israel of God" (Gal. 6:16). Such imagery indicates that "the church extends the mission of Israel. While no longer defined by its claims on the land and on its physical descent from Abraham, the church is nevertheless the community that has fallen heir to the gift and the call of Israel."[67] We might be tempted today to think we live in a different time and a better political climate: worship of Caesar is not required. True, our challenge might be different than that of the early Christians, but it is no less political, a politics that is ultimately discovered in and through worship. As early Christians discovered the identity of Christ in worship, they "found that political subversion was both necessary and possible."[68] The point, however, is not simply to be subversive but to discover more fully what it means to be God's people, God's "holy nation," in our world today and thus to discover what is authentically political. From this perspective, "it is life outside the Christian community which fails to be truly public, authentically political. The opposition is not between public and private . . . but between political virtue and political vice."[69]

To modern liberal/pluralist ears, such a statement might well sound oppressive and hegemonic. How can anyone make such an exclusive claim? As we have seen, liberal politics embraces the idea that there is not *one* end but many. But such pluralism in reality serves the good of the market and the nation-state. The politics that forms the lives of Christians ought ultimately to serve the body of Christ rather than any secular nation. Such politics has to do with ordering the lives of persons who are members one of another, rather than arranging the lives of individuals.

138

As frequently noted, a liberal polity that focuses only on individual rights (and the nation-state as the guarantor of those rights) creates over time a society of self-interested individuals and, eventually, a society of *strangers*. So understood, individuals enter society through social contract, to protect person and property. Since such a polity trains us to see others as strangers and potential threats, the apparent harmony of liberal pluralist rhetoric actually conceals conflict and fragmentation.[70] Just recently, my children wandered into a neighbor's yard. My daughter knew the young girl who lived there. The family had recently bought a new trampoline, and my son immediately ran toward it. Before I let him jump, I asked the onlooking mother (standing at her window) if he could jump, to which she responded, "I don't want to be sued!" I was taken aback by her response, but it is an understandable one given the kind of politics that has come to dominate our lives. Since we have no common good, we easily become a society of strangers bound only by our mutual fears and need for protection from potential threat. Our increasing willingness to sue one another witnesses to the degeneration of ways of political living that make the practice of hospitality possible.

That strangers might generate fear in us is a possibility we all face, and certainly we are to be wise and discerning in the ways we relate to and welcome strangers. Yet Christians' lives are to be determined by our loves rather than our fears. If fear of the stranger had been determinative of the lives of the first disciples, they would never have received and followed Christ, since Christ was a stranger before he was a friend. As Christians, we "cannot afford to let ourselves be defined by what we are against" or by what we fear. "Whatever or whomever we are against, we are so only because God has given us so much to be for."[71]

The politics of Christian colleges and universities, then, must counter the politics that dominates our culture. Understood as the art of living (rather than what governments and states do), such politics is grounded in and oriented toward the love of God. The vocation given to Christian institutions is the same one given to Christians individually. It is, in the words of the encyclical *Veritatis Splendor*, a "vocation to perfect love." Such a vocation is not voluntaristic in character: it is not realized by human effort alone. Therefore perfect love does not imply a kind of naive perfectionism. It does, though, personalize the end or goal of education. The purpose of education is not only to acquire knowledge or skills, important though these are, but to become a particular kind of person. So understood, education is transformative, but the transformation is not to serve false ideologies that ultimately disfigure the church. Rather, true education seeks to transform persons in light of the true end of education: love and service of God.

That the end of education is love of the triune God might sound odd, impractical, and even exclusive. One cannot force love; love comes as a gift. Yet as a virtue, love is also a habit, a way of being formed. And all education is ultimately formation in love of something. As Augustine states, "Whether for good or for evil, each man lives by his love."[72] Therefore, we need to ask, what kind of love does our politics produce? Is it the Kantian "good" of autonomously achieving freedom and rationality? Is it the utilitarian "good" that makes desire of satisfaction central? Is it the "good" of relativism (we each choose our own good) that can quickly degenerate into indifference? In the words of Catholic philosopher Josef Pieper, "The true antithesis of love is not hate but despairing indifference, the feeling that nothing is important."[73]

Naomi Riley, among others, has noted this despair and malaise among many college students who can be described as "souls without longing." One student, Jeffrey Lorch, a sophomore at Columbia, had no "real problem" but needed "an unknown quantity of Prozac to get through the day." Reflecting on his college experience, Jeffrey said, "There have been times when I've felt like every conversation [I've had at school] was a sham." Jeffrey is living in a world of strangers, a world where a shared love of the true and the good is absent. Emory professor Robert Bartlett describes an educational malaise that is evident in the "narrowness of students' frame of reference or field of vision; in the pettiness of their daily concerns; . . . in the mediocrity of their ambitions. . . . The world could be their oyster, but they tend to stare back at it, pearls and all—and yawn."[74] When education is not formation in how to love the good, it easily degenerates into supporting ways of life in which no good is worth loving.

In our educational practice, we are often influenced by a natural-scientific ideal of knowledge in which education is simply the impartation of facts and information. From this perspective, the Jeffreys of the collegiate world need to go see a counselor. While counseling may or may not be called for, the selection of what "facts" are taught and why already draws from something other than strict facts. Some prior sense of the good always drives the way we structure the curriculum, even though this may be unacknowledged. Stated differently, all education serves something or someone.

Use of the word *love* in our dominant cultural context can ring all sorts of bells. *Love* easily brings to mind sentimental and romantic connotations; *love*, from this perspective, refers to our private emotional lives and desires. Christian love does not negate desire. In fact, as David B. Hart has emphasized, divine beauty inflames desire, stretching one "out toward an ever greater embrace of divine glory." Thus, the "trinitarian love of God—and the love God requires of creatures—is eros and agape at once."[75] Education has to do with cultivating the right kinds of desires, the right kinds of loves. Hart thus rightly concludes that for Christian thought "delight is the premise of any sound epistemology."[76]

In the sixth century, in fact, Gregory the Great, one of the four Latin doctors of the church, wrote, "Love is itself a form of knowledge." Such a claim can sound bizarre to modern ears, but Gregory is drawing from an understanding of education as formation such that one needs to be a certain kind of person in order to know certain things. In other words, Gregory is focused not first of all on the question *what can be known?* but on *what must I be in order to know?*[77] Robert Wilken states that for Gregory, as well as for all the great thinkers of the early church, "thinking about the things of God, like grammar, was not an end in itself; its aim was the love of God and holiness of life." Gregory, Wilken adds, "did not construct a world of ideas for others to admire but one to live in."[78] The idea that something like grammar, let alone biology or economics, has to do with holiness of life might seem a long stretch to us today. Yet more recently, philosopher Simone Weil claimed that attention and reception of a gift are as important to the life of study as to the life of prayer.[79] For both Gregory and Weil, "school studies with a view to the love of God" (Weil's phrase) have to do with developing the capacity to receive a gift—the love of God and the corresponding world into which such love draws us to live.

The politics that both Gregory and Weil presuppose differs drastically from that of political liberalism. As we have seen, such liberal politics sees the nation-state as the bearer of politics, regards religion as apolitical, and underwrites a view of society constituted by strangers and fragmentation. Above all, such a politics depends upon the ideology of individualism, where persons are in essential or potential conflict with each other.[80]

That we are created for communion with God and others means that we are part of a tradition in which we are dependent on others (including those not explicitly within our tradition) to demonstrate to us what we are to be. Such a politics does not depend on individualism but rather on *friendship*. It depends less on the language of rights and more on the language of *gift*. In fact, education made possible by friendship can be described as *the circulation of gift,*[81] which is also a way to describe hospitality.

Wes Avram tells about receiving a gift on Valentine's Day that completely surprised him and his wife. It was a white box inside of which was a wiggling lobster, especially significant for them since they had recently moved from Maine, where lobsters even appear on the license plates. Avram felt a bit uncomfortable, since they had not bought their friend anything; he admits to being drawn to the rules of "interpersonal commerce," the rules of the marketplace. Later, he is asked to give encouragement in the form of a letter to a young boy in need. While initially wondering if he has time for this, he writes the letter and realizes that he is "responding to one gift with another, directed elsewhere, to a place the first giver knows nothing of. It's the chain of gift giving, both mundane and significant, that makes life full."[82]

Avram rightly indicates that hospitality involves taking delight in the dynamics of giving and receiving such that we become more fully capable of delighting in the love of God. Without such hospitality, friendship is not possible. An understanding of God as triune, with God's own life constituted by giving and receiving, forms such a view of friendship, hospitality, and education. God's own life involves the circulation of gift. The Father, Son, and Holy Spirit give and receive without remainder, such that their identities are entirely constitutive and therefore dependent on each other: the Son is the Son only in relation to the Father and vice versa, a communion that takes place in the Spirit. So understood, the Trinity generates a politics because it generates a notion of the good (as well as the true and the beautiful) known through communion, *koinonia*, and friendship. As Aquinas says, "Charity signifies not only love of God, but also a kind of friendship with Him, which adds besides love a returning of love for love along with a certain communing of one with another."[83]

Like hospitality, friendship today is often regarded as apolitical and as something people search for to fulfill their private lives. Yet friendships of virtue or charity, as Aristotle knew, were political in that they trained persons to love the common good, and thus to become a *polis* oriented to that good. For an example of such friendship in the academy, we can turn to a third-century account by a pupil, Gregory Thaumaturgus, of his brilliant teacher Origen (185–254). When Origen first received Gregory, he was a bright young student intent on a career in law. The encounter with Origen, however, changed Gregory's life. In his *Panegyric* in praise of Origen, Gregory focuses not so much on his teacher's erudition as on recounting how Origen "in accepting as his students Gregory and his brother *first made friends* with these young men—and did it as if it were a valuable achievement on Origen's side to have such friends. Gregory felt like Jonathan embraced by this academic David."[84] That Origen saw friendship as a cornerstone of education indicates that he understood education as formation in a way of life. "The teachers of Alexandria were not interested solely in conveying knowledge or transmitting intellectual skills. They were interested in moral and spiritual formation. . . . The school of Alexandria was a school for training in virtue."[85] Such formation in fact led Gregory to drop his career in law; he went on to become a well-known bishop.

This kind of formation can seem far removed from our lives today. More often than not fragmentation marks the life of the academy as well as other institutions. While this fragmentation no doubt has numerous causes, embrace of a plurality of goods (like a plurality of goods on the market) is surely a leading one. Given this fragmentation, how can friendship oriented toward the Good be possible? While I have no easy answers to this question, such friendship will be more likely when Christian colleges and institutions see how counterpolitical they need to be in our context. Being able to name the good or end of education, and the politics and fragmentation that would obscure this end, begins to make possible a different politics and education, one that will enable Christian hospitality, a giving and receiving of the good (and true and beautiful), to flourish.

Important questions remain: Am I not being hegemonic in my identification of the good with the triune God? How are Christians to relate to and understand those who do not believe in God or who worship a different God? Or, even, how do we relate to fellow Christians who differ radically from us, who believe, for example, that capitalism is the best form of economics or that abortion is a free choice? A common response, as indicated, is that we must be tolerant of those who differ from us. Yet it is helpful to consider how Christian hospitality *differs from* tolerance, which is the form of "hospitality" offered by liberal democracy.[86] The meaning of *tolerance* has been contested; at its best, perhaps, it means "restraint," while at its worst it means "indifference." In the popular imagination, tolerance means something like "letting be." The dictum referred to earlier, "We agree to disagree," reflects this understanding of tolerance as a mode of getting along.

As philosopher Scott Moore observes, however, Christian hospitality denies the "allegedly neutral space within which tolerant political discourse longs to move. Since there is *no such thing as neutral space* to begin with, this means that hospitality is also more honest."[87] The irony of tolerance, as others have pointed out, is that it is intolerant of intolerance. Or stated differently, invocations of "tolerance" presuppose some assumptions about the good life and thus how to understand "tolerance" *and* how to regard those who don't share such assumptions as "intolerant." Murray Jardine notes that if we all have different perceptions and values, "then there is no reason why we should all agree on the principle of tolerance, or nonimposition of values, and even if we did, we would not be able to agree on what constitutes an imposition of values."[88] Locke's *Letter concerning Toleration*, as we saw, makes specific kinds of "value" and political assumptions. Tolerance can thus easily foster a kind of self-deception. As Moore points out, "My gallant exercise of tolerance can become self-congratulatory evidence for my own enlightened state. At the same time, my enlightened tolerance easily cultivates an inaccurate and harmful view of the other as 'irrational' or 'unbalanced.'"[89] One thinks of the comments from Rawls and Rorty with which this chapter began.

Practitioners of Christian hospitality are not, of course, immune from self-congratulation and false humility. Yet the tradition that gives shape to such hospitality requires that practitioners see others not as irrational or unbalanced but as persons created in God's own image and as members or potential members of the body of Christ. This latter description is not intended to suggest that the non-Christian has worth only as a potential member of Christ's body but to emphasize that here, too, is one for whom Christ lived and died. In the practice of hospitality, exercising the virtue of love, we are to give and receive from the "other" (or stranger) as Christ would. So understood, hospitality is at once more receptive and more active than tolerance, receptive in that it sees the other as gift and active in that it seeks lovingly to live, speak, and hear the truth in any given situation. The faithful practice of hospitality requires that we see ourselves as both guests, receiving from the other, and hosts, offering ourselves to the other. Such hospitality acknowledges that truth and insight may come from "strange" quarters. For example, a person who is mentally handicapped is not simply deficient but can give gifts that might well transform our lives. Even more, Christian hospitality understands that lack of truth or half-truth can still be a kind of gift. Christian heresy, for example, when faithfully engaged and named, can enable Christians to see themselves, the world, and God more truthfully. Hospitable truth seeking and speaking is admittedly messy, inconvenient, and sometimes thankless. But hospitality does not aim for merely getting along, as does tolerance. Rather, it serves the good of communion with God. This friendship with God and others enables us to be a people capable of truthful speech in the first place.

Our focus on hospitality, love, and higher education ends with an emphasis on speaking the truth in love. I have probably been drawn to this focus because I find truth speaking incredibly difficult to practice in the academy today. Giving and receiving truth can be disruptive[90] and frightening. But without the truth we are not free. And surely we need each other to be able to name the false ideologies and politics that deform, domesticate, and distort education, the church, and our very lives. If education can even begin to initiate us into a politics that allows for truthful speech, then it is on the right road. Then we may recover a more robust hospitality to offer the world; then we may learn more fully how to give and receive from others, even strangers. Then, too, we may be able to say about our lives and our institutions, "My love is my weight; where it goes I go."[91]

Part 3

Hospitality as a Unifying Practice

■ In this final section, I consider hospitality as a necessary practice for the unity of the body of Christ. The modern assumptions outlined in the previous section about science and economics, ethics, politics and education have wreaked havoc on our understanding of what it means to be church. Thus today we easily conceive of the church as a group of like-minded individuals; if for some reason we come to a different mind from others in our congregation, then we readily assume our only alternative is to leave. Such a mentality is often underwritten by seeing and even celebrating the disunity of the church as a necessary diversity rather than as a deep wound on the body of Christ.[1]

Our unity, however, comes not through common political agendas for the nation-state, nor through common economic advantages or status. Neither does our unity come through tolerance of everyone's opinion. Rather, faithful unity emerges through the "fire of Christ's cross," which transforms us to be one body.[2] Perhaps nowhere is the fire of Christ's cross more dramatically enacted than at the Lord's Table, where we become Christ's body as together we eat and drink this holy meal. The meal remains a deep mystery, not only because of its identification with Christ but also because of its ongoing manifestation of divisions in the church. The Eucharist reveals that our house of hospitality is divided. This itself, we must not forget, is a gift. Only as we see and accept our brokenness can we allow the Spirit to heal and transform us. Satisfaction with division is not a faithful option, as Pope Benedict has rightly stated: it is "not unity that requires justification, but the absence of it."[3] How does and can the Eucharist transform and unify such that we practice hospitality from an undivided place?

Having looked at hospitality as liturgical, countercultural, and eucharistic, the final chapter looks at how two particular communities, the Church of the Saviour and L'Arche, have embodied a faithful hospitality in our time. These communities give us ways to imagine the faithful practice of hospitality in the mundane and ordinary circumstances of our lives. Involving small deeds and gestures done with faith, hope, and love, hospitality entails a whole way of life made possible by God's surprising abundance.

6

A Divided House?

Hospitality and the Table of Grace

■ This chapter returns to the conviction that worship is hospitality: when we gather to worship, we participate most fully in the triune hospitality of God. Perhaps nowhere is this more visibly apparent than when we gather around the table of the Lord, feasting upon the self-giving of the Son in the body and blood and united with Christ to become his body for the world. In this light, then, I wish not to look at the relation between hospitality and the Lord's Supper but rather to approach the Lord's Supper as an *intensification* of our participation in divine hospitality.

And yet perhaps nowhere else than at the Lord's Table is it more apparent that we live in a divided house. We do not eat of one loaf; we do not drink from one cup. A divided house compromises our practice of hospitality because it signals a failure to participate as fully as we might in the holy giving and receiving that constitute the life of God. The fact that we cannot share together in God's hospitality means that our hospitality in and for the world is compromised. Jesus prays that his disciples may be one: "As you, Father, are in me, and I am in you, may they also may be in us, so that the world may believe that you have sent me" (John 17:21). Disunity makes it more difficult for Christians to participate in God's triune hospitality, and thus more difficult to receive and give hospitality in the world.

Christians, then, have a deep incentive to discern ways we might receive the unity that our triune God desires to give, a unity that counters the economic, political, and ethical divisions that domesticate or destroy hospitality. In what follows, then, I seek to describe the Eucharist as a place of hospitality and unity. Like others who have written on these topics, I have found no easy or straightforward solutions to eucharistic unity. A conviction rather than a solution drives my argument: that the church is one, and that such oneness is crucial to the faithful practice of Christian hospitality.

"Many Mansions" or a Divided House?

Years ago, I worked as a chaplain in a large state mental hospital. Two other student chaplains and I used to visit patients, housed in some twenty buildings, both to spend time with them and to conduct worship services. In these services, we could always count on one patient to shout out the same Bible verse: "In my Father's house are many mansions; if it were not so, I would have told you" (John 14:2 KJV). This passage pictures a great spaciousness in the house of God, an expansiveness that no doubt held deep significance for this mentally handicapped woman.

In God's house, there are many mansions; there are many dwelling places. Teresa of Ávila, in the sixteenth century, made famous this image of a beautiful mansion or castle, at the center of which dwells the living God, a castle that in fact we already are. Teresa thus writes, "There can be no question of our entering it. For we ourselves are the castle: and it would be absurd to tell someone to enter a room when he was in it already! But you must understand that there are many ways of being in a place."[1] Some remain on the outside, but if they enter they discover a castle of diamonds: no matter which of the countless rooms they are in, they can see through to the middle, where God is. According to Teresa, the Christian life consists of journeying through the castle, meandering through the different rooms, allowing God to draw us more fully into communion with him.

While Teresa applies her imagery to the journey of the individual soul, we can also apply it more broadly to the church. After all, the church is frequently identified as "the house of God." In scripture, in fact, it is not so much that Christians have a house as that they *are* a house (1 Peter 2:4–6); they are knit together in the Spirit into a "dwelling place for God" (Eph. 2:22). Teresa's vivid imagery gives us a helpful way to think about what kind of house this is: expansive, beautiful, the very dwelling place of the triune God. At this same time, this "dwelling" requires pilgrimage, since Christians are at home in no nation.[2] Varmints and other pests may trouble those who enter. The dwellers may become mired down by any number of illusions and be tempted to cease journeying. The church is, then, a moving dwelling place, "embracing sinners in her bosom," "at the same time holy and always in need of being purified, and incessantly pursu[ing] the path of penance and renewal."[3] And as Teresa beautifully describes, as one journeys closer to the triune God, a more profound freedom and joy mark one's life. The journey of "life together" as God's dwelling is one of freedom and delight.

We have already seen in chapter 3 how the *oikos* that is the body of Christ frees the church to practice a different economics (*oikonomia*) from that of market capitalism. Yet our efforts to be this *oikos* are at best partial and broken. We easily exchange the spaciousness of the church and its many dwelling places for isolated units having little to do with each other. Perhaps the most glaring example of our brokenness is our inability to share Christ's body with each other.

In this chapter, I focus on the Lord's Supper as a practice necessary for the faithful practice of hospitality. In the Eucharist, as in worship more broadly understood, the Spirit gathers us and enables us to participate in the communion the Son has with the Father.[4] Thus the Eucharist does not simply motivate Christians to practice hospitality; rather, it is our participation in God's hospitality, as through this celebration we are enabled to become eucharistic, extending God's offering and gift to the world.

But why focus on the Lord's Supper, rather than baptism or preaching or even hymn singing?[5] More than any other liturgical action, the Lord's Supper is the place where our disunity is most obvious, where our lack of communion is most visible. It is possible to sing hymns together, listen to preaching together, and even (with some exceptions) acknowledge each other's baptism. It is not now possible, however, for Protestants, Catholics, and Orthodox to commune together at the Lord's Table.

The connection between hospitality and food is well known and practiced in a variety of cultures; "secular parables" of the Lord's Supper abound.[6] As a young child growing up in the South, I would often visit our elderly neighbors, knowing that they would always offer me something good to eat. And at the large Baptist church I grew up in, "dinner on the grounds" was a great feast: rows of tables stretching across the lawn, filled with an abundance of all kinds of meats, casseroles, salads, and desserts. A rule of hospitality, at least in the South, was always to have more than would be needed—an understanding of abundance surely shaped by the biblical stories of the loaves and fishes and of the early Christian agape meals.

In the Lord's Supper or Eucharist (terms I use interchangeably), the church engages in a particular kind of feeding and feasting. So determinative is this eating and drinking that Henri de Lubac has classicly claimed that "the eucharist makes the church."[7] That is, according to de Lubac, the church receives *itself* through the reception of Christ's body. "Fed by the Body and Blood of the Saviour, his faithful thereby all 'drink of the same Spirit' who truly makes of them one Body."[8] We may support de Lubac's emphasis with Paul's question to the Corinthians, "The bread that we break, is it not a sharing (*koinonia*) in the body of Christ?" (1 Cor. 10:17). From this perspective, the Eucharist is not a "miracle to believe" but the defining source of the church.[9] This means that the Eucharist is not merely edification for the individual but makes the church the body of Christ, so that "Christians are never *not* members of Christ's Eucharistic social body."[10]

The problem, of course, is that the body is broken, the table is divided. Such disunity diminishes the practice of hospitality and no doubt contributes to the various distortions prevalent today. Conversely, a fuller, more united eucharistic practice would make possible the discovery of a richer Christian hospitality.

Mere Ritual?

Yet I am not convinced that simply "understanding" the deep mystery of this sacrament is necessarily the key. Such an emphasis can easily throw the significance of the Lord's Supper back on the individual, as if the subject must feel or think the right meaning in order for the Lord's Supper to be significant. This is one of the worst traps we face today in regard to worship, as if worship can really happen only if we conjure up the right kinds of interior thoughts or emotions. More important than this rationalistic or emotional approach is recovering the Lord's Supper as a liturgical and political drama in which we participate, one that offers an alternative to other dramas that easily determine our lives.

In many ways, what we "understand" about the Lord's Supper has to do with how we position our bodies when we gather. In my own tradition (Baptist), the typical way that the supper is served is by passing plates down the aisles, first a tray of small "shot glasses" of grape juice and then a plate of small "chiclets" of hard bread. Everyone remains seated. Some have argued that the passing of the plates to one another reflects the nonhierarchical emphasis in Baptist life. True, Baptists are known for a supposedly nonhierarchical polity (a fact that is at least as negative as it is positive).[11] But the practice is also highly individualized, as each person picks up her own little cup and her own already cut piece of bread. Each participant remains seated, there is little exchange with others, and the "celebration" is quickly done. There are, of course, complex historical and theological reasons for contemporary Baptists' coming to celebrate the Lord's Supper in this way, which some have persuasively argued is a departure from earlier Baptist traditions.[12] But clearly in the way the community enacts and celebrates the Lord's Supper, the richness of God feeding and nourishing the community so that they become the body of Christ is diminished. Without powerful gestures, rich prayers, significant movements, and bread that can be tasted, it will be difficult for the Lord's Table to be seen as a participation in divine hospitality in which, through the gift of Spirit, we participate in the unity of love between the Father and Son.

While other traditions, such as Roman Catholic, have maintained the centrality of the Eucharist, it is nonetheless the case that in our culture all Christians are faced with the trivialization of this practice, a reflection of the broader reduction of religion to the private sphere. A significant number of the Catholic students at Saint Mary's College (where I used to teach) talked about the bread and wine in symbolic terms rather than in terms of "real presence." And at least some students attended Mass as if it were a private ritual, leaving quickly after they received the bread only. In 1994, a news story reported that a majority of North American Catholics favored "symbolic reminder" over "real" when describing the eucharistic mystery.[13]

Dom Gregory Dix locates the decline of the social and corporate nature of the Eucharist as early as the late Middle Ages, as the subjective devotion of the worshipper in her own mind began to prevail. During this time, according to Dix, private devotion often came to be seen as more important than corporate worship. "The part of the individual layman . . . had long ago been reduced from 'doing' to 'seeing' and 'hearing.' Now it is retreating within himself to 'thinking' and 'feeling.' He is even beginning to think that over-much 'seeing' (ceremonial) and 'hearing' (music) are detrimental to proper 'thinking' and 'feeling.'"[14] In other words, ritual becomes a distraction to true worship.

William H. Poteat detects a similar bias but locates it in the time of the Enlightenment, when ritual and ceremony came to be seen as "the meaningless residues of a tradition" that reasonable people wished to abandon. "There is no doubt that these 'trappings,' as we are tempted to call them, come to lose all authority, are emptied of meaning and come to veil reality from us."[15] An understanding of ritual as "mere" easily underwrites the idea that individual thoughts and feelings are the real and primary sources of meaning. The weight of the eucharistic "meaning" falls on the individual, who consumes not the body and blood of Christ but an immaterial and apolitical spirituality.

151

Eucharist as Remembering

When modern dramas, such as those alluded to by Dix and Poteat, come to dominate our imaginations, we suffer from a kind of liturgical amnesia. Oliver Sacks, in *The Man Who Mistook His Wife for a Hat*, writes about Jimmy G., a man who suffered from severe retrograde amnesia and could remember virtually nothing since 1945, when he was nineteen. He had served in World War II and continued to serve in the U.S. Navy until 1965. As Sacks tells us, Jimmie could form no new memories. "If a man has lost a leg or an eye, he knows he has lost a leg or an eye; but if he has lost a self—himself—he cannot know it, because he is no longer there to know it."[16] Reflecting on this sad story, Gilbert Meilaender writes, "If we cannot say who we have been, we can never know who we are."[17] The same is true of our lives as liturgical creatures, made for communion with God. If we cannot say who we have been, if modern conceptions of time and space easily erase our eucharistic memory, then we cannot know who or, even more, *whose* we are.

In Christian worship, we gather to remember. Yet such remembering is not simply calling to mind a past event. Liturgical theologian James White, discussing the Lord's Supper, suggests that "commemoration . . . has the power of reliving the event in all its power to save and it frees us from our captivity to the present by making all God's saving acts present for us to appropriate."[18] Is such commemoration like remembering a happy occasion shared with a good friend so that it is *as if* she were present? This weak sense of remembrance is a problem for two reasons: (1) there is nothing of the "as if" about the presence of God when we gather to worship (God in fact gathers us), and (2) worship does not depend ultimately upon our remembrance of God but upon God's remembrance of us.

The Jewish roots of Christian worship provide fertile ground for understanding worship as commemoration and so also for understanding the eucharistic *anamnesis* (remembrance, as in "Do this in remembrance of me," 1 Cor. 11:24–25). When Jews celebrate Passover, they *are* contemporaries of their forebears, the Hebrew slaves, in their escape from slavery; they *are* on the banks of the Red Sea fleeing Pharaoh and his armies. The youngest child, on every Passover night, asks, "Why *is* this night different from all other nights?" The Mishnah explicitly requires that every one of the participants in the Passover meal "see oneself as one who has come out of Egypt."[19] This is not, as Jean-Luc Marion states, "the subjective memory of the community [of] a past fact that would be defined by its nonpresence."[20] In this Passover drama, rather, God's saving power is as present to those who observe it as it was to the ancient Hebrews. The event "remains less a past fact than a pledge given in the past in order, today still, to appeal to a future—an advent, that of the Messiah—that does not cease to govern this today from beginning to end."[21] This liturgy is contemporaneous with the exodus past and messianic future not by virtue of the Jewish ability mentally to recover a time that is no longer or not yet. Rather, it is made possible by God, whose saving acts are not bound by a sealed-off past or an unavailable future. God's continuous and faithful presence to his covenant people makes possible their participation in the cosmic story of salvation. They worship the same God now that their ancestors worshipped, and this God continues to give his people time to become a visible light to all nations.[22]

While the common tendency is to think about liturgical remembrance as what *we* do, Joachim Jeremias states that the more frequent practice of Judaism in Jesus's time would have been to use *anamnesis* not for human remembrance but for God's remembrance.[23] We see such use, for example, in Exodus 2, where the Hebrew slaves' cry for help "rose up to God. God heard their groaning, and God remembered his covenant with Abraham, Isaac, and Jacob" (vv. 23–24). This emphasis on divine remembrance has, according to Jeremias, a twofold significance. First, it means that something must be brought before God, and second, its purpose is that God may remember, either mercifully or in judgment. But such divine remembrance is always "an effecting and creating event," so that when Luke 1:72 ("Thus he has shown the mercy promised to our ancestors, and has remembered his holy covenant") says that "God remembers his covenant, this means that he is now fulfilling the eschatological covenant promise."[24] Following this line of thought, Jeremias argues that "Do this in remembrance of me" should be translated and understood as "This do, *that God may remember me*."[25]

With particular insight, Jeremias sees that the *anamnesis*, and more broadly the Lord's Supper, is not primarily something *we* (or even worse *I*) do. Rather,

> the command to repeat the rite is not a summons to the disciples to preserve the memory of Jesus and be vigilant ("repeat the breaking of the bread so that you may not forget me'"), but it is an eschatologically oriented instruction: "Keep joining yourselves together as the redeemed community by the table rite, that in this way God may be daily implored to bring about the consummation on the parousia." By coming together daily for this table fellowship . . . and confessing in this way Jesus as their Lord, the disciples represent the initiated salvation work before God and they pray for its consummation.[26]

In the Lord's Supper, then, we make ourselves willing participants in God's redemptive work even as we ask for God's remembrance of us. God gathers us, God feeds us, and in so doing God remembers us, making us the body of Christ as we await the eschatological consummation of God's salvation.

We might be tempted to ask: Why does God need to be reminded of anything? Why ask God to remember? As indicated, "remembering" when applied to God refers to God's creative action. In asking God to remember, we beseech God to make present the fullness of his kingdom, past, present, and future. Our own remembering is rightly formed (our amnesia overcome) as we are drawn into this time of salvation. Jeremias's emphasis reminds us that it is God rather than the community or individual that is the primary actor when we gather at the Lord's Table. God's remembering (God's creative action) is always prior and makes possible our remembering response as we eat the bread and drink the wine.

Jean-Luc Marion captures this rhythm of divine, then human, remembrance: "The Christian Eucharist does not recall to memory the death and the resurrection of Christ—would we be 'Christians' if we had forgotten them?—it relies on an event whose past reality has not disappeared in our day (the Ascension belongs intrinsically to the death and resurrection), in order to ask with insistence—eschatological impatience—that Christ return, hence also that his presence govern the future as much as it is rooted in the past."[27] Such an account puts the emphasis where it belongs: on the presence in time of the resurrected Christ, whose love and power we invoke so that the fullness of God's kingdom might be made known. The penitent thief no doubt expected such loving action when he said, "Jesus, remember me when you come into your kingdom" (Luke 23:42). "Remembering" is not in this instance mental recall. Rather, the thief's desire is that God will re-create him (forgive him) so that he might participate in God's reign.

Temporality and Real versus Symbol

The past and the future are both really present in the eucharistic celebration. Just as in celebration of the Passover, Jewish celebrants are contemporaneous with the ancient Hebrew slaves, in the Lord's Supper not only Passover but also Jesus's final meal with his disciples (a Passover meal) and other New Testament meals (such as the feeding of the five thousand) are made present. The future is likewise present in the Eucharist. As Geoffrey Wainwright emphasizes, the eschatological reality is present as taste, sign, image, and mystery of the kingdom.[28] In fact, in the Lord's Supper we are gathered before Christ, into the past, present, and future that Christ himself transforms and creates. The church across time and into the future is thus Christ's "new creation,"[29] the "first fruits" of God's creatures (James 1:18).

154

We might be inclined to think that the presence of the past and the future are unique to the eucharistic (or Passover) liturgy, but to draw this conclusion would be a mistake. The past and the future are always really present, so that making this claim for only the Eucharist (or for liturgy more generally) can easily leave a piece of modern fiction in place, so that the Eucharist itself seems like fiction, a "magical" or only symbolic intrusion into an otherwise real world.

The work of Poteat helps us understand this. "Is there not," Poteat asks, "a sense in which the future is quite as real—not a fiction—as the past? It's just different." We might accept this claim but believe that the past and especially the future are present only in a weaker sense. Poteat himself notes that perhaps it might not seem so odd "to say yesterday's actuality is a present actuality in the ligatures of . . . my present mind-bodily being. It *seems* more problematical however to say that for my temporally distended mindbody in the present tomorrow's *possibility* . . . is a *present actuality*."[30] For the modern sensibility, the future seems only possible, not real. Yet consider how we go about playing a piece of music. If the future notes were not actually present in the playing of a song or sonata, we would be unable to play. Their actuality is present in a different way, as *anticipated*, but this makes their presence no less real. In the words of Poteat, we are creatures in whose "primitive worldliness . . . the weight and authority of myth are founded." This means that even in our "artless uses of the past and future tenses in ordinary speech," the "past and future are present as we speak." If this were not so, if we embodied no future (just as if we embodied no past), we would become completely disoriented. Poteat can thus conclude that "there is, then, nothing of the *as if* . . . about our references to the future, no want of an 'ontological' ground for it; even if that ground is different from my retrotended past acts in the present."[31] While this may seem like an abstruse point, Poteat is rightly challenging the common notion that the present is real while the past and future are not. As we saw with Jimmie G., when he lost much of his past, he also really lost himself, and so also what he could anticipate became greatly diminished.

The import of Poteat's claim is absolutely crucial for moving beyond constricted understandings of the Lord's Supper. Many (especially Protestants, perhaps) approach the Lord's Table with the conviction that Christ is not *really* present. Various dichotomies shape our imaginations: metaphorical-literal, figurative-direct, symbol-real. From this perspective, one is tempted to say, "But the bread is not literally the body of Christ!" (Or as an Anabaptist once famously said to his interrogators, "I know nothing of your baked God.")[32] This perspective easily leads one to "demythologize" (Rudolf Bultmann) or "deliteralize" (Paul Tillich) Christianity in order to arrive at real truth.[33] Such positions draw a clear line between the mythical and the literal such that the "literal and direct is what is serious and real; all the rest of our talk is, however pleasing and even irresistible, secondary or tertiary."[34] Yet if Poteat's description of time is valid, then the "real" is always situated in the actuality of past, present, and future time. The deeper question to ask is not *symbol or real?* but rather, *which reality is shaping the past, present, and future of our lives?*

To understand the past, present, and future as real is also to see that some mythos always forms our understanding of the "real." Thus, as Poteat indicates, buying bread at the store is no more direct or real than eating bread that is the body of Christ. Or asking a clerk for bread is as real (as bound by myth and by a really present past and future) as praying, "Give us this day our daily bread." We never abandon ritual and myth, even in our seemingly quotidian lives. We can say more fully, then, that how we understand space (or location) is always temporal.[35] When we eat and drink "bread" and "wine," we are always doing so in particular contexts and times, none of which is more "real" than another. Certain contexts, however, may more fully deny or embody the truth of who God calls us to be.

The idea that things are given *in themselves* (apart from time) is, as Poteat puts it, really "a fantasy of (visual) space," a kind of "dead slice of visual space." To find an analogy for Poteat's point, imagine that you can look at one picture frame of an unfamiliar movie and understand the plot-line. And yet a dominant philosophic tradition "identifies the *real as such* with that which is exhaustively mediated in reflection through number, (written) word, and concept."[36] Left out of this view are *temporal images* "that represent us as speakers who, however incompletely and inconstantly, own our words before one another, who make and sometimes keep promises, as transcendent spirits, incarnate persons—in granting these images an only secondary authority, the philosophic tradition deprives us of these resources for doing philosophical anthropology."[37] Such "anthropology," in other words, fails to acknowledge its roots in a particular past, present, and future. Poteat himself in his account of speech is drawing from the Hebraic and, even more, Christian traditions, in which speech, word, and logos are central motifs. God speaks the world into existence *ex nihilo* (for Christians). Humans are given the gift of speech: naming, making promises, asking forgiveness, demanding justice, lamenting, and much more. Human words (which are also deeds) can destroy or create contexts of faithfulness (Peter's denial creates a context of sorrow and repentance; Jesus's forgiveness reestablishes communion). Speaking as deed comes to fruition when Jesus is identified as the Word become flesh (John 1). When our gift of speech (in response ultimately to God's Word) is given only secondary authority (in contrast, say, to the triumph of mathematics as the paradigmatic language or in contrast to speech as responsive to distorted political or economic realities), then our promises, our prayers and petitions, our words before one another will easily be seen as less than real, especially when contrasted with the "scientific," "mathematical," or "economic" real.[38] From this perspective, the real-symbol dichotomy is better understood as a dichotomy shaped by our erroneous assumptions about the nature of the real. The Lord's Supper draws us into a story where "real" is not determined *over against* ritual and story (a false option in any case) but by the story of the life, death, and resurrection of Christ, ritualized and entered into in the eucharistic celebration.

So understood, this sacrament, as Barry Harvey importantly notes, exegetes "the idea of the autonomous individual as a tragic character within the dramatic work of fiction that is the world as ordered by the power of the state and the principality of the market."[39] The Lord's Supper, in other words, challenges the false realities of the state and market that maintain the fiction of "autonomous individual" for the sake of consumerism and state power. Rather, the eucharistic drama propels us out of our alleged autonomy and *really* unites us with the body of Christ. Liturgical time, which is real time oriented by gathering around Word and Table, enables us to live more fully in the time of God's saving events in history that stretch back to the formation of Israel and forward to the consummation of the kingdom of God. In so doing, we enter God's space where the gathered community and the bread and wine become Christ's body for the world. Of course, the body of Christ that is the church is still divided, and we still easily tend to live our lives as if we were autonomous individuals, in control of our identities and plans. But it is precisely our identity as the body of Christ, an identity we receive as pure gift, that enables us to see ecclesial division as a distortion, as *not* the deepest truth about ourselves.

Two aspects of God's time are particularly pertinent at this point. First, Gerhard Lohfink reminds us that God is not in a hurry; Abraham, for example, moves from one encampment to another. "God takes time," says Lohfink, "but it is not empty time." God is doing a new thing. And while in light of the world's problems "the movement of a wandering Aramean and his concerns for tent and flock seem positively laughable," nonetheless "in *one* place in the world now faith is being practiced."[40] God's patience meant that Abraham's descendents did indeed, across generations, become as numerous as the stars. We can extend Lohfink's comments to the Eucharist. While the seemingly ordinary gathering to celebrate the Lord's meal can seem laughable or inconsequential in light of the world's problems, this liturgical time is by no means empty or wasted. Wainwright affirms, "Because the Blessed Trinity is Lord of time, the one Christ who came and who is to come can come even now at the eucharist in answer to the church's prayer, in partial fulfillment of the promise and therefore as its strengthening, even though the moment of the final coming remains a divine secret."[41] The apparent insignificance of gathering to worship and to celebrate this meal belies the momentous thing that God is doing: creating a people to be Christ for the world.

Second, then, worship, and the Eucharist specifically, does not remove us from the movement of time. The word *eucharist*, thanksgiving, names our dependence on God's self-giving in Christ in time. Because of this, the time of the Lord's Supper and hence all time is marked by an attitude of thanksgiving as well as anticipation, "anticipation of that 'knowing even as I am known' which keeps Christian life in motion and free of solipsism."[42] The Eucharist enables us to live in a time marked by Christ's self-giving. Our part is learning to receive Christ, learning how to be "re-membered"[43] so that we desire to be who Christ desires us to be. Because Christ comes to us in time, this ecclesial journey takes time as we allow ourselves to be placed, clay vessels that we are, in the great drama of God's cosmic salvation.

Not Just "in the Head": Eucharist as Play

So far, we have emphasized God's remembrance of us; we have contrasted God's time with the modern fictions of time (and thus space) that easily rule our lives. My primary reason for discussing memory, time, and space has been to move beyond imagining the Lord's Supper as either some internal head game (as in the idea that the Lord's Supper or religion more broadly is only as real as one can believe it to be) or an alien magical intrusion into time and space. We can also move beyond such misconceptions by looking at the formation of liturgical "bodies."

That the Eucharist does not depend upon our mental recall (or understanding) is especially evident when we consider the participation of children or those with mental handicaps,[44] where "understanding" may not be a possibility. Even "reflecting" and "paying attention" may be difficult for parents who are preoccupied with small children (as I have personally discovered!). At the other end of the age spectrum, the elderly can sometimes not "understand" because of physical or mental disabilities. One elderly man who comes faithfully to our church can seldom hear the sermon or prayers, but he nevertheless shows up every Sunday. His presence would make no sense if understanding were the primary point.

While I do not wish to deny the power of gaining intellectual insights, the aim of worship is not "getting something out of the service," whether understanding or emotional uplift. The "aim" is rather, as John Milbank says about the church itself, a "sociality and conviviality itself, a *telos* which subverts teleology, because in the continuous 'music' of community, no aspect of life is merely a stage on the way to a final outcome." Milbank is arguing that the church is unlike the antique *polis* in having fixed roles for individuals. Childhood, for example, is not simply training for adulthood, when a child will "understand" and thus worship more fully. Rather, childhood (like being mentally handicapped or elderly) is a "mode of being as directly and absolutely related to the creative action of God (which being eternal, does not seek a goal or follow a plan, but simply happens as a spontaneous, perfectly existent 'excess') as any other."[45] Children, the elderly, and those with mental handicaps have as much access to God's extravagant abundance as do those of us who are "normal" adults (I return to the question of normality in the final chapter). All whom God gathers are therefore able to display and participate in God's excess. This emphasis on the creative and excessive action of God frees us to see liturgy not as simply something somber and controlled but as "playful," like the serious play of children.[46] Our aim is not simply to get something out of the service, but to participate—playfully and joyfully—in what God is doing in our midst with these particular people whom God has gathered.

Understood in this light, the Lord's Supper is not so much about mental apprehension as about our participation in a cosmic drama much larger than ourselves or our individual thoughts—a participation we rightly call a celebration, since we are given our true purpose and identity in the life of God. Through such participation, we can even say that bodies become "reconfigured."[47] Ben Quash gives us an example of reconfiguration from the Peto Institute in Hungary where, he writes,

> severely handicapped children are "conducted" repeatedly through certain motions. They submit to the control of another whilst their limbs are guided to certain positions and through certain sequences of action. In this way, they begin to acquire a greater control over their own bodies and a capacity to initiate action themselves. . . . The eucharist itself [is] conductive in some comparable way. And the movement through which [it] conducts [its] participants is the decentring movement of *ekstasis* and *kenosis*—the loving movement of the Trinity itself.[48]

For a key description of the decentering movement that Quash is referring to, we can turn to the familiar passage from Philippians 2, thought originally to be an early Christian hymn. Christ empties or humbles himself (*kenosis*) even unto death, yet this movement is met with a countermovement: God highly exalts him, bestowing on him "the name that is above every name" (v. 9). The resurrection is ecstatic, the joyous realization that Christ, the Son of God, is alive. In a similar way, Quash observes, our bodies "exercise" a decentering movement, dying and receiving new life, in the Eucharist. To participate, to eat the body and blood of Christ, is to give up, to let go, to sacrifice who we are apart from our identity with Christ. There is thus a dying to self. Yet in letting go we receive new life. We allow ourselves to be fed and nourished by Christ and in so doing receive—ecstatically and delightfully—our very life as gift.

In the Eucharist, then, bodies are reconfigured as we submit to others and to a story much larger than ourselves. Such bodily configuration, however, is not unique to the Peto Institute or the Eucharist; we daily allow our bodies to be configured in all sorts of ways, as we watch advertisements on TV (thereby allowing certain desires to be formed) or drive (usually alone) hurriedly to and from work (often allowing such work to determine our identity). Or more broadly, as noted in the previous chapter, our modern liberal political polity configures our bodies such that we easily maintain a split between the personal, private realm of religion and the public realm of politics, such that we might feel embarrassed—a bodily sign—to talk about our faith "in public," especially if we have been configured to believe faith is a "personal choice." In these instances, both the market, with its emphasis on consumer freedom, and the state, with its private-public dichotomy, deeply form our bodily habits of imagination. Harvey summarizes our situation as follows: "In virtually every corner of the globe men, women and children are being carefully scripted as 'individuals,' that is, as interchangeable integers of consumption and production, making choices from a wide range of options which are controlled by institutions they cannot see, and managed by people they never meet face-to-face."[49] And this now applies to software engineers as well as lettuce packers.

That our bodies are so deeply configured in ways antithetical to the body of Christ could be a cause for despair. But Christian resistance entails not despair but repentance, a repentance we enact within the wider eucharistic context of Christ's presence as we kneel or bow our heads and confess our sins. We repent rather than despair because we learn to embody the truth that God has not abandoned us but remains present, a material presence celebrated and welcomed as we gather around the Lord's Table.

To speak of the body's being configured differently, then, is to name ways our bodies themselves become liturgically formed. Of course, we can and often do just "go through the liturgical motions" and remain unchanged. That this happens, that we ourselves resist God's grace, means that we have allowed our bodies to be formed or configured by other stories and other dramas. For all of us, conversion into the divine liturgical drama is an ongoing process.

Two body signs in particular reflect a deeper conversion or reconfiguration into the eucharistic unity of the church. One of these has to do with how we "taste" the bread and wine. This may sound odd, but ecumenical theologians such as Ephraim Radner and George Lindbeck have both written that "the eucharist tastes bitter in the divided church."[50] Radner compares the taste of the Eucharist in a divided church to vinegar and gall.[51] The pain of division, and even more the fact that we are contributing to the brokenness of Christ's body, leaves a bitter taste. By contrast, Radner notes, the "easy conscience of embraced Eucharistic participation often [goes] hand in hand with the denial of ecclesial separations, indeed, with the interiorization and individualization of the Christian life altogether, against which the whole reality of ecclesial suffering [holds] little relief."[52] If the bread and wine do not taste bitter, or if they do not taste like much of anything, this might well be due to a cultural formation that vaporizes religion into an interior sphere or makes acceptable a variety of ecclesial bodies. Yet in the context of the Eucharist, nature alone—the bread and wine alone apart from the presence of Christ—produces a lack, one that is "like salt on the tongue, leaving us thirsting for something more; not for more salt, but for the water that alone quenches our thirst."[53] That the bread and wine do not taste bitter, do not remind us of the brokenness of the people of God, is a sign of how adjusted we have become to disunity and division. The liturgical drama ought so to configure our bodies that we *desire* communion with Christ's whole body. This might seem an entirely negative observation, but dissatisfaction and yearning are ways God draws us toward himself (as expressed by Augustine's classic statement "My heart is restless until it rests in Thee, O God").

Another significant sign of liturgical reconfiguration is, as odd as it might sound, our willingness to be embarrassed. In his book on the Eucharist, P. J. Fitzpatrick gives the following provocative subtitle to one section: "I Blush, Therefore I Am." Embarrassment, he says, should not be eliminated from our thinking about the Eucharist; he maintains even that "embarrassment is the best starting-point" for trying to understand this ritual.[54] The temptation today among some is to domesticate accounts of the Eucharist in order to release us from such embarrassing unmodern notions as sacrifice or the real presence of Christ.

Embarrassment or humiliation can therefore be a kind of bodily sign of eucharistic transformation. Hans Urs von Balthasar discusses the role of humiliation in the "eucharistic thought" of John's Gospel in the washing of the feet. Recall that Peter says in shock, "Lord, are you going to wash my feet?" (13:6). Von Balthasar reminds us of the inappropriateness of Jesus's act, as it was something only a slave would do. While people today might be mildly embarrassed to have their feet washed by another, for Peter this is inconceivable. He is deeply humiliated because he is willing "what *he* in no way wants . . . the Lord's being a slave." He wills what he does not want because his willingness is rooted in the desire to obey.

Jesus has told him, "Unless I wash you, you have no share with me" (13:8). "This sharing (*meros*) alludes to the eucharistic word *koinonia*."[55] In the language I have been using, Peter's "reconfiguring" consists in a kind of humiliation as he allows Jesus to wash his feet. Von Balthasar draws this conclusion: "Unity can be brought about only in such a way that we are *forced* by him into humiliation, on the basis, to be sure, of a once freely given consent of faith, but then in a being overwhelmed by *his* will to self-humiliation in obedience to the Father."[56] Peter's humiliation consists in his allowing Christ to become a slave on his behalf. Peter knows he in no way deserves this; he does not *want* to be in this role. But it is precisely his recognition (however incomplete) that Jesus is the Messiah that enables Peter to allow Christ to override Peter's own sense of worthlessness and social custom. Just as Peter was humiliated by Jesus's desire to wash his feet yet at the same time "overwhelmed" into obedience, so also is the Eucharist our sharing in the Son's obedience to the Father and an overwhelming by the unitive love of God into obedience. Such love makes possible a willingness to go against the grain of the proper and expected thing to do, against even the grain of our sense of unworthiness, which is signaled by a willingness to be embarrassed.

Modern habits train us to resist such embarrassingly enthusiastic responses as the one Peter finally gives to Jesus: "Lord, not my feet only but also my hands and my head!" (John 13:9). Instead, creatures of modernity that we are, we easily practice "a religion of civility." We are "complexly aware of our religious appearances *to others*."[57] As we saw in chapter 1's discussion of a privatized hospitality, a "decorum of democratic culture" emphasizes sophisticated tastes and bars "crude" religious conviction from polite discourse. In short, no one wants to be embarrassed. And yet a willingness to be embarrassed—to allow Jesus to wash our feet or to feed us with his body and blood—might well signal the birth of something new: the liturgical reconfiguration of our bodies into a fuller manifestation of the body of Christ.

The Eucharist and Unity

The claim of this chapter is that a divided house prevents the full practice of Christian hospitality. Thus we have looked to the Lord's Supper as a uniting practice, where we are remembered by God, where we enter God's time and space, and where our bodies are reconfigured. In doing this, I have wanted to break down the easy slide that the Lord's Supper can take into interiority (for some Protestants) or magical intrusion into otherwise "normal" time and space (often associated with Catholics). While these emphases might shore up misleading conceptions of the

Eucharist, we are still left with the seemingly intractable fact of disunity. In what follows I want to bring to bear these various threads, particularly the emphasis that God rather than the individual is the primary actor in worship, on the eucharistic unity of the church.

In doing so, I will look briefly at Anabaptist and Roman Catholic understandings of the Lord's Supper. These are, of course, large topics; my purpose will be to focus on this sacrament as a reconfigurative practice with an eye to building up the unity of the church and thus making possible a more faithful practice of hospitality.

Ulrich Zwingli and, later, the Anabaptists regarded the Lord's Supper as an expressive rite: it proclaimed or expressed the community's faith. Anabaptist leader Conrad Grebel, for example, stated that "the Supper is an expression of fellowship, not a Mass or a sacrament. Therefore none is to receive it alone, neither on his deathbed nor otherwise."[58] So much did Grebel emphasize the oneness of the body and desire to be "true brethren with one another" that he believed receiving Communion alone would deny the very nature of the Supper as communion fellowship. Grebel's understanding that the Lord's Supper is not simply an individual devotional affair but requires a gathered community living in peace with each other is theologically powerful.

While Grebel's strong emphasis on communion is particularly important (especially in light of the strong Anabaptist witness to communion as embodying the peace of Christ), it limits the *Lord's* Supper to an expression of a prior faith (Zwingli) or of a prior fellowship (Grebel). While the Anabaptists especially place a strong emphasis on "brotherly love," the liturgical celebration of the meal itself is not unitive or binding but representative of a prior unity. The Lord's Supper is not a participation in the self-offering of Christ but a *symbol* of a unity already achieved.

In an odd way, this pattern can also be seen in the Catholic understanding of the Mass, even though the Catholic emphasis on real presence (as transubstantiation) differs from the Anabaptist understanding. Protestant and Orthodox bodies are denied table fellowship unless they are in full communion with the Catholic Church. Thus John Paul II states that "celebration of the eucharist . . . cannot be the starting point for communion; it presupposes that communion already exists, a communion which it seeks to consolidate and bring to perfection."[59] While moving toward unity of belief and doctrine is no doubt crucial, this approach, like the Anabaptist approach, fails to acknowledge that the Eucharist as the acknowledged real presence of Christ might be itself a source of unity, not because of human agreement but because of Christ's real presence and desire to unite us with himself. Because of Christ's self-giving, the Eucharist can itself be "creative."[60] I realize such an approach is fraught with potential problems, perhaps the chief of which is for substantial theological differences to be watered down or seen as unimportant. While acknowledging that eucharistic fellowship is a good thing and an expression of the yearning for unity, Pope Benedict XVI has warned that it must not become "atrophied into a kind of communal act of socialization."[61]

And yet we must take into consideration the kind of argument that Bruce Marshall puts forth in "The Disunity of the Church and the Credibility of the Gospel," as he analyzes John 17. Marshall suggests that the church's visible unity has a number of dimensions: a unity of faith, as displayed in worship and confession; a unity of mutual love and service; a unity in a common baptism; and a unity of shared participation in the Eucharist. Marshall focuses particularly on the latter unity, which he says has a distinctive twofold function: it visibly unites the church with Christ as the one risen Christ's own body and blood, and the church is united both temporally and spatially "by the gift and reception of Christ's body and blood, from Pentecost to the parousia and from Jerusalem to the ends of the earth."[62] Thus Marshall acknowledges that the Eucharist itself has a creative and unitive function. Marshall further claims that the church's unifying participation in God's own life "happens not primarily in the minds and hearts of individuals (though it does of course happen there), but in the public Eucharistic celebration by which Christ joins individuals to himself and so makes of them his own community."[63] The unity of the church is the unity of God: "God makes the church one by bringing human beings to share in his own unity; Christ through the promised Spirit will draw the church into the unity of being and love he has with the Father, assimilating the church to the unique bond that exists between them."[64] Thus Marshall emphasizes a unity located not primarily in the minds of individuals but in worship (prayer, confession, baptism) and particularly the public celebration of the Eucharist itself. Such eucharistic visibility is the way the triune God displays to and in the world his own eternal life, "that the world may believe" (John 17:21). The statement that is most significant in light of our analysis is the following: "If the reading of John 17 just sketched is right, then Eucharistic fellowship does not manifest the unity of the church; it *is* (though not all by itself) the unity of the church. What it manifests is the unity—and thereby the reality—of God."[65]

By emphasizing that the Eucharist *is* our unity, our participation in the triune life of God, rather than simply *manifesting* a unity, Marshall lifts up a crucial dimension of real presence: the Eucharist itself is creative of unity. This claim, rather than emphasizing the Eucharist as representative of a prior communion, provides a theological rationale for celebrating the Eucharist across divisions in the church, even when such communion is still imperfect.[66] This approach does not mean being inclusive as if inclusivity were all that mattered. Rather, it elevates the *real* presence of

Christ as ultimately unitive; it confirms de Lubac's classic saying, cited earlier, that "the eucharist makes the church."

We can acknowledge, however, that an understanding of the Eucharist as "creative" or "causative" might not necessarily be unitive, at least in the short term. Radner, in fact, claims that this causative power is not to be understood in the first instance as unity itself. Instead, it might first lead to the taste of the bitterness of disunity. "Where a willing reception of such taste may lead us and how it will do so in the near term is hardly clear, however; nor is it necessarily benign."[67] Radner's comments can be understood in light of Paul's concern that participants not eat and drink unworthily or "eat and drink judgment against themselves" (1 Cor. 11:29).

Hospitality as an Exclusive Discipline

While I think an emphasis must fall on the creative and potentially unitive power of the Lord's Table, at the same time we must embrace the conviction that the Lord's Supper expresses a genuine communion as well.[68] In Matthew's Gospel we read, "So when you are offering your gift at the altar, if you remember that your brother or sister has something against you, leave your gift there before the altar and go; first to be reconciled to your brother or sister, and then come and offer your gift" (Matt. 5:23–24). How are we to approach the Table so that we are not eating and drinking judgment against ourselves?

In this light, it is important to see the Lord's Supper and hospitality as disciplinary practices. To our modern ears, *discipline* has primarily a negative connotation, such that discipline and hospitality hardly seem compatible. Hospitality, it is commonly assumed, should be about "welcome," not discipline or, even worse, exclusion.

In response to such a seemingly commonsensical approach, however, I must emphasize two points. First, any practice of hospitality (or the Lord's Supper) is going to be exclusive in some sense. Since such practice will always be rooted in a broader tradition regarding the way the world is and regarding the good and the true, it is going to necessarily exclude other kinds of hospitality. For example, a consumeristic hospitality that promotes "choice" will exclude an Aristotelian hospitality that is oriented toward the good of the *polis*. So understood, a consumeristic hospitality "disciplines" its "guests" in very particular and often subtle ways—to desire to look younger, to desire certain kinds of experiences (staying in nice hotels), to possess certain things. As noted earlier, a hospitality formed by political liberal assumptions disciplines its practitioners to live in two spheres: the private sphere of values and "spirituality" and the public sphere of politics. To ignore the sophisticated and complex ways we are in fact already disciplined is to deceive ourselves. So the more basic question is not whether or not we will live by discipline but rather *which* disciplines we will give ourselves over to.

Second, without discipline, a practice will quickly atrophy or devolve into something else. For example, the ongoing threat of gnosticism to Christianity has made possible an interiorization of belief such that the spiritual world becomes separate from the material world of bodies, politics, and economics. The Lord's Supper then easily becomes simply a symbol of an interior conviction, and the visibility of the church is compromised.

This last point brings us to our chief concern: the church as the visible body of Christ. Discipline is always for the sake of Christ's body, that the church might become more fully itself. Reflecting on 1 Corinthians 11:27–32, William Cavanaugh writes, "What Paul seems to mean by 'discipline' is essentially the authority over the body which produces a visible body of people set apart from the world by their conduct."[69] Without disciplinary ways of living as the body of Christ, the church risks becoming a collection of individuals who might share common beliefs or common likes but who cease to be a visible, political body. Undisciplined hospitality easily becomes superficial, often judging poorly out of false desires, such as the desire to be liked.[70]

Rightly understood, discipline need not be entirely negative. Discipline is similar to training, and the right kind of disciplines—the discipline of praying or of playing the piano, for example—are ultimately sources of joy. Even such an extreme discipline as excommunication ultimately has a positive purpose that could be described as medicinal: "Its purpose was not to forsake the sinner but to cure him," Cavanaugh states.[71] In fact, if partaking of the bread and cup in an unworthy manner and without discerning the body leads to judgment against oneself and even death (1 Cor. 11:27–32), then Cavanaugh states that it would be "positively cruel" to allow a person to continue to do so. "As an invitation to reconciliation . . . excommunication done well is an act of *hospitality*, in which the church does not expel the sinner, but says to her, 'You are already outside our communion. Here is what you need to do to come back in.'"[72] Failure to excommunicate the notorious sinner results in leaving her to eat and drink to her own condemnation. The hope is then that excommunication, like all disciplines, will bring about a kind of retraining, enabling one to become reconciled with God and others.

In discussing excommunication, Cavanaugh is obviously talking about a disciplined hospitality *within* the church: how the body of Christ is to practice hospitality toward its own members, particularly when persons refuse to repent for sins against the church itself. "Excommunication, by definition, is for ecclesiological offenses," a fact borne out by the 1983 Code of Canon Law. While excommunication certainly has the potential to be abused, it is also true, as Raymond Brown says, that "from the earliest days and with the approval of its most notable spokesmen the Church has exercised the power of exclusion, especially in doctrinal and moral matters. And so a protest against all excommunication is not simply a protest against canon law but against the preachers of the Gospel."[73]

When we raise the issue of discipline, however, a number of difficult practical kinds of questions come to mind. Who is going to discipline? For which offenses? In response to the first question, Cavanaugh argues that the discipline of excommunication resides in the office of bishop, whose role is to produce and preserve unity and who is head of the eucharistic community. Such a role does not place the bishop above the people; rather, "the celebrant stands as the Lamb who was slain"[74] and is therefore a servant, one who also as a successor to the apostles is to preserve continuity with Jesus. To the second question, Cavanaugh responds that excommunication has been for ecclesiological offenses, those sins that would threaten the visibility of the body of Christ, such as sins against human life or against the unity of the church.[75]

In terms of Cavanaugh's analysis, one difficulty for some Protestant traditions is that there is no bishop. Excommunication, of course, should be a rare discipline, carried out only after "extensive consultation with laypeople and other bishops."[76] For those churches with a congregational polity (which usually are loosely connected in an association), a similar kind of consultation could be a possibility between pastors and laypeople. Disciplinary practices have historically been a rich part of various Christian traditions. Christopher Ellis, for example, notes that historically Baptists have seen the Lord's Supper as a place where the church acknowledges its "identity as a community before God with obligations of mutual care." He continues that historically "this care was sometimes exercised in the form of discipline. All members of a local congregation were expected to attend worship on a regular basis. . . . Absence was seen not only as disobedience to a divine ordinance and a lack of loyalty to Jesus Christ but also as a sin against the fellowship."[77] Absentees were visited and attendance and ways of life examined. Even more, in the early centuries of Baptist life, a member could be excluded from the Table because of some public sin "from which they needed to repent and which dishonoured the Church." The exclusion was seen as a pastoral measure with the intention of eliciting repentance and was usually justified by reference to Matthew 18:15–18.[78]

The key point here is that discipline is not antithetical to hospitality but an expression of it. As indicated earlier, every kind of hospitality relies upon some sort of discipline. Christian hospitality relies upon the discipline of faithfully gathering around the Lord's Table. In so doing, we are refusing to be disciplined by market and political forces that would relegate hospitality to a choice or private gesture. We are also embodying the conviction that the presence of Christ is both saving and judging. As Ernst Käsemann states, "When the Lord comes on the scene, it is also the universal Judge who appears. . . . His presence never leaves us unaffected. We do not, by our own disrespect, render his gift ineffective or make the presence of Christ unhappen. . . . Where the Saviour is despised, the universal Judge remains present and shows himself in that very place as the one from whose presence there is no escape."[79] Failure to repent or to see Christ's presence does not lead to the absence of Christ but to the presence of Christ as Judge—present to save us from our blindness and refusal to repent.

In the wider liturgical drama, participants are given (or should be given) opportunity for repentance and confession. The kiss of peace was traditionally placed before the service of the Table, a unitive and reconciling gesture that disciplined participants to approach the Table in and through the Spirit of peace. The discipline of gathering around the Lord's Table involves a rich assortment of other disciplines: praying, singing, hearing the preached Word, offering gifts, and allowing these and other practices to saturate the common life. Such ongoing training and retraining (excommunication being the extreme example) make possible the faithful practice of hospitality, both inside and outside the church, as we learn to bear one another's burdens, share one another's joys, delight in each other's gifts, and, in doing so, become people capable of recognizing and receiving Christ. So understood, hospitality is exclusive in the sense that it can be practiced well only by those who are rightly disciplined and who are trained to recognize and receive Christ in all his guises.

The Eucharist as the Wound of Hospitality

We cannot be in the presence of the Lord and remain unscathed. Two dramatic scriptural narratives capture this fact:

The Lord suddenly appears to Moses in a burning bush (Exod. 3). It doesn't occur to Moses to say, "Is this real?" Instead he feels fear, even perhaps humiliation. His life has been disrupted.

Jacob struggles with a mysterious stranger on the banks of the Jabbok (Gen. 32). The presence of his divine opponent is so intense that Jacob cannot let go unless he is blessed. He receives a blessing—a new name— though not without a wound.

In these accounts, Moses and Jacob are interrupted, surprised, and afraid; they struggle, and Jacob leaves "limping because of his hip" (Gen.

32:31). Such stories ought to make us think twice about imagining God's presence as comfortable, pleasing, and nice. To the contrary, as testified throughout scripture, it can be terrifying.

As we have seen, hospitality too is easily tailored to fit our images of a nice God who supports our spiritual lives while powerful economic and political forces determine our lives in the material world. Within this deformed hospitality, the Eucharist seems to have little political or economic relevance.

I am, however, arguing that hospitality depends upon the Eucharist, or even more, that the Eucharist *is* the hospitality we receive and extend to others. This book's discussion of Eucharist and hospitality as disciplines signals that these are communal acts that call for bodies willing to give and receive the abundance that is God.

Even more, Christian hospitality is always cruciform. It has the shape of the life, death, and resurrection of Christ. Taking this seriously can be frightening. Who wants to suffer? Yet I think the deeper question to consider is, are we suffering or willing to suffer for the right things? A cruciform hospitality does not seek after suffering as such but seeks to live out of the death and resurrection of Christ.

This cruciform life of hospitality is exactly what we perform and pre-figure when we gather to celebrate the Lord's Supper. As Wainwright recounts, an eschatological view of the Eucharist provides three chris-tological dimensions. First, life in the final kingdom will be life *in Christ*, as expressed by St. Paul. Second, it will be life *with Christ*, as Jesus tells the thief on the cross, "Today you will be with me in paradise." Finally, it will be Christ living *in us* (Gal. 2:20). These represent, respectively, the divine transcendence, the distinction between God and creature, and the immanence of God.[80] Each of these dimensions may be found in the Lord's Supper: Christ is the host (transcendent), Christ is the companion (a table fellow), and Christ is also the food (immanent).[81] Christ is both the giver and the gift, a fact that makes sense only in the triune economy of salvation. Christ is the host, the One who through the Spirit in com-munion with the Father creates the church and nourishes her. At the same time, Christ is the gift, the One who gave himself unto death (the body and blood) in obedience to the Father and who now gives us a share in his resurrected life.

By being in and with Christ, and Christ in us, we become his body; we participate or share in the body and blood of Christ. "The cup of blessing that we bless, is it not a sharing in the blood of Christ? The bread that we break, is it not a sharing in the body of Christ?" (1 Cor. 10:16). The concern always lingers that somehow in making this claim we are ignor-ing the sinfulness of the church. The church of course is by no means perfect. "It is not only the Church of the saints, but always the Church of sinners as well. And yet," as Lohfink says, "it is the real and physical presence of Christ in history."[82] The practice of the Eucharist signals that our faithlessness cannot overcome the faithfulness of God. When we gather, Christ is present both as Savior and as Judge. David Ford notes that at the Last Supper, Jesus is incorporating a community that betrays, denies, and abandons him. "He forms a community for them without their trust or understanding. He does the trusting, obeying, suffering and dying. This lack of presumption that they have to do anything right to be the recipients of the bread and wine makes it an Archimedean point of receptivity—and, therefore, of potential gratitude."[83]

Ford's amazing insight signals not that God does everything, and humans nothing, or that humans are mere puppets. He is rather drawing our attention to the fact that our trust or lack of trust, our understanding or lack of understanding, does not ultimately determine our identity as the body of Christ. To receive the bread and wine (to be baptized) is to be *marked* by Christ, a fact that we can only truly receive with gratitude.

The gift of our lives, of our identities as members of Christ, is not a one-time gift to be taken and then controlled. The nature of our eucharistic feeding is ongoing; we gather again and again to receive the body and blood of Christ. Our lives are always gifts of God; the divine spring continually supplies what we need. There is never a time when we can sit back and say, "Ahh, now my life is mine." Such a way of thinking distorts not only our lives but more fundamentally the nature of God, whose superabundant giving never ceases because it lies at the heart of God's triune identity. The well never runs dry. What this means for us is that our lives are always gift. There are no moments when we can step out of this, because to speak of our creation (and re-creation) is also to speak of God's giving, and to speak of God's giving is also to speak of God's creating.

From this perspective, gifts "cannot be owned without ceasing to be themselves."[84] Rather, as Ford indicates, we learn to live our lives as gifts to the extent that we live in gratitude. The eucharistic gifts we receive, therefore, are not "ours" to hoard for personal devotion or simply to strengthen personal piety. Rather, to receive the Eucharist is already to give back. To receive faithfully is to give thanks (*eucharist* means "thanksgiving"). This is how we are to see our lives as members of Christ's body. To receive the body and blood is to accept with our mouths, hands, and knees—our whole body—that we live only by receiving from God. We are sinners but also forgiven; our lives are total gifts made possible by the gift of the Son.

Hospitality, then, is not moral do-goodism. In fact, in the Eucharist we are being asked to *give up* trying to be good, to *give up* trying to be hospitable. Such a statement may sound scandalous, especially in a book on hospitality. But faithful worship always involves a giving up of ourselves, even a giving up of *our* goodness, since goodness is never ours (as a possession) anyway. Discussing Martin Luther (who himself stressed the giving up of good works),[85] Milbank states that Luther's message is essentially that of Augustine:

> Without the virtue of worship, there can be no other virtue, for worship gives everything back up to God, hangs onto nothing and so disallows any finite accumulation which will always engender conflict. Confident worship also knows that in offering it receives back, so here the temporal world is not denied, but its temporality is restored as gift and thereby rendered eternal.[86]

Worship involves giving up even our own "goodness." In the Eucharist, we offer our lives in unity with the offering of Christ. This is the cruciform dimension we enact as we participate in the movement of uniting our lives with Christ in the bread and wine. Even as we give up, however, we are confident that we will receive our lives back as gift. Our offering, made possible by God's grace, is already a receiving, since it is God's grace that makes our worship possible in the first place.

To see worship in this light is to see, with Augustine and Luther, that worship is the virtue that makes all other virtues possible. Without worship, there can be no Christian hospitality, since such hospitality receives and extends God's own gracious plentitude, a plentitude known and realized most fully in worship, where our giving is always restored as gift. Milbank writes that "the confident man, believing in plentitude, does not steal, and does not need to tell lies to protect himself." So also, we could say, the confident Christian believing in plentitude does not need to hoard (time, gifts, or possessions) or to live in fear (of the neighbor, stranger, or even the enemy) but is free to live a life of Christlike hospitality. Such a way of life, as Milbank notes, is not an exact copying of Christ or the saints but rather involves improvisation, like that of an artist, all the while "trusting the perfect maker of all things." Thus, the Christian "gives up trying to be good." Paul encourages the Romans to cease trying to be self-sufficient and instead become good at "first receiving from the all-sufficiency of God, and acting excessively out of this excess."[87] A cruciform hospitality gives up self-sufficiency, even the self-sufficiency of our own goodness. In scriptural language, we can call this a "death to self." But this giving up, this dying, is confident that Christ is present as friend, as Savior, and as the giver of new life. The wounds of Christ do not disappear but are rather transformed.

Finally, we come to the woundedness of the church. Lohfink has called the disunity of the church one of the greatest wounds on the body of Christ. As we have seen, various economic, political, and ethical distortions have created divisions within the church and domesticated Christian hospitality. The memory of the unity of the church, of the Table, has faded so that it has become easy for us to forget our brothers and sisters in Christ, whether they are in other parts of the world (Iraqi Christians, for example), in our own cities, or in other "communions" (Orthodox, Roman Catholic, or Protestant). For those who see the brokenness of Christ's body in the divisions of the church, Jean-Jacques von Allmen has noted that there are at least three temptations. The first temptation sees ecclesial unity as an Edenic state, one quickly abandoned when the church began to engage in worldly struggles. A second temptation holds that unity will be accomplished only at the end of time, when God restores all things. A final temptation is fatalistic, recognizing the intractability of our present Christian differences.[88] In light of the New Testament, however, Lohfink rightly states that the splintering of the people of God cannot be regarded in any other way than as a "broken mirror that distorts the image of Christ."[89] He cites Ephesians 4:3, "[Make] every effort to maintain the unity of the Spirit," and Jesus's prayer in John 17, "That they may all be one . . ."[90]

From this perspective, the Lord's Supper disrupts *all* false unities: the false unities of the nation-state and the market, and unities based on personal likes and tastes. At the Table, all baptized Christians—rich and poor, Iraqi and American—are gathered. The less privileged are even to be given places of honor (1 Cor. 12).

But what if the shadow of the United States flag falls over the bread and wine, as it does in many churches? What unity prevails? To the extent that we are willing to kill other Christians (and non-Christians) on behalf of our nation-state, it certainly seems as if the Eucharist is merely symbolic, in the negative modern sense of that word. It's just a symbol; another reality dominates our lives. If this is so, however, we enter the eucharistic drama at our peril, possibly eating and drinking "judgment against [our]selves" (1 Cor. 11:29). But such a judgment, if received as gift, enables us to see the false unities of this world for what they are. The eucharistic drama draws us into the divine hospitality so that we ourselves are enabled, by God's grace, to become Christ to each other and the world, a becoming that might well look like crucifixion and resurrection.

Strange Hospitality to the Stranger

■ We have looked at various ways hospitality becomes distorted. We have considered the political, economic, and ethical assumptions that shape these distortions. We have understood worship, particularly the Eucharist, as our participation in God's own triune self-giving and receiving. We have emphasized that through the gifts of faith, hope, and love (gifts that when received over time become part of who we are), we participate in God's hospitality.

Yet a gap remains. The economic and political forces that dominate our culture inevitably shape the contours of our lives. How can we avoid the seduction of the market? How can we be formed so that we genuinely desire not the consumption of possessions and experiences that dominates our culture but the giving and receiving that constitute the life of God? How do we overcome the alienation that easily marks our lives and that leads us to see others as competitors and threats? Finally, how do we build up the church so that its hospitality is not domesticated but is a communal embodiment of life together in Christ? In theory, the kind of Christ-centered hospitality described in this book may sound intriguing; in practice, the obstacles can seem paralyzing.

As mentioned earlier, my husband pastors a small United Methodist church located in the Virginia countryside. The twenty-five or so of us who attend usually do not see each other except on Sunday morning. We gather for worship, we pray for each other (some are ill, some have lost jobs, some are having hard times with their children), and then we go our separate ways. This relatively brief time together hardly seems transformative when measured against the time we spend doing other things. Our current culture, fascinated with conspicuous consumption and "supersize me" opportunities, would lead us to ignore the significance of such a small gathering. Yet Christ never said our gathering together as his body had to be large. By contrast, Jesus lifted up the deep significance of the few and apparently insignificant. "Where two or three are gathered in my name, there I am." He chose only twelve disciples; he did not begrudge the interruptions of small children (Mark 10:13–16). Many of his parables focus on the few and the little: the mustard seed, the lost sheep, the lost coin.

During announcement time at our church, our four-year old son used to raise his hand eagerly to announce the latest adventure on his favorite computer game, Bugdom. "Rolly McFly defeated King Ant!" he would shout out. Finally, my husband told him that this was not the time for those kinds of announcements, to which he replied, "Oh—okay . . . I got one. God's love is real." As insignificant and small as our gathering is, he has nonetheless learned to name, even if in a small way, the presence of God.

The faithful practice of hospitality must begin (and also end) with what our society will tend to regard as of little consequence. Waiting for the earthshaking event or the cultural or even ecclesial revolution can paralyze us. We are rather, as the gospel reminds us, called to be faithful in the small things. Hospitality is a practice and discipline that asks us to do what in the world's eyes might seem inconsequential but from the perspective of the gospel is a manifestation of God's kingdom.

So in this final chapter, I want to emphasize hospitality as a practice of small gestures. In fact, when we look at faithful practitioners of hospitality, without exception they emphasize the importance of the small, the apparently insignificant, the vulnerable, and the poor. The tendency to focus on large-scale success inhibits the faithful practice of hospitality, since the significance of small gestures can fall through the cracks. Faithful hospitality forms us to see that the destination and the journey cannot be separated. If hospitality is our participation in God's own giving and receiving, then as scripture testifies, this gift and reception is always particular, concrete, and seemingly insignificant. Jesus calls a band of ordinary disciples to follow him; they must have seemed relatively inconsequential to many observers. The familiar verse "God so loved the world that he gave his only Son . . ." indicates that God's love, as universal as it is, nonetheless became fully revealed in one particular place and time and in one particular person.

An emphasis on the small gesture, the seemingly insignificant act, could seem to suggest that I am endorsing a way of practicing hospitality that leaves everything as it is. Such hospitality might be perceived as a Band-Aid approach that fails to challenge systemic political and economic powers. I am not, however, claiming that hospitality is "synonymous with romantic notions of personalistic politics that seek change by means of individual, one-on-one acts of kindness to the exclusion of . . . communal efforts."[1] Hospitality is not simply individual acts of kindness—and this is a theological claim. God desires to have not autonomous individuals loosely connected to each other via "rights" but a people (Israel and the church), a body in the world witnessing to the love and mighty deeds of God.[2] God gathers us for a purpose much larger than our self-interest. As we will see more fully below, a romanticized, individualistic politics obscures Christian hospitality as the task and calling of a people whose lives are marked by a story different from one that would have us believe we can be "individuals" apart from the body of Christ.

In response to the possible concern that small gestures make no difference, consider the following illuminating example. Challenging our narrow conception of politics as policy making, Philip Kenneson writes,

> If Christians lobby Congress to restrict the amount of violence on television, this is considered "real political action." If Christians put their television sets in the closet, however, this is considered a private matter, a personal lifestyle choice, a simple apolitical preference. But certainly if all people who consider themselves Christians did the latter, this action would have a sizable impact on the social order we call the United States of America. Isn't such ordering of the social the traditional concern of politics?[3]

Hospitality, like the Christian life more broadly, is a practice of the "little way," a phrase made famous by St. Thérèse of Lisieux. God takes the little things we are capable of and transforms them. Waiting for the great opportunity or the path to success can blind us to our daily reliance upon God's bread and the ordinary ways we can give this bread to others. Through small and often ordinary acts of faith, hope, and love—however faltering and weak these might be—God makes the church visible in the world.

We can particularly see how hospitality is marked by small, faithful gestures in two remarkable Christian communities in our time: the L'Arche communities, founded by Jean Vanier, and the Church of the Saviour, founded by Gordon and Mary Cosby. The L'Arche communities, begun by Vanier in 1964, are places where those with mental handicaps live in communion with those without such handicaps. Initially, Vanier invited Raphael Simi and Philippe Seux to live with him in a small house in France that he was able to purchase with the help of friends. Raphael and Philippe had been shut up in a "rather violent" institution after the deaths of their parents. "My intention," Vanier writes, "was to create community with them," a community rooted in the conviction that "God chose what is foolish in the world to shame the wise, God chose what is weak in the world to shame the strong" (1 Cor. 1:27).[4] Today there are more than one hundred L'Arche communities in twenty-five different countries. In 1947, Gordon and Mary Cosby began the Church of the Saviour in Washington, D.C., out of a desire to live more intentionally as the body of Christ for the world. To this end, there has been a strong emphasis on the inward journey (prayer, worship, discernment of call) and the outward journey (commitment to the poor, the broken, and the vulnerable). The church today consists of twelve faith communities, each focused on a particular ministry in the inner city of Washington. Members commit themselves to specific disciplines, including prayer (usually one hour each day), gathering for worship, proportional giving beginning with a tithe, and working with a particular mission.

I am drawn to these communities as living embodiments of hospitality for a number of reasons. First, on a personal note, I have had the opportunity to meet both Jean Vanier and Gordon Cosby. A deep and profound holiness marks the lives of both. In a recent conversation with Gordon Cosby, he told me that people sometimes refer to him (in contrast to his wife) as a "porcupine," a description that might not sound particularly holy. But his willingness to risk, to speak the truth in love in radical ways, and to simply be present to others exemplifies the presence of God in his life. Years ago, on a visit to the church, I was walking down the street with him when a jobless man sitting out on the sidewalk looked up at me and said with great conviction, "You're walking with a powerful man." Those words capture the power that comes from a life of deep faithfulness to God.

I met Jean Vanier during a very dark period in my life that had required me to take a leave of absence from Saint Mary's College. Vanier was in town to receive a service medal from the University of Notre Dame, and one of my students offered to take me to his lecture, a gesture I can now grasp as a profound gift. I communicated with Vanier briefly afterward (primarily about how his lecture touched me and about my illness and the uncertainties surrounding it), and he responded with several beautiful notes to me. Like Cosby, Vanier is a powerful man, one whose power no doubt comes from a deep communion with God, especially through communion with those who have mental handicaps.

Both of these men would be the first to point out that the "success" of their respective communities is not primarily about them but about God's desire to be visibly and tangibly present in the world: healing our brokenness, reconciling us to each other, and drawing us into God's own triune life. They share a vision of the church that highlights receiving the "stranger" as Christ would. The stranger may be someone with a mental handicap, a homeless person, someone in your community whom you may not like, or even yourself (the broken, wounded parts of yourself that you might want to reject). The hospitality of both L'Arche and the Church of the Saviour is public and communal; no single individual possesses the practice. Christian hospitality has "naturally" become a part of who they are in their life together.[5] I place *natural* in quotation marks because the kind of hospitality these communities offer is not natural to the uninformed. Indeed, it can seem strange. Why live in a home with those who are mentally handicapped? Why "waste" so much time praying when there are a lot of other really important things to do? Why seek downward rather than upward mobility? The new visitor to either of these communities might be inclined to ask these and similar questions.

Here we will consider the strange ways of Christian hospitality manifested in these communities. Such hospitality is strange because, as these communities testify, God does strange things when we open our lives to him. Christian hospitality cannot be domesticated or managed; it takes us on an adventure, and both L'Arche and the Church of the Saviour show us that this adventure can be truly remarkable. Both of these communities are gifts to the church universal. Like all of God's gifts, we are called to receive them and allow them to build up the whole body.

Normal versus Holy

Hospitality, faithfully practiced, challenges our assumptions about what it means to be normal. Thus the word *strange* captures an important aspect of Christian hospitality. We are not required to fit into a predetermined mold supplied by culture or family or even our own expectations. We are free from the diverse cultural expectations, examined earlier, that would have us practice a domesticated hospitality. We are free to be faithful, to live joyfully, and becoming faithful makes us more free.

Perhaps nowhere is this challenge to "normal" more apparent than in L'Arche communities, where many members simply are not able to live up to certain standard expectations. As we saw in the earlier discussion of economics, ethics, and politics, it seems normal to succeed by competing with others; it seems normal to be the sole determinator of our identity; it seems normal to seek security through demanding our rights. As Vanier emphasizes, however, people with mental handicaps cannot compete in society to achieve such normalization. They simply are unable to hide their weaknesses, their vulnerabilities, and their "failures." "In our competitive societies, which put so much emphasis on power and strength, they have great difficulty in finding their place; they are losers in every competition."[6] They cannot be "autonomous individuals." To some, their behavior may seem strange or even scary.

One popular response to the "tyranny of the normal" has been to claim, as does Nicholas Harvey, that "all humans are just different from each other, that there is no norm and that the question of abnormality [ought] not arise." In defending his position, Harvey reflects on Nick Vereker, a severely handicapped person in L'Arche who was Anglican and was not therefore allowed to receive Communion at a Roman Catholic Mass.[7] He writes, "My suggestion is that the episode is an example of the extreme difficulty all humans have in transcending notions of what it is to be normal."[8] Harvey implies that we can transcend the tyranny of the normal by claiming that our differences ought not to matter. Yet our differences *do* matter. The challenge, in terms of hospitality, is to discern when our differences ought to be embraced and when they need to be transformed. My lust for power or money, for example, is not a difference that Christian hospitality ought to embrace; rather, faithful hospitality would seek to challenge and transform this difference, so that together we might dwell more fully in God's own giving and receiving.

Vanier's response to the question of "being normal" differs dramatically. Vanier discusses becoming acquainted with a "theory of normalization," initially through the Scandinavian vision of people with handicaps. This approach equates "normal" with individual autonomy and securing certain rights and is certainly informed by the political assumptions discussed in chapter 5. It focuses on the rights of people with mental handicaps to be able to go to school, local swimming pools, movies, and so on like everyone else. Vanier admits learning a great deal, particularly from people in North America who were enthusiastic about this theory: "love should never be opposed to the competence necessary for the development of each person's potential." Yet, Vanier asks, "isn't there another danger in taking normalization to an extreme?" When our societies speak of "normality," what do they really mean? "Are they not rather pushing us towards extreme individualism, infidelity in relationships and the primacy of pleasure and economics?"[9] Here Vanier rightly questions an economics of competition and survival of the fittest as well as a politics that relegates ethics to personal choice.

While growth toward greater independence and renewed dignity is important, Vanier also muses, "Maybe normalization does not sufficiently consider the deepest needs of persons with handicaps and the special gifts they give to society. . . . While it is true that people with handicaps are called to develop and grow towards greater autonomy, they need above all a whole network of friendships and a community that gives them security and a sense of belonging, awakens each one's gifts, encourages growth, and develops love and a sense of service."[10] Now Vanier is advocating a different politics, one that does not rest on the assumption that we are individuals essentially in conflict with each other, pursuing our self-interest. Rather, Vanier zeroes in on *friendship* centered on a shared good: love of God, service, and discernment of gifts. Such friendship, as we saw earlier, is itself a kind of politics as it enables us to live toward our common end: to love and enjoy God.[11] Vanier notes that "L'Arche is founded on the gospel. For people with handicaps, even more important than 'normalization' is their growth in love, openness, service and holiness, which is the ultimate purpose of each human person."[12] The alternative to "normality" is not transcending difference or acting as if it did not matter (so that, as in our globalized economy, difference becomes *mere* difference) but living lives of faithfulness around a shared good, namely love of God. We can go further and say that the L'Arche embodies in a powerful way that we are not called to be "normal" but to be holy. But such holiness is never an individual achievement; it is a byproduct of belonging to one another in and through Christ and seeking to extend that belonging to others. Holiness is therefore inherently communal as we learn to participate in the dynamics of God's giving and receiving. It does not ultimately matter if we are "normal" by distorted cultural standards; what matters is that we delight in the politics of belonging to each other and Christ, a politics that certainly might make us look strange to the modern/postmodern world.

But, perhaps we might think, are mentally handicapped people capable of holiness? It seems as if they are limited in many ways, both physical and mental. Often when we think of holiness, we think of the great saints: the apostle Paul or Mother Teresa, people who have done amazing things. But here again, L'Arche brings to our attention that holiness is located in vulnerability and seemingly small gestures. (Even Mother Teresa, who for twenty years took a train through Calcutta, watching suffering people from the window, admits that she would never have ministered to thousands of dying if she had not stopped one day to help one lonely man on the street.) Vanier tells the following story about "Mr. Normal" and a mentally handicapped young man.

> I don't know whether around here you have some normal people, but I find them a very strange group. I don't know—I remember—well, one of the char-acteristics of normal people is that they have problems. They have family problems, they have financial problems, they have professional problems, problems with politics, problems with church, problems all over the place. And I remember one day a "normal" guy came to see me and he was telling me about all his problems. And there was a knock on the door and entered Jean Claude. Jean Claude has Down's syndrome and, relaxed and laughing . . . he just shook. I didn't even say, "Come in." He came in, and he shook my hand and laughed and he shook the hand of Mr. Normal and laughed

and he walks out laughing. And Mr. Normal turned to me and he said "Isn't it sad, children like that."

He couldn't see that Jean Claude was a happy guy. It's a blindness, and it's an inner blindness which is the most difficult to heal.[13]

In his spontaneous and joyful way of being, Jean Claude radiates a kind of holiness, a holy hospitality that by its very oddness enables us to see the presence of God. "Mr. Normal," on the other hand (who probably represents many of us), is so caught up in living by society's "normal" expectations and demands that he is unable to see the beauty of Jean Claude.

Wasting Time

One of the common assumptions about hospitality is that it is primarily about doing something and getting certain results. I once was a board member of an organization that advocated for people with mental handicaps, and occasionally I visited our "clients." Even though I had come to think of myself as welcoming and supportive, I remember, on one such visit to a severely handicapped person, thinking, *Why am I here? This person can't even tell that I am in the same room. What difference could my being here possibly make?* Though I am not happy to admit it, I saw the person in the bed in terms of "usefulness." Since my time was not bringing results, it seemed a waste. My own way of being, more than I care to admit, was marked by a "McDonaldized" economy of efficiency and results.

Yet "wasting time" in this way is exactly what the hospitality of L'Arche is about. It is not so much focused on efficiency and results as on simply being present to others. Vanier writes of spending time earlier in his life in the navy and then the academy (he earned a Ph.D. in philosophy and taught for a while). In both of these worlds "weakness, ignorance and incompetence were things to be shunned—efficiency was everything."[14] But then, Vanier writes, he entered a "third phase" of life when he discovered people who were weak, fragile, and poor. He began to discover what he refers to as the "thirst for communion." Such communion, he writes, is not the same thing as collaboration, where people work for a similar goal but are not personally vulnerable to one another. Neither is communion the same thing as generosity. "Generosity consists in doing good to others, in giving our time or money, in devoting ourselves to others and to their good. Generous people are in a strong position: they have talents, power and wealth; they do good things for others but do not receive from them. They are not vulnerable to love."[15]

While the larger society would have us hide our vulnerability and weaknesses, those with mental handicaps simply cannot. Yet Vanier says that it is precisely their vulnerability that is their great gift to the church and the world. In their vulnerability and poverty, they can teach all of us not to hide our own weaknesses but rather to see these as places of grace, where we see our *need* for others and for the grace of God. Hans Reinders, in his essay "Parenting the Mentally Disabled," includes some reflection on the L'Arche communities. Reinders confirms that people who have been part of these communities realize that the most important thing is not "doing for" but "being with." "Doing for" is characteristic of those who want to do something for the disabled—the professional or the teacher—whereas "being with" refers to the notion of "wanting to share your life with somebody." "It is the distinction between professional intervention and personal presence."[16] From this perspective, the greater challenge is in learning how to receive than in rushing to give: "The dominant theme of the spiritual journey is not 'giving to' but 'receiving from.'"[17] The emphasis falls upon our receiving from the other, the stranger, and behind this lies learning to see the other as a gift. And behind this lies a willingness to give up concern with efficiency and results and to "waste time." In this context, the focus of hospitality is not so much our giving, though it does involve that, as our receiving from the other whom we learn to see as gift.

This difference between "being with" and "doing for" is evident in the familiar story of the transfiguration. Jesus ascends to a high mountain with Peter, James, and John; his "clothes [become] dazzling white, such as no one on earth could bleach them" (Mark 9:3), and Elijah and Moses appear and talk with Jesus. Peter's initial response is terror. As in the testimony of some who live in L'Arche communities, there is the desire to flee. And Peter also wants to "do for" Jesus by making three dwellings, one for Jesus, one for Moses, one for Elijah. Yet God's call at this point is for the disciples not to do anything but to be with Jesus as the Messiah, "my Son, the Beloved; listen to him!" This stern command may seem out of keeping with the spirit of a hospitable "being with." Yet those in L'Arche who have learned the hospitality of "being with" do not gloss over the difficulties and challenges. Odile Ceyrac writes that "in the life we share together, we soon discover that they are our 'teachers'; they give us more than we can ever give them, in terms of acceptance of our human condition, in the discovery of what is essential in our lives. This is a *terribly demanding discovery*."[18] The gift or discovery involves a deeper conversion to who we are called to be (rather than what we are called to do).

According to Vanier, one of the "demanding discoveries" that comes from being and living with those with mental handicaps is discovering our own poverty. To the uninitiated, the discovery of poverty might not sound like much of a gift. But Vanier proceeds to tell us about Lucien, a severely handicapped man who could not speak, walk, or look after himself and was also incontinent. For thirty years, his loving mother had cared for him. When she had to be hospitalized, Lucien came to live at L'Arche. Without his mother, Lucien was in deep distress. Vanier describes how he would have terrible moods and emit high-pitched screams of anguish. These cries, writes Vanier, "pierced me like a sword. I could not bear them. . . . And this anguish in me became anger and violence and hate. I would have liked to have killed Lucien, to have hurled him out of the window. I would have liked to have run away, but I could not because I had responsibilities in the house. I was filled with shame and guilt and confusion."[19] Reflecting on this experience, Vanier writes that discovering our capacity for hate and harm is humiliating. We realize that we are "not part of the elite, far from it!" Such humiliation is a good thing, however, as it "puts us in touch with our true selves, our poverty. And only the truth can set us free."[20]

Vanier uses "poverty" to refer to the shadows within us, our brokenness and our inner demons. We might even call this the stranger in ourselves that we want to ignore or deny. In Vanier's account, the discovery of our poverty and brokenness enables us to rely not on our own strength and efforts but on the healing and forgiving grace of God. The realization of need, a gift given in this instance by Lucien, draws Vanier into deeper communion with God and others.

When we conceive of hospitality as communion, as does Vanier, we also can see that the challenge is not "moral perfection," a notion that typically turns the focus to individual effort. Rather, in Reinders's words, those who live in L'Arche come to see that the "most important thing to know is not how to love and be good, but how to be loved despite our faults and failures. The most important thing is not to strive toward your own perfection but to learn to live with your imperfections."[21] Encouragement to "learn to live with your imperfections" can sound like a counsel to mediocrity. Aren't we supposed to strive to be holy? Yet as Reinders elaborates, "living with their imperfection is what mentally disabled people have been doing all their lives. That is how they become healers."[22] This may sound counterintuitive; how can those with imperfections become healers? By having to live without illusions, those with mental handicaps witness to the fact that God does not call us to be "perfect," at least as society defines perfection. Rather, God calls us to lives of faithfulness in communion with each other. Faithfulness rather than perfection enables us to welcome the weak and the vulnerable even as we accept our own vulnerabilities, acknowledging our limitations as places of deep grace. Such hospitality is far from moral do-goodism. That we are limited and weak means we *need* others; we depend on others in order to receive, discover, and be the healing presence of Christ in the world. "We have discovered that we have a common spirituality of humility and presence, close to the poor and the weak; a common call to live with them, not to change them, but to welcome them and share their gifts and their beauty; to discover in them the presence of Jesus—Jesus, humble and gentle, Jesus, poor and rejected."[23]

An emphasis on "being with" fits with our understanding of worship itself as hospitality (chapter 2). Worship is "being with" God. In worship we are welcomed and received, through Christ and the Spirit, into God's triune communion. Worship is thus a pure gift; it displays God's desire *to be with* us. God gathers us, not the other way around. This does not make us simply passive subjects, any more than "being with" in the L'Arche communities results in subjective passivity. There is rather a kind of patient waiting, allowing the other the space to take initiative, so that we might respond. Receptive waiting must be nourished and deepened. In worship too there is receptive waiting as we make room for God to invade our lives, through Word and Table, through song, prayer, and offering as Christ unites our gifts with his own. It takes time and patience for us to see that we are part of something much larger than ourselves. While being with the mentally handicapped and gathering to worship may seem like a waste of time in a world geared toward efficiency, it is actually a time of abundance that comes from embodying more fully God's own hospitality.[24] L'Arche members practice economics as a way of life (versus a system or science) so secure in God's abundance that they are willing to waste time.

A Gospel Interlude

I have described Christian hospitality as "strange" in order to counter the many ways we are tempted to domesticate or distort hospitality. As discussed earlier, our dominant politics and economics see the "other" as primarily a rights-bearing creature, with the right to do as she wishes as long as she does not infringe on the rights of another. But such a view forms us to see others as potential threats and deepens our sense of alienation. Since we have no common good other than certain rights that the state oversees, we have no real reason to need one another. We become a society of strangers; gated communities, security systems, and avoidance of the stranger become our ways of coping.

But don't we need to protect ourselves and our children from potential threats? Is hospitality really realistic in this day and age when you can't trust others, especially strangers? We have all heard stories of people who were taken advantage of or even abused while trying to help someone in need.

While scripture does tell us to be "wise as serpents and innocent as doves," Jesus decisively calls into question a withholding and calculating demeanor. In the well-known parable of the sheep and the goats (Matt. 25:31–46), the sheep are rewarded for their uncalculating generosity. So "natural" is their hospitality to the stranger and their love of God that they seem unaware even that they are practicing hospitality: "When was it that we saw you a stranger and welcomed you, or naked and gave you clothing?" (v. 38). The response is familiar to most of us: "Truly, I tell you, just as you did it to one of the least of these who are members of my family, you did it to me" (v. 40). In relation to hospitality, we can glean at least two key points from this powerful parable. First, the "sheep" have simply become a hospitable people. So much is hospitality a part of who they are that their responses to others are not discrete acts but the overflow of who they are. Second, love and service to the stranger are so integrally linked to love of God that they are essentially the same. "As you did it to one of the least of these . . . you did it to me." In light of this parable, we can say that hospitality involves relating to others (particularly those in deep need) not out of fear or scarcity but as those who are "bearers" of Christ.[25]

The emphasis on spontaneous doing in Matthew 25 seems to stand in some tension with another passage often cited in relation to hospitality: Luke 10:38–42. Here Mary and Martha both seek to welcome Jesus. Mary sits at the Lord's feet listening to his teaching, while Martha is distracted by "much serving," so much so that she complains, "Lord, do you not care that my sister has left me to do all the work by myself?" (v. 40). And Jesus responds, "Martha, Martha, you are worried and distracted by many things; there is need of only one thing. Mary has chosen the better part, which will not be taken away from her" (vv. 41–42). This passage may be unsettling to us because Jesus seems to commend "doing nothing" ("being with"?) over serving and preparing for the guest. Meeting the physical needs of the guest is surely a vital facet of hospitality. Even more, Martha seems to be doing exactly what Matthew 25 commends: giving Christ something to eat. Yet, taken together, Matthew 25 and Luke 10 illustrate key facets of hospitality that L'Arche embodies: not calculating and hoarding, and a willingness to "waste time" being with the other (Christ).

Teresa of Ávila adds to our analysis of Luke 10 by saying that the Lord needs *both* Mary and Martha. "Believe me, Mary and Martha must walk together when they offer the Lord lodging, and must have Him ever with them, and they must not entertain Him badly and give Him nothing to eat."[26] *Lodging, eat, entertain*: all are words reminiscent of hospitality. According to Teresa, "being with" and service are not in conflict with each other, as serving Christ requires being with him. The role of women in Teresa's time was rigidly circumscribed. She imagines her fellow Carmelite sisters saying they are unable to do great things like the apostles, such as teaching, preaching, and leading souls to God. While we do not live in Teresa's time, we may equally feel that our lives and talents are for various reasons so limited that we cannot be a Mother Teresa or a Jean Vanier. Yet Teresa of Ávila powerfully responds: "The Lord does not look so much at the magnitude of anything we do as at the love with which we do it." Offer the Lord what we are able to give, "though our actions in themselves may be trivial," and "His Majesty will unite it with that which He offered to the Father for us upon the cross."[27] We hear across the centuries from Teresa a reminder that the kingdom of God rests not in the great achievement but in the small and particular gesture, a gesture done with the love we are given as we seek to be a hospitable dwelling for Christ.

Accountable Hospitality

Such gospel themes are at the heart of the Church of the Saviour. We can see this most fully in its emphasis on the inward and outward journey,[28] or what is classically known as the contemplative and active life. Prayer, scripture study, and silence are as central as mission and outreach. Mary Cosby remembers how liturgical silence was initially unfamiliar to many in the Church of the Saviour. In the Baptist church, where Gordon Cosby was raised, "if there was silence after a hymn, we wondered if the preacher had become ill."[29] Yet mostly because of the ecumenical spirit of the Church of the Saviour, the community has been exposed to a range of traditional Christian practices that have gradually become a deep part of their lives together.

The most striking aspect of the inward/outward journey as embodied in the Church of the Saviour is how deeply it is rooted in accountability and community disciplines. In our day, "spiritual journey" usually means the reflections and meanderings of a solitary soul. The Church of the Saviour aims for something very different. As Elizabeth O'Connor writes, "The Church of the Saviour . . . was founded on the conviction that the greatest contribution the church can make in any time is in *being the church*—'a fellowship of reconciled and reconciling men,' a community of the Holy Spirit, a people in which Christ dwells . . . [a] new society into which others can be drawn."[30] Its members have rightly recognized that "being the church" will not happen without discipline and accountability. Consequently, there is a period of training (six months to two years) during which potential members involve themselves in the life of the community. For those who are members, four key disciplines mark their lives together: one hour of daily prayer, weekly worship together, involvement in one of the corporate missions, and giving money. Members also pledge to confess and seek help from the fellowship should they fail.

Such disciplines, O'Connor notes, are not another form of perfectionism, "a holy rule by which one is self-justified."[31] If anything, there is a strong emphasis in the Church of the Saviour on giving each other the freedom to fail. As Gordon Cosby emphasizes, one of the qualities of leadership "is a willingness to fail and to let others fail."[32] O'Connor considers that the willingness to take risks arises out of a conviction that God is doing a new thing; along the way some may go off on tangents, but there is also a lot of growing. Faithfulness rather than perfection is the aim, and the disciplines help "keep us open to the love of God; [they help] keep our feet upon the pilgrim way."

Gordon Cosby tells of one wealthy businessman who became involved in the Church of the Saviour over a significant period of time. He had gone through the classes of preparation and come to the place of wanting to become a member. Talking with him about the principle of accountability, Cosby said, "You'll have to bring your total life to our group so that we can look at it."

The man asked, "You mean that I, who am running this big corporation worldwide, [am] going to bring those decisions to this group?"

Cosby said, "Yeah."

The man said, "Well, I can't belong."[33]

Reflecting on this and the church more broadly, Cosby asks, "How do you become accountable so that all of life is lived out in faithfulness and obedience to Jesus Christ who is the head of the church?" In a conversation I had with Gordon Cosby, he interpreted this story, as odd as it might sound, as an act of hospitality. He emphasized that hospitality flows out of identity and that if you do not know who you are, you cannot offer hospitality. In this instance, Cosby was telling the man "who we were" and giving him the opportunity to become more fully a part of the church's life together, but he was also extending to him the freedom not to do so. In light of the previous chapter's discussion of hospitality and discipline, we could also say that Cosby was calling attention to the disciplines that determined this man's life. In what ways does our attitude to money discipline or shape how we live? The Church of the Saviour, in its willingness to bring this discipline to light, is at least seeking ways to subvert an economics based on scarcity and hoarding.

Cosby says about being the church, "We try to make it as difficult for a person to merely attend our church as possible, because we feel this can be detrimental and contribute to the soul's disease rather than the soul's health."[34] Certainly the Church of the Saviour welcomes people to attend their services and to become involved in their missions, but there is also a deeper welcoming to not merely attend but to become part of an ecclesial journey grounded in God's wealth rather than only our own.

O'Connor discusses a kind of crisis that took place in the Church of the Saviour in 1969. It had to do with one of the disciplines of the church: the requirement that every member be involved in one of the communal missions. "Some felt that the inward-outward structure of the mission groups defined the church as a servant people called into existence to be the community for others. Many contended that this was too narrow a definition and that one was often better able to live out one's servanthood in individual mission. To this cry came back, 'Where then is the place of accountability?'"[35] After much discernment, they ended up deciding that if a member dropped out of one of the small groups on corporate mission, they dropped out of membership in the church. O'Connor reflects on the alternative: "Because we do not want to exclude anyone, we bend to everyone's wish and in the end have no style of life which is noticeably different from that of any other grouping of people. We give no one anything to be up against. We have been transformed by the world—not by the secular outside us but by the secular within us, that part that believes so fervently that something can be had for nothing and that we should not have to choose."[36]

Such training and discipline may sound harsh. But one is reminded of the early church requirements of the catechumen before he or she could be baptized. Sometimes the period of training lasted as long as three years. Many professions were considered unsuitable. As Gerhard Lohfink states, "The awareness that acceptance of the faith means entry into a new creation, a new form of society, is evident not only in the Pauline letters. The whole of the ancient Church was sustained by that knowledge, and for that reason it was also aware of the great significance of baptism."[37] What O'Connor writes about the church today was true of the ancient church as well. The refusal to grapple with the issue of "entrance into the Christian Church is not tolerance; it is betrayal of the gospel which we preach."[38] The Church of the Saviour has deeply absorbed the reality of the church as a new creation, one that therefore looks different from the surrounding society, not for the sake of looking different but for the sake of being more fully the church.

What does all of this have to do with hospitality? The exchange between Gordon Cosby and the businessman might sound like inhospitality if one is imagining hospitality in terms of any of the distortions discussed in chapter 1: a privatized, sentimental, marketed, and pluralistic hospitality. But Cosby was concerned enough about this man to remind him that Christian discipleship involved his whole life. Surely such truth speaking is fraught with difficulty, but to avoid accountability is to exchange genuine hospitality for mere pleasantry. Accountable hospitality is the way we bring our gifts and weaknesses to the table, trusting that the Holy Spirit provides for the whole body as we learn to be members one of another and so also are enabled to welcome the stranger in our midst.

Being Ordinary

We cannot practice hospitality on our own any more than we can be Christians on our own. Yet we live in a society that tells us to be independent and to choose and achieve the goals we set for ourselves. We are formed from an early age to position ourselves over against one another and to see others as competitors. So much is this way of thinking a part of who we are that we may have difficulty seeing it as a problem. Shouldn't we determine our own goals? Don't we want our children to be independent? And competition is not necessarily a bad thing, especially if it is "healthy" and inspires us to greater heights. Yet Jesus tells his followers to become as children, to imitate their trust and willingness to depend on another. We hear Jesus tell his disciples not "Think for yourselves," but "Follow me." And the spirit of competition toward which the disciples begin to gravitate is deeply challenged, as when James and John want to sit with Jesus in glory, "one at your right hand and one at your left" (Mark 10:37). Jesus tells them rather that "whoever wishes to be great among you must be your servant, and whoever wishes to be first among you must be slave of all" (Mark 10:43–44).

To practice hospitality well, we are not called to be moral heroes, great individuals who summon the willpower, courage, and strength to achieve certain goals. Christian hospitality does not require such heroes. One of the chief problems with the hero approach is that the focus is on the self and our own efforts and talents. Samuel Wells contrasts the language of *hero* with that of *saint*, noting that *hero* is not found in the New Testament, whereas *saint* occurs sixty-four times. While the hero's story is about the hero, the saint "is always at the periphery of a story that is really about God."[39] The definitive hero is the soldier who is willing to risk death in battle, much like our modern politics. "The story assumes that in a world of limited resources [like our modern view of economics], there is bound to be conflict at some stage so that good may prevail." Wells notes that the story of saints, however, does not involve learning to fight over competing goods, "because Christ has fought for and secured the true good, and the goods that matter now are not limited or in short supply. Love, joy, peace, faithfulness, gentleness—these do not rise or fall with the stock market."[40] Finally, whereas the hero stands out from the community, "the story of God tells how he expects a response from his disciples that they cannot give on their own: they depend not only on him but on one another for resources that can sustain faithful lives, and they discover that their dependence on one another is not a handicap but is central to their witness."[41] Wells then notes, significantly, that of the sixty-four references to saints in the New Testament, all are in the plural.

This contrast between heroes and saints helps us see more clearly that hospitality, like all Christian practices, is not a matter of heroic self-effort. Hospitality is always first of all about who God is and about learning to live out of God's triune abundance in the *ekklesia* that God has called into being. But how does such learning take place? Both L'Arche and the Church of the Saviour witness to the fact that hospitality is not something we accomplish but a life we are given as we grow in dependence upon God and one another. Both of these communities witness to the fact that dependence is not a handicap (as in an ethics of autonomous choice) but central to what it means to be the body of Christ, the church. In fact, from this perspective, the one who is truly handicapped is the one who tries to be a hero, invulnerable and living in isolation from the larger body.

At this point, it is important to acknowledge that writing and reading about Christian hospitality can take us only so far. As I read about L'Arche and the Church of the Saviour, I found myself wanting to be part of communities like these. But then, I must confess, I realized that these kinds of communities seemed "out of reach" to me. I have a family, children; we're settled in the place where we are. L'Arche and the Church of the Saviour can seem extraordinary in comparison to our very ordinary lives. Yet members of these communities would be the first to say that they are very human: they have feet of clay, they keep falling into various pits, and they struggle with setbacks and disillusionments.[42] It is easy to fall into the illusion that we could practice hospitality well only if we were in better church communities. There is no doubt that certain ecclesial communities are more faithful than others in building up the church universal, but Christian hospitality is not so much about the extraordinary deed (or community) as it is about allowing God to invade our very ordinary lives. The wisdom we glean from the hospitality that shapes L'Arche is the holy significance of the ordinary, small gesture. Vanier tells of bathtime with Eric, an emotionally disturbed and severely handicapped child who had spent twelve years in a psychiatric hospital. This simple occasion becomes a special moment for building communion: "Eric's tiny body relaxed in the warm water. He was so happy to be held and washed. . . . And in touching him, I received from him the trust and tenderness that he wanted to show me."[43] Any of us and any particular congregational body seeking to be faithful to God are capable of this "little way."

When asked about the future of the church, Gordon Cosby exhibited real wisdom: "I have never had a helpful answer to that question. Have no idea. I do not know what the judgments of God are or what will be the breakthroughs of God's power. . . . I'm glad to leave it to God's sovereignty. It is his church—not mine."[44] These words place the emphasis where it should be. The church is not ours but God's; we are therefore free from the seduction of trying to save the church and the world in extraordinary ways. Those in the Church of the Saviour readily confess that they are ordinary, fallible people. Yet many creative missions (health care, low-income housing, homes for the homeless, job training, a coffeehouse, and more) have grown out of their church. "The good news is that the glimmering structures prefiguring another world are the work of ordinary folk."[45] This emphasis on the ordinary frees us to be faithful rather than heroic, trusting that God will provide. Such provision, as the Church of the Saviour readily acknowledges, may come in the way of failure. In fact, success or failure does not ultimately matter, since God can use both. From this perspective, our life together involves not heroic self-determination but being with each other in our brokenness and rejoicing in our gifts. Hospitality calls us to allow God to create a people who can live and witness to his love in ordinary and particular ways.

We receive the gift of L'Arche and the Church of the Saviour not by placing it on a shelf to admire but by hearing God's call to practice a more faithful hospitality in the ordinary small deeds we are given to do. Even this hospitality, done well, is simply our willingness to be drawn into "the heart and the love of the Trinity."[46]

Washing Feet: The Way the Church Moves

In reading books about L'Arche and the Church of the Saviour, listening to a number of tapes, and talking with some members of these communities, I was struck by how often the story of Jesus washing the feet of his disciples came up. In some ways, this might be expected: both communities emphasize humble service. O'Connor writes about the Church of the Saviour, "We exist under the lordship of One who took a towel and a basin and told us to do likewise. . . . We have to overcome that in ourselves which keeps our groups from taking the form of the suffering servant."[47] Particularly important is O'Connor's emphasis that suffering servant is a communal role. Elsewhere she writes, "The little band of disciples came back to Jesus, and all that they had done was to go into the homes of people and talk to them about the good news of Christ, the richness of their faith. And when they came back Jesus said, 'I saw you. I saw what was happening. Satan fell like lightning from the sky.' This is the drama, but it is the drama of quiet suffering and quiet serving. This is *the way the church moves*."[48] Foot washing, a concrete gesture of hospitality, is identified with the very movement of the church.

In a similar vein, Vanier writes, "The washing of feet is a sign. . . . Jesus is asking us to live and act constantly with a humble and loving heart in regard to other. But at the same time, Jesus insists on the importance of washing, of touching each other's feet."[49] In fact, in the L'Arche communities, the "paraliturgy" (as Vanier calls it) of footwashing has become a part of members' liturgical life together. It is an act of worship. Typically, they sing a hymn, hear a gospel reflection, and then wash each other's feet. The one whose feet has been washed places her or his hands on the head of the person who washed the feet, and they pray silently. "This signifies the gratitude and desire to live in communion with the one whose feet have been washed."[50] Then the one whose feet were just washed turns and washes the person next to him or her, until all have been washed. They conclude with the Lord's Prayer. Though in some L'Arche gatherings the Eucharist cannot be a visible sign of unity, everyone can wash each other's feet. Footwashing is thus a liturgical act that unites, embodies gift and reception, and thus makes possible a fuller expression of Christ's hospitality.

We are familiar with Peter's objection to footwashing: "Lord, do you wash my feet? . . . You shall never wash my feet" (John 13:6, 8). Peter sees this action as scandalous; it was the work of a slave. Yet, as Vanier notes, Jesus had already had his own feet washed by a woman's tears, a woman who was a sinner (Luke 7:36), and he must have "felt in his own heart all the love contained in this gesture."[51] Jesus's washing of his disciples' feet is a gesture of great love (John 13:1). St. Bernard even referred to footwashing as a sacrament. "Do you want to know why this act of Jesus has the value of a sacrament and not just an example? Pay attention to his words to Peter: 'If I do not wash your feet you will have no part with me' (John 13:8)."[52] The disciples become more fully united with Jesus when they allow him to wash their feet; through the water and the healing touch of Christ, they receive his love. The footwashing "paraliturgy" thus unites and creates. As a sacramental gesture, it creates a unity in Christ, enabling the disciples to become more fully Christ for the world. The disciples are enabled to "wash the feet" of others; "If I then, your Lord and Teacher, have washed your feet, you also ought to wash one another's feet" (13:14).

That this is strange is perhaps displayed most fully in our own resistance to it. What's so special about washing feet? Who even wants to have his or her feet washed or to wash the dirty, calloused feet of another? Having our feet washed places us in a vulnerable position; someone else will see our ordinary feet, our feet of clay. Furthermore, washing someone else's feet can also be humbling as it exposes our desire, however faltering, to participate in the love of Christ.

In the front of one of the missions of the Church of the Saviour, a health-care mission for the homeless, sits a large figure of Jesus washing feet.

Apparently the figure has received all sorts of attention; alcoholics have placed their empty bottles in Jesus's hands, and once a street person placed an old Christmas tree next to the figure. The one criticism leveled against the footwashing Christ figure is that it should not have been placed at street level; it should not be in such a vulnerable place and thus easily subjected to sacrilegious gestures. It should be raised up. As Gordon Cosby reflects on this figure, however, he appreciates such vulnerability and reckless abandonment. "How do we become vulnerable? . . . We're talking about the incarnation of love assuming the servant shape not as an occasional act [but] . . . so that we are ready for martyrdom in whatever form martyrdom will come to us."[53] Martyrdom might seem like an alien concept in our contemporary situation. Who is being asked to die for their faith?

But in the footwashing liturgy, and in worship more broadly, we encounter the reckless, abundant, even terrifying giving of God in Christ. When we receive this abundant giving through the power of the Spirit, we ourselves become vehicles of this grace for others. And when we open our lives to this divine hospitality, we do not know where it will lead. We might be given a more truthful economic vision, as has happened in the Church of the Saviour, whose members have learned to free themselves from an addiction to money. We might be given a more truthful political vision as embodied in the L'Arche communities, a vision focused not on individual rights but on friendship with the vulnerable and the weak. We might be given a more profound vision of the church as the real body of Christ, such that we have to take seriously how the brokenness and division in the church are a deep and bleeding wound on this body, affecting all of our lives.

May we together, like Peter and countless others, find the courage to practice this extraordinary hospitality until our feet, hands, and head overflow with the love of God.

Notes

Introduction

1. John Bunyan, *Grace Abounding to the Chief of Sinners* (Chicago: Moody Press, 1959), para. 244.
2. Ibid., my emphasis.

Part 1

1. Geoffrey Wainwright, *Doxology: The Praise of God in Worship, Doctrine, and Life* (New York: Oxford University Press, 1980), 23.

Chapter 1

1. For a book centered on an apophatic approach, see D. Brent Laytham, ed., *God Is Not . . .* (Grand Rapids: Brazos, 2004). Laytham's own chapter, "God Is One, Holy, Catholic, and Apostolic," provides an especially helpful analysis of the importance of analogy for talk about God. Following Thomas Aquinas, Laytham states that our words for God are neither univocal (our words for finite things and for God mean the same thing) nor equivocal (our words for finite things and for God are unrelated). Rather, analogy means that "words drawn from the finite realm mean different but not entirely unrelated things when affirmed of something finite and of God" (121). Further, Laytham highlights two reasons we can speak about God: (1) God has already spoken to us, and (2) our speech participates in the "ongoing conversation of the Son and Spirit with the Father" (118).

2. Craig Dykstra, "Reconceiving Practice in Theological Inquiry and Education," in *Virtues and Practices in the Christian Tradition: Christian Ethics after MacIntyre* (Harrisburg, PA: Trinity Press International, 1997), 170. Dykstra, influenced by Alasdair MacIntyre, cites MacIntyre's familiar definition of a practice: "Any coherent and complex form of socially established cooperative human activity through which goods internal to that form of activity are realized in the course of trying to achieve those standards of excellence which are appropriate to, and partially definitive of, that form of activity, with the result that human powers to achieve excellence, and human conceptions of the ends and goods involved, are systematically extended."

3. Alasdair MacIntyre, *After Virtue* (Notre Dame, IN: University of Notre Dame, 1984), 188.

4. MacIntyre observes that only as one seeks faithfully to engage in a practice will he or she come to an awareness of a particular kind of life. Thus, "the artist discovers within the pursuit of excellence in portrait painting—and what is true of portrait painting is true of the fine arts in general—is *the good of a certain kind of life*" (ibid, 190).

5. Jonathan R. Wilson, *Gospel Virtues: Practicing Faith, Hope, and Love in Uncertain Times* (Downers Grove, IL: InterVarsity Press, 1998), 44–45.

6. Dykstra, *Virtues and Practices*, 172.

7. Robert Louis Wilken, *The Spirit of Early Christian Thought* (New Haven, CT: Yale University Press, 2003), 239.

8. Stanley Hauerwas, *Christian Existence Today: Essays on Church, World, and Living in Between* (Durham, NC: Labyrinth, 1988; repr. Grand Rapids: Brazos, 2001). Hauerwas goes on to say that "the church is but God's gesture on behalf of the world to create a space and time in which we might have a foretaste of the Kingdom. It is through gestures that we learn the nature of the story that is the very content and constitution of that Kingdom. The way we learn the story, after all, is not just by hearing it. . . . We must be taught the gestures that help position our bodies and our souls to be able to hear rightly and then retell the story" (106).

9. William H. Poteat, *A Philosophical Daybook: Post-critical Investigations* (Columbia: University of Missouri, 1990), 54, my emphasis. Poteat uses the term *mindbody* to undermine all the ways we might be tempted to think in a "disincarnate" way; "mindbody" reminds us that all our thinking and doing comes from our incarnate places in the world.

10. Ibid., 58.

11. *"The Iliad" and "The Odyssey" of Homer*, trans. by Richmond Lattimore (Chicago: Encyclopaedia Britanniaca, 1996), 437.

12. Ibid., 391.

13. Barry Harvey, *Another City, An Ecclesiological Primer for a Post-Christian World* (Harrisburg, PA: Trinity Press International, 1999), 19. Harvey is quoting Nicholas Lash's *Theology on the Way to Emmaus*.

14. Kierkegaard uses this phrase to describe "Christendom" in his day in "The Point of View for My Work as an Author," in *A Kierkegaard Anthology*, ed. Robert Bretall (Princeton, NJ: Princeton University Press, 1946), 330.

15. Henri Nouwen, quoted in Christine Pohl, *Making Room: Recovering Hospitality as a Christian Tradition* (Grand Rapids: Eerdmans, 1999), 3.

16. Rodney Clapp, *A Peculiar People: The Church as Culture in a Post-Christian Society* (Downers Grove, IL: InterVarsity Press, 1996), 19.

17. G. K. Chesteron, quoted in John Murray Cuddihy, *No Offense: Civil Religion and Protestant Taste* (New York: Seabury, 1978), 46.

18. Parts of the following analysis are taken from my earlier article "Flannery O'Connor and the Practice of Hospitality," *Perspectives in Religious Studies* 32, no. 2 (Summer 2005): 135–47.

19. Flannery O'Connor, "A Good Man Is Hard to Find," in *The Complete Stories* (New York: Farrar, Straus, and Giroux, 1979), 118.

20. Ibid., p. 122.

21. Ibid., p. 123.

22. Ibid., p. 119.

23. Flannery O'Connor made this observation: "I've talked to a number of teachers who use this story in class and who tell their students that the Grandmother

is evil, that in fact, she's a witch, even down to the cat. One of these teachers told me that his students, and particularly his Southern students, resisted this interpretation with a certain bemused vigor, and he didn't understand why. I had to tell him that they resisted it because they all had grandmothers or great-aunts just like her at home, and they knew, from personal experience, that the old lady lacked comprehension, but that she had a good heart." *Mystery and Manners* (New York: Farrar, Straus, and Giroux, 1962), 110.

24. Reinhard Hütter, "Hospitality and Truth: The Disclosure of Practices in Worship and Doctrine," in *Practicing Theology: Beliefs and Practices in Christian Life*, ed. Miroslav Volf and Dorothy C. Bass (Grand Rapids: Eerdmans, 2002), 207.

25. Ibid., 215.

26. L. Gregory Jones, *Embodying Forgiveness: A Theological Analysis* (Grand Rapids: Eerdmans, 1995), 54.

27. D. Stephen Long, "God Is Not Nice," in *God Is Not . . .* , ed. D. Brent Laytham (Grand Rapids: Brazos, 2004), 44.

28. Ibid., 49–50.

29. O'Connor, "A Good Man Is Hard to Find," 127.

30. Ibid., 127, 132.

31. Ibid., 132.

32. Ibid., 133.

33. O'Connor, *Mystery and Manners*, 111, my emphasis. The *New Catholic Dictionary* defines "anagogical sense" as follows: "(Greek: *anagogikos*, that which leads up; e.g., the teachings of the Bible lead to eternal life) That division of the typical sense which includes blessings to be hoped for, and which refers particularly to the future life. The rest which the Israelites found in Canaan is anagogically typical of eternal rest in heaven (Psalm 94; Hebrews 4). Jerusalem in its anagogical sense is typical of the Church triumphant." Accessed online: www.catholic-forum .com/saints/ncd00486.htm.

34. Hütter, "Hospitality and Truth," 218.

35. John Thorne, "Martha Stewart," in *Outlaw Cook* (New York: Farrar Straus Giroux, 1992), 271.

36. John Murray Cuddihy, *No Offense: Civil Religion and Protestant Taste* (New York: Seabury, 1978), 2.

37. Ibid., 13.

38. Flannery O'Connor, *Collected Works* (New York: Library of America, 1988), 977.

39. Cuddihy, *No Offense*, 100.

40. Stanley Hauerwas, *Sanctify Them in the Truth: Holiness Exemplified* (Nashville: Abingdon, 1998), 79.

41. This recalls an earlier way of thinking—even a current one in some places—that it is "bad manners" to recognize the *existence* of servants. For example, in a scene from the film *Remains of the Day*, the gentlemen speak of the butler as if he can't hear them.

42. Nicholas Boyle, *Who Are We Now? Christian Humanism and the Global Market from Hegel to Heaney* (Notre Dame, IN: University of Notre Dame, 1998), 154.

43. Murray Jardine, *The Making and Unmaking of Technological Society: How Christianity Can Save Modernity from Itself* (Grand Rapids: Brazos, 2004), 123.

44. Søren Kierkegaard, *A Kierkegaard Anthology*, ed. Robert Bretall (Princeton, NJ: Princeton University Press, 1946), 105.

45. Robert N. Bellah et al., *Habits of the Heart: Individualism and Commitment in American Life* (New York: Harper and Row, 1985). According to the authors,

Walt Whitman exemplifies "expressive individualism" in its clearest form. His life centered not so much on material interest as on rich experience and the freedom to express oneself against all conventions and constraints.

46. Jardine, *Making and Unmaking of Technological Society*, 92.

47. Ibid., 90.

48. Boyle, *Who Are We Now?* 152.

49. Ronald Beiner, *What's the Matter with Liberalism?* (Berkeley: University of California Press, 1992), 32. Beiner is here describing and criticizing liberalism more broadly, a point to which I return in chapter 5.

50. Stanley Fish, "Boutique Multiculturalism: or, Why Liberals Are Incapable of Thinking about Hate Speech," *Critical Inquiry* 23 (Winter 1997): 379. In this essay, Fish distinguishes between boutique, strong, and really strong multiculturalism. The first cannot take particularity seriously; the second cannot really honor diversity insofar as it refuses to be "generous"; and the third goes to the wall with a particular instance of diversity, but then is not multicultural.

51. Ibid., 380.

52. William T. Cavanaugh, *Theopolitical Imagination: Discovering the Liturgy as a Political Act in an Age of Global Consumerism* (London: T & T Clark, 2002), 109.

53. Beiner, *What's the Matter with Liberalism?* 23.

54. Boyle, *Who Are We Now?* 152.

55. Ibid., 153.

56. The full title is William R. Leach, *A Country of Exiles: The Destruction of Place in American Life* (New York: Pantheon, 1999).

57. Jardine, *Making and Unmaking of Technological Society*, 256.

58. Cited in ibid., 268. Jardine adds that in our expressive-individualistic culture, "for professional people, work is their primary means of self expression, so they tend to work long hours."

59. Immanuel Kant, "What Is Enlightenment?" in *The Philosophy of Kant*, ed. and trans. Carl J. Friedrich (New York: Random House, 1949), 132.

60. William H. Poteat, *The Primacy of Persons and the Language of Culture* (Columbia: University of Missouri, 1993), 39.

61. Ibid., 27.

62. Ibid., 31. Poteat notes that "Cartesianism as an explicit philosophical doctrine is virtually without effect in this culture. It functions however at a tacit level like a repetition compulsion; it is ubiquitous and pervades the atmosphere of our life like chronic depression." In a line of argument in some ways similar to Poteat's, Boyle, referring to Nietzsche, says, "The eye of Zarathustra does not even have a body, let alone a beginning" (*Who Are We Now?* 155).

63. Blaise Pascal, quoted by Poteat, *Primacy of Persons*, 34.

64. Blaise Pascal, *Pensées* (New York: Penguin, 1966), 310.

65. Isak Dinesen, quoted by Hannah Arendt, *The Human Condition* (Chicago: University of Chicago Press, 1958), 175.

66. Philip Cushman, "Why the Self Is Empty," *American Psychologist* 45 (May 1990): 600.

67. Ibid., 606.

68. "Anyway, I kept walking and walking up Fifth Avenue, without any tie on or anything. Then all of a sudden, something very spooky started happening. Every time I came to the end of a block and stepped off the goddam curb, I had this feeling that I'd never get to the other side of the street. I thought I'd just go down, down, down, and nobody'd ever see me again." J. D. Salinger, *The Catcher in the Rye* (Boston: Little, Brown, 1951), 200.

69. Cushman, "Why the Self Is Empty," 599. In a similar vein, theologian Harvey notes that "the pioneers of modernity sought to uncover an understanding of the self that was prior to and independent of the contingencies of particular times and places, which offer rich and thick contexts for becoming and staying human, but precisely for that reason are often messy and fraught with uncertainty and ineluctable mystery. But what they actually bequeathed to us was a self without substance, frantically searching for something, anything, to fill it up" (*Another City*, 8).

70. Isak Dinesen, "The Roads around Pisa," in *Seven Gothic Tales* (New York: Vintage Books, 1972), 185.

71. Harold Bloom, *The American Religion: The Emergence of the Post-Christian Nation* (New York: Simon and Schuster, 1992), 49.

Chapter 2

1. Vicki Hearne writes that Hans Winkler, a brilliant trainer of horses, must have had "a story about how what appears to be horse insanity may be—even must be, most of the time—evidence of how powerful equine genius is, and how powerfully it can object to incoherence, and he must have had a story like that about Halla which would move him to keep thinking and trying when things got rough. . . . The stories we tell matter, and not only do stories reclaim the beauty of crazy horses but also stories lead to insanity in the first place." From *Adam's Task*, quoted in William H. Poteat, *A Philosophical Daybook: Post-critical Investigations* (Columbia: University of Missouri, 1990), 109.

2. In the turn to worship, both theologically and ethically, I have been especially influenced by Geoffrey Wainwright (see especially *Doxology: The Praise of God in Worship, Doctrine, and Life* [New York: Oxford University Press, 1980]) and Stanley Hauerwas. For a helpful introduction, see Stanley Hauerwas and Samuel Wells, "Part I: Studying Ethics through Worship," in their jointly edited *Blackwell Companion to Christian Ethics* (Oxford: Blackwell, 2004), 1–50. Here they argue that "ethics" is not a subject "that can be distinguished if not isolated from the liturgical life, daily habits, and elementary practices of the Church" (34). For the turn to thinking about worship itself as Christian hospitality, I am especially grateful to my husband, Jon Baker.

3. By contrast, Rev. Terry Hamilton-Poor tells of a divorced woman who became pregnant and the father dropped out of the picture. As she began to show, she felt she could not go to church anymore. "After all, here she was, a Sunday School teacher, unmarried and pregnant." She called a friend, who ended up sitting with her every Sunday at church. Eventually the church rallied around the woman, whose little girl became "a child of the parish." Recounted in "Abortion, Theologically Understood," in Stanley Hauerwas, *The Hauerwas Reader* (Durham, NC: Duke University Press, 2001), 606–7.

4. Martin B. Copenhaver, Anthony B. Robinson, and William H. Willimon, *Good News in Exile* (Grand Rapids: Eerdmans, 1999), 95.

5. Rodney Clapp states, "A premium is put on altering and reinventing church rituals so that they will serve individual emotional fulfillments." The church becomes "nothing but an interest or affinity group." Rodney Clapp, "On the Making of Kings and Christians," in *The Conviction of Things Not Seen*, ed. Todd E. Johnson (Grand Rapids: Brazos, 2002), 121.

6. E. Y. Mullins, *The Axioms of Religion* (Philadelphia: Judson, 1908), 55, my emphasis.

7. Philippe Beneton, *Equality by Default: An Essay on Modernity as Confinement* (Wilmington, DE: ISI Books, 2004), 128.

8. Gabriel Marcel, quoted in ibid., 127.

9. Beneton, *Equality by Default*, 16.

10. Ibid., 15.

11. Ibid., 22.

12. Ibid., 23.

13. Ibid., 21, my emphasis.

14. "Seeker-friendly" worship allows those who know the story least well to be the ones who dictate how it shall be told.

15. As Stanley Hauerwas states, "If we are to learn to think differently, we must have our bodies repositioned." *Sanctify Them in the Truth: Holiness Exemplified* (Nashville: Abingdon, 1998), 89.

16. In fact, I admit that I may feel the weight of this question more than some others because I come out of a free church tradition. As Clapp points out, "There are those, especially those in Free Church (so-called nonliturgical) traditions, who sometimes protest the emphasis on worship. After all, they say, corporate worship occurs for only two or three hours a week; can we really believe it has much of an effect on changing the minds, behaviors, and attitudes of even the most faithful worshipers?" "On the Making of Kings and Christians," 110.

17. Hauerwas and Wells, "Part I," 6.

18. Josef Pieper, *Leisure, the Basis of Culture* (Indianapolis: Liberty Fund, 1952), 51.

19. We are enriched by God "with all speech and all knowledge . . . so that [we] are *not lacking* in any spiritual gift" (1 Cor. 1:5, 7, New Oxford Annotated Bible).

20. Pieper, *Leisure*, 17, my emphasis.

21. James B. Torrance, *Worship, Community, and the Triune God of Grace* (Downers Grove, IL: InterVarsity Press, 1996), 20.

22. M. Craig Barnes, "It's Not about You," in *Fire and Wine: The Holy Spirit in the Church Today*, ed. Joseph D. Small (Louisville, KY: Geneva, 2002), 137.

23. Torrance, *Worship, Community*, 44.

24. Ibid., 46.

25. Ibid.

26. Alexander Schmemann, *For the Life of the World* (Crestwood, NY: St. Vladimir's Seminary Press, 1963), 25, my emphasis.

27. Ibid., 16.

28. Ibid., 18.

29. Ibid., 26.

30. Geoffrey Wainwright, *Worship with One Accord: Where Liturgy and Ecumenism Embrace* (New York: Oxford University Press, 1997), 24.

31. Beneton, *Equality by Default*, 116. He adds that time too becomes one dimensional: "All is functionalized, even time, which is cut off from natural rhythms. In the cities composed of large, sterile building complexes in North America, there is no more evening, no more morning, no more spring, and no more winter. Time is homogenous and uniform."

32. William F. Arndt and F. Wilbur Gingrich, *A Greek-English Lexicon of the New Testament and Other Early Christian Literature* (Chicago: University of Chicago, 1979), 561.

33. See also Acts 7:44–50.

34. The three ways of being relevant are identified by Erik Peterson and described by Reinhard Hütter in "The Church as Public: Dogma, Practice, and the Holy Spirit," *Pro Ecclesia* 3, no. 3: 350.

35. I return to the church as *polis* later in the chapter.

36. Hütter, "Church as Public," 352.

37. John Milbank, *Theology and Social Theory: Beyond Secular Reason* (Cambridge, MA: Blackwell, 1990), 364–69.

38. Ibid., 364, 368.

39. Ibid., 403.

40. Hütter, "Church as Public," 347.

41. Ibid., 348.

42. Gerhard Lohfink, *Does God Need the Church? Toward a Theology of the People of God* (Collegeville, MN: Liturgical, 1999), 263.

43. Ibid., 290–308.

44. Philip Kenneson, "Gathering: Worship, Imagination, and Formation," in *The Blackwell Companion to Christian Ethics*, ed. Stanley Hauerwas and Samuel Wells (Oxford: Blackwell, 2004), 66. Kenneson uses *ekklesia* to highlight the fact that church is not simply a building for "religious" gatherings but is the community of disciples of Jesus Christ.

45. Hütter, "Church as Public," 357.

46. Hauerwas and Wells, "The Gift of the Church," 18.

47. Beneton, *Equality by Default*, 168. He goes on to cite Tocqueville, who dreaded what he saw forming on the horizon: "an innumerable crowd of men alike and equal whose lives revolve around themselves without respite in order to procure the little and vulgar pleasure with which they stuff their souls."

48. Debra Dean Murphy, *Teaching That Transforms: Worship as the Heart of Christian Education* (Grand Rapids: Brazos, 2004), 14. Murphy notes that this was not the worship of her childhood. The same is true for me. While in the Baptist church the Word was and continues to be central, worship tends to deemphasize the sacraments and so is not in continuity with the historic pattern that rightly saw the sacraments as central in authentic worship. I return to a discussion of this in chapter 6.

49. Don Saliers, *Worship as Theology: Foretaste of Glory Divine* (Nashville: Abingdon, 1994), 105. He is quoting Johannes Metz and Karl Rahner, *The Courage to Pray.*

50. Wendell Berry, *Life Is a Miracle: An Essay against Modern Superstition* (Washington, DC: Counterpoint, 2000), 27.

51. Odo Casel, *The Mystery of Christian Worship* (New York: Crossroad, 1999), 40.

52. Gregory of Nyssa, quoted in Robert Louis Wilken, *The Spirit of Early Christian Thought: Seeking the Face of God* (New Haven, CT: Yale University Press, 2003), 302.

53. Karl Barth, quoted in Scott Bader-Saye, "Listening: Authority, and Obedience," in *The Blackwell Companion to Christian Ethics*, ed. Stanley Hauerwas and Samuel Wells (Oxford: Blackwell, 2004), 168. The quotation is from *Church Dogmatics*, 4/3. Stanley Hauerwas also says the church enables us to see the world rightly. See, for example, coauthored with William H. Willimon, *Resident Aliens* (Nashville: Abingdon, 1989).

54. Rowan Williams, *Teresa of Avila* (Harrisburg, PA: Morehouse, 1991), 140.

55. I return to this insight from Teresa of Ávila more fully in chapter 7.

56. Wainwright draws from Von Allmen in his opening paragraph of "The Church as a Worshiping Community," in Wainwright, *Worship with One Accord*, 19.

57. Kelly S. Johnson, "Praying: Poverty," in *The Blackwell Companion to Christian Ethics*, ed. Stanley Hauerwas and Samuel Wells (Oxford: Blackwell, 2004), 229.

58. The nineteenth-century French saint Thérèse of Lisieux, for example, is well known for her emphasis of "the little way." The little way focused not on great dreams of sanctity and martyrdom but on living life as it actually is and doing even the tiniest deeds with detailed care and love. For an especially provocative account of Thérèse, see David F. Ford, *Self and Salvation: Being Transformed* (Cambridge: Cambridge University Press, 1999).

59. John Milbank, *The Word Made Strange: Theology, Language, Culture* (Cambridge, MA: Blackwell, 1997), 228.

60. I am especially thankful to Therese Lysaught for emphasizing this point.

61. Milbank, *Word Made Strange*, 230.

62. Fergus Kerr, *Theology after Wittgenstein* (New York: Blackwell, 1986), 183, my emphasis.

63. Mother Teresa, *A Simple Path* (New York: Random House, 1995), 35.

64. Gilbert I. Bond, "Liturgy, Ministry, and the Stranger," in *Practicing Theology: Beliefs and Practices in Christian Life*, ed. Miroslav Volf and Dorothy Bass (Grand Rapids: Eerdmans, 2001), 137–56.

65. Helen Keller, *The Story of My Life* (New York: Dell, 1961), 67.

66. Schmemann, *For the Life of the World*, 11.

67. Susan J. White, *The Spirit of Worship: The Liturgical Tradition* (Maryknoll, NY: Orbis, 1999), 46.

68. L. Edward Phillips, quoted in Frederick C. Bauerschmidt, "Bodies and Abortion," in *The Blackwell Companion to Christian Ethics*, ed. Stanley Hauerwas and Samuel Wells (Oxford: Blackwell, 2004), 259.

69. L. Edward Phillips, *The Ritual Kiss in Early Christian Worship* (Cambridge: Grove, 1996), 15. Phillips adds, "This would explain the kiss of Judas—and why the early church remembered the betrayal kiss as such a heinous violation of trust, and it would explain how the kiss could later be understood as a part of initiation into the church, as was the case in some areas" (ibid.).

70. Vincent J. Donovan, *Christianity Rediscovered*, 2nd ed. (Maryknoll, NY: Orbis, 2003), 94.

71. Here we can see that the offering of grass was not a sign of something that is absent, like a sign that says Richmond is 60 miles away. Rather, it is a causal sign in that it brings about a reality, like the words "I pronounce you husband and wife."

72. Randy Cooper, *Being Subject to One Another as We Sing*, Ekklesia Project, Pamphlet 11 (Eugene, OR: Wipf and Stock), 13. The quotation is from John Wesley's instructions on hymn singing.

73. Ibid., 4.

74. When the Masai gathered for worship, some dances could be performed at the Eucharist. But there were other dances the Masai were ashamed to bring into the Eucharist. Donovan writes: "By that very fact, a judgment had been made on them. Such dances should no longer be part of their lives at all" (*Christianity Rediscovered*, 94).

75. Cooper analyzes Ephesians 5:18–21 and argues that the Greek text holds together verse 21 ("Be subject to one another out of reverence for Christ") with the previous paragraph. Furthermore, "be subject" is not an imperative but a present participle, "being subject." He thus concludes that "being subject" is the last of

five present participles in this passage: "speaking," "singing," "making melody," "giving thanks," and "being subject to" (ibid., 4–5).

76. Ibid., p. 6.

77. Christine Pohl, *Making Room: Recovering Hospitality as a Christian Tradition* (Grand Rapids: Eerdmans, 1999). See especially "Hospitality from the Margins," 104–24.

Part 2

1. M. Therese Lysaught, "Eucharist as Basic Training," in *Theology and Lived Christianity*, ed. David M. Hammond (Mystic, CT: Twenty-third, 2000), 277.

Chapter 3

1. M. Therese Lysaught, "Eucharist as Basic Training," in *Theology and Lived Christianity*, ed. David M. Hammond (Mystic, CT: Twenty-third, 2000), 265.

2. Ibid.

3. After the cleansing of the temple, the "disciples remembered what was written, 'Zeal for you house will consume me'"(John 2:17). This quotation is taken from Psalm 69:9.

4. My experience is confirmed by Elisabeth Kübler-Ross in *On Death and Dying* (New York: Macmillan, 1969): "In modern hospitals the moribund patient is an object of great medical interest, and incidentally also of enormous financial investments ('He will get a dozen people around the clock, all busily preoccupied with his heart rate, pulse, electrocardiogram . . . his secretions or excretions'), but the patient will not succeed, no matter how much he insists, in persuading a single one of these busy people to pause for a minute and listen to a question, let alone answer it." Quoted in Josef Pieper, *Faith, Hope, and Love* (San Francisco: Ignatius, 1992), 196.

5. Hannah Arendt, *The Human Condition* (Chicago: University of Chicago Press, 1958), 6.

6. Ragan Sutterfield, *God's Grandeur: The Church in the Economy of Creation*, Ekklesia Project, Pamphlet 12 (Eugene, OR: Wipf and Stock, 2004), 8.

7. Ibid.

8. David Matzko McCarthy, *The Good Life: Genuine Christianity for the Middle Class* (Grand Rapids: Brazos, 2004), 15.

9. Wendell Berry, *Life Is a Miracle: An Essay against Modern Superstition* (Washington, DC: Counterpoint, 2000), 25.

10. Wendell Berry, "A Defense of the Family Farm," in *Home Economics* (New York: Farrar, Straus, and Giroux, 1987), 162–78.

11. Dale Gish, member of the Church of the Sojourners, San Francisco, in a panel discussion at the Ekklesia Project, July 20, 2005.

12. Edward O. Wilson, quoted in Berry, *Life Is a Miracle*, 33.

13. Marjorie Greene, "The Personal and the Subjective," *Tradition and Discovery: The Polanyi Society Periodical* 22 (1995–96): 7.

14. Philosopher of science Michael Polanyi stands out as one who has argued for an alternative understanding of science. Particularly in his book *Personal Knowledge, Towards a Post-Critical Philosophy* (Chicago: University of Chicago, 1958), Polanyi argues that scientific knowing involves tradition and apprenticeship (hence authority!), personal commitment (contra objectivism), and a reliance upon truth as both tacit (embodied) and heuristic (true in that it has potential to

reveal more truth to future eyes). I describe Polanyi more fully in the following chapter.

15. H. A. Nielsen, "A Meeting of Minds on Water," in *The Grammar of the Heart*, ed. Richard H. Bell (San Francisco: Harper and Row, 1988), 75.

16. Wittgenstein, quoted in ibid., 75.

17. Ibid., 78.

18. George Macdonald, quoted in ibid., 81.

19. http://en.wikipedia.org/wiki/Evolution.

20. It is significant that the supernatural is equated, and thus reduced, to origins. From a Christian theological position, any full account of God as Creator will discuss what this means not only in the past but also in the present and future.

21. Charles Darwin himself drew out certain implications from this story. For example, he writes, "man scans with scrupulous care the character and pedigree of his horses, cattle, and dogs before he matches them; but when he comes to his own marriage he rarely, or never, takes any such care. . . . Both sexes ought to refrain from marriage if they are in any marked degree inferior in body or mind; but such hopes are Utopian and will never be even partially realized until the laws of inheritance are thoroughly known. Everyone does good service, who aids toward this end." Charles Darwin, *The Descent of Man*, Great Books of the Western World 49 (Chicago: Encyclopaedia Britannica, 1996), 596. This is a nice example of how the story of Darwinian evolution gives little reason for why "weaker" or inferior humans should survive.

22. David Bentley Hart, *The Beauty of the Infinite: The Aesthetics of Christian Truth* (Grand Rapids: Eerdmans, 2003), 256–57.

23. Augustine of Hippo, *The Augustine Catechism: The Enchiridion on Faith, Hope, and Love* (New York: New City, 1999), 41.

24. John Milbank, "Can Morality Be Christian?" in *The Word Made Strange: Theology, Language, Culture* (Cambridge, MA: Blackwell, 1997), 229.

25. Milbank interprets Paul as writing to the Romans, "Cease to be self-sufficient in the face of scarcity. . . . [Receive] from the all-sufficiency of God, and [act] excessively out of this excess" (ibid., 231).

26. This paragraph is taken from my article "Theology and Science without Dualism," *Center for Theology and the Natural Sciences Bulletin* 17, no. 1 (Winter 1997): 15–23; reprinted in *Cross Currents* 48, no. 1 (Spring 1998): 34–48.

27. Loyal Rue, "Redefining Myth and Religion: Introduction to a Conversation," *Zygon* 20 (September 1994): 316–17.

28. Ibid., 318.

29. Ibid., 319.

30. William H. Poteat, *A Philosophical Daybook: Post-critical Investigations* (Columbia: University of Missouri, 1990), 72.

31. I do not think these two have to be exclusive. Rue, however, would see creation by God as unacceptable since it is "somebody's" story.

32. John Hick, quoted in Kenneth Surin, "A 'Politics of Speech': Religious Pluralism in the Age of the McDonald's Hamburger," in *Christian Uniqueness Reconsidered: The Myth of Religious Pluralism*, ed. Gavin D'Costa (Maryknoll, NY: Orbis, 1990), 200. Hick is perhaps the best-known pluralist theologian. His Kantian approach posits divine noumena reflected in multiple or plural phenomena; the noumenal transcendent is common to all religions.

33. Lesslie Newbigin, *The Gospel in a Pluralist Society* (Grand Rapids: Eerdmans, 1989), 9.

34. Ibid., 10.

35. Surin, "Politics of Speech," 200–201.

36. Douglas Wilson, "The Emerging American Empires: Mammon *Versus* Allah," *Chronicles: A Magazine of Amerian Culture*, June 2005, 14–15.

37. It might seem to the reader as if I have been unfair to pluralism. After all, the pluralist is rightly concerned about Christian triumphalism and rightly desires to engage the other. Yet even though well intended, the pluralist approach ends up undercutting Christian hospitality. Am I then an inclusivist (one who thinks others are "anonymous Christians") or an exclusivist (one who sees Christ alone as the way to salvation)? I am not convinced that these common descriptions are adequate. After all, every position is exclusive in that it excludes other positions that contradict it. Rather, I think Paul's "all things to all people" is a provocative way to move forward. Paul writes, "For though I am free with respect to all, I have made myself a slave to all, so that I might win more of them. To the Jews I became as a Jew, in order to win Jews. To those under the law I became as one under the law (though I myself am not under the law) so that I might win those under the law. . . . To the weak I became weak, so that I might win the weak" (1 Cor. 9:19–20, 22). Paul is not setting forth a "position" here as much as he is describing a way of being with others. We might at first be repelled by Paul's "blowing with the wind" approach. But I think it is more accurate to the sense of the Corinthian letter to say that Paul is practicing a hospitality that seeks to be where people are, not in spite of the gospel but for the sake it. Paul desires to live such that he does not "put an obstacle in the way of the gospel of Christ" (9:12). For Paul, hospitality entails living in such a way that nothing obstructs Christ; as he writes to the Philippians, "For, to me to live is Christ . . ." (1:21).

38. Ched Myers, *Economics and the Gospel of Mark*, audiotape (Albuquerque, NM: Center for Action and Contemplation, 1988).

39. Sharon Daloz Parks, "Household Economics," in *Practicing Our Faith*, ed. Dorothy Bass (San Francisco: Jossey-Bass, 1997), 44.

40. For the connection between economics and household, see ibid. Parks notes, "Like the words *ecumenical* and *ecology*, *economics* is rooted in the Greek word *oikos*, meaning household, and signifies the management of the household—arranging what is necessary for well-being" (44).

41. Daniel M. Bell Jr., "What Gift Is Given? A Reponse to Volf," *Modern Theology* 19, no 2 (April 2003): 272–73.

42. Murray Jardine, *The Making and Unmaking of Technological Society* (Grand Rapids: Brazos, 2004), 132.

43. Ibid.

44. Ibid., 133. Jardine's analysis of our current political and economic context is much more sophisticated and thorough than I am able to recount here. He provides a thorough analysis of liberal capitalist democracy with an eye to offering a Christian critique and response.

45. William H. Poteat, *Recovering the Ground: Critical Exercises in Recollection* (New York: State University of New York Press, 1994), xvii.

46. Michael L. Budde, "Global Culture Industries," in *The Blackwell Companion to Christian Ethics*, ed. Stanley Hauerwas and Samuel Wells (Oxford: Blackwell, 2004), 129.

47. George Ritzer, *The McDonaldization of Society*, 4th ed. (Thousand Oaks, CA: Sage, 2004), 12.

48. Alan Sica, *Max Weber and the New Century* (New Brunswick, NJ: Transaction, 2004), 114.

49. Ibid., 13.

50. Ibid., 15–16.

51. Philippe Beneton, *Equality by Default: An Essay on Modernity as Confinement*, trans. Ralph Hancock (Wilmington, DE: ISI, 2004), 86–87.

52. Ibid., 87. On how globalization replaces genuine catholicity, see especially William T. Cavanaugh, "The Myth of Globalization as Catholicity," in *Theopolitical Imagination: Discovering the Liturgy as a Political Act in an Age of Global Consumerism* (New York: T & T Clark, 2002), 97–122.

53. Ritzer, *McDonaldization of Society*, xiv.

54. Hans S. Reinders, "Being Thankful: Parenting the Mentally Disabled," in *The Blackwell Companion to Christian Ethics*, ed. Stanley Hauerwas and Samuel Wells (Oxford: Blackwell, 2004), 436.

55. Jacques Ellul, *Money and Power* (Downers Grove, IL: InterVarsity Press, 1984), 20.

56. Gilbert I. Bond, "Liturgy, Ministry, and the Stranger," in *Practicing Theology: Beliefs and Practices in Christian Life*, ed. Miroslav Volf and Dorothy Bass (Grand Rapids: Eerdmans, 2001), 142.

57. Ibid., 143.

58. The title of this section is inspired by Alasdair MacIntyre's *Whose Justice? What Rationality?* (Notre Dame, IN: University of Notre Dame Press, 1988).

59. Beneton, *Equality by Default*, 58.

60. Ibid., 64.

61. Ibid., 65; quotation from Edmund Burke.

62. Max Weber, quoted in Sica, *Max Weber and the New Century*, 119.

63. Ibid., 123.

64. Ritzer argues that McDonaldization has led to disenchantment: "efficient systems have no room for anything smacking of enchantment," and "predictability is inimical to enchantment" (ibid., 132–33).

65. David Matzko McCarthy, *The Good Life: Genuine Christianity for the Middle Class* (Grand Rapids: Brazos, 2004), 75.

66. Jake Silverstein, "Grand Opening: Ronald McDonald Conquers New Spain," *Harper's Magazine*, January 2005, 74.

67. Ibid., 70.

68. Ray Kroc, quoted in Eric Schlosser, *Fast Food Nation: The Dark Side of the All-American Meal* (Boston: Houghton Mifflin, 2001), 37.

69. Livio Melina, *Sharing in Christ's Virtues: For a Renewal of Moral Theology in Light of "Veritatis Splendor"* (Washington, DC: Catholic University of America, 2001), 61.

70. Gerhard Lohfink, *Does God Need the Church? Toward a Theology of the People of God* (Collegeville, MN: Liturgical, 1999), 17.

71. Sutterfield, *God's Grandeur*, 3, my emphasis.

72. John D. Zizioulas, *Being as Communion* (Crestwood, NY: St. Vladimir's Seminary Press, 1985), 39.

73. Melina, *Sharing in Christ's Virtues*, 147.

74. Alexander Schmemann, *For the Life of the World* (Crestwood, NY: St. Vladimir's Seminary Press, 1963), 42.

75. For an interesting discussion of the dangers and temptations of modernity and postmodernity in relation to Christian faith, see Jonathan Wilson, *Gospel Virtues: Practicing Faith, Hope, and Love in Uncertain Times* (Downers Grove, IL: InterVarsity Press, 1998), 53–60.

76. Jean-Luc Marion, "They Recognized Him, and He Became Invisible to Them," *Modern Theology* 18, no. 2 (April 2002): 145.

77. Ibid., 146.

78. Sometimes "having" faith and other times not is really better understood as a kind of competition between different kinds of faith/stories.

79. Marion, "They Recognized Him," 147.

80. Ibid., 150.

81. Lohfink is here writing about the seeing of the "glory of the Lord" in Isaiah and the Gospel of John (*Does God Need the Church?* 142).

82. Robert Louis Wilken, *The Spirit of Early Christian Thought* (New Haven, CT: Yale University Press, 2003), 165.

83. John Milbank, "Can a Gift Be Given? Prolegomena to a Future Trinitarian Metaphysic," *Modern Theology*, 1995, 152. Milbank is here writing against Jacques Derrida and Martin Heidegger's "mystical atheism."

84. Lohfink, *Does God Need the Church?* 145.

85. Ibid.

86. Ibid., 143.

87. Ibid., 149.

88. Wilson, *Gospel Virtues*, 61.

89. Melina, *Sharing in Christ's Virtues*, 150. "One is incorporated in Christ always and only through the sign of, and in the measure of, a 'con-corporation' into the mystery of the Church."

90. Beneton, *Equality by Default*, 163.

91. Bell, "What Gift Is Given?" 273.

92. Wilson, *Gospel Virtues*, 63. Wilson states more generally that the task of Christian ethics is to describe not a better life but a new life.

93. Lohfink, *Does God Need the Church?* 149.

94. Bell, "What Gift Is Given?" 273–74.

95. In the words of Brent Laytham: "It may be due to the church's captivity to capitalism, unable or unwilling to imagine the abundance of God's economy." "God Is One, Holy, Catholic, and Apostolic," in *God Is Not . . .* , ed. D. Brent Laytham (Grand Rapids: Brazos, 2004), 129.

96. Stanley Hauerwas, *Sanctify Them in the Truth* (Nashville: Abingdon, 1998), 222.

97. Lohfink, *Does God Need the Church?* 150.

Chapter 4

1. Josef Pieper, *Faith, Hope, Love* (San Francisco: Ignatius, 1997), 113.

2. Karl Barth, quoted in John C. McDowell, *Hope in Barth's Eschatology* (Burlington VT: Ashgate, 2000), 153.

3. Paschasius Radbertus describes this as follows: "Christ is held by the hand of hope. We hold him and are held. But it is a greater good that we are held by Christ than that we hold him. For we can hold him only so long as we are held by him." Quoted in Pieper, *Faith, Hope, Love*, 105.

4. William H. Poteat, *A Philosophical Daybook: Post-critical Investigations* (Columbia: University of Missouri Press, 1990), 5.

5. I use the term *postmodernism* cautiously to point out general tendencies in contemporary thinking. I tend to agree with those who maintain that postmodernism is not a radical departure from modernity but a logical conclusion of modern thought. For a good brief summary of modernity and postmodernity, see Murray Jardine, *Speech and Political Practice: Recovering the Place of Human Responsibility* (New York: State University of New York Press, 1998), 1–15. Douglas Sloan makes

a helpful distinction between constructive and deconstructive postmodernism in *Faith and Knowledge* (Louisville, KY: Westminster John Knox, 1994), 212–37.

6. Jardine describes the egalitarian political position of such thinkers as Michel Foucault and Jacques Derrida, sometimes referred to as "postmodern," as follows: "For these thinkers, the recognition that reality is a chaos of interpretations implies that one who wants to live most fully should be open to 'otherness'—that is, to other interpretations of the world and their practical manifestations that bourgeois rationalism has suppressed and silenced" (*Speech and Political Practice*, 5).

7. John Milbank, *Theology and Social Theory: Beyond Secular Reason* (Cambridge, MA: Blackwell, 1990).

8. Stanley Fish defines this as "the multiculturalism of ethnic restaurants, weekend festivals, and high profile flirtations with the other." Quoted in Barry Harvey, *Another City: An Ecclesiological Primer for a Post-Christian World* (Harrisburg, PA: Trinity International, 1999), 2–3.

9. Pieper refers to our status of being on the way (*status viatoris*), a reality that is "part of the very foundation of being in the world for the Christian" (*Faith, Hope, Love*, 91).

10. Ibid., 98.

11. Robert W. Jenson, *Systematic Theology*, vol. 1, *The Triune God* (New York: Oxford University Press, 1997), 71. Jenson adds in a note that postcanonical Judaism did "affirm [the life of the blessed's] deification materially if not formally. . . . 'In the World to Come . . . the righteous sit with their crowns on their heads enjoying the effulgence of the *Shekinah*.'"

12. Stanley Hauerwas and James McClendon have also influenced my analysis in this chapter, though I do not cite them directly.

13. For a discussion of the connection between MacIntyre and *A Canticle for Leibowitz,* see Ralph Wood, "Lest the World's Amnesia Be Complete: A Reading of Walter Miller's *A Canticle for Leibowitz*," *Perspectives in Religious Studies* 27, no. 1 (Spring 2000): 83–97. Wood also provides an excellent theological analysis of Miller's novel.

14. Alasdair MacIntyre, *After Virtue* (Notre Dame, IN: University of Notre Dame Press, 1984), 5.

15. Jardine nicely summarizes the impact of an Enlightenment epistemology as follows:

> The application of the Enlightenment model of acceptable knowledge has thus had the effect of progressively shrinking the domain of intelligible human experience. In the seventeenth and eighteenth centuries, what is now called "religious belief" conflicted with the model of exact, impersonal knowledge and was relegated to the realm of mere opinion; by the late nineteenth century, morality, which the Enlightenment philosophers had thought could be placed on a firm, secular footing by skeptical rationalism, was in serious danger of becoming a matter of subjective value; and by the mid-twentieth century it had become an open question whether even the hardest sciences could meaningfully be described as objective. (*Speech and Political Practice*, 2)

16. Alasdair MacIntyre, lecture, Culture of Death conference, University of Notre Dame, South Bend, IN, October 13, 2000. A videotape of this lecture is available from the Notre Dame Center for Ethics and Culture.

17. William James, quoted in George Marsden, *The Outrageous Idea of Christian Scholarship* (New York: Oxford University Press, 1997), 46. Marsden at this point is not criticizing James but finds his image "quite congenial."

18. Ibid., 47.

19. According to Stanley Hauerwas, James assumed "that the hotel corridor he imagined could be maintained nonviolently." Hauerwas continues, "Yet we have learned that no such corridor exists, even in universities," *With the Grain of the Universe: The Church's Witness and Natural Theology* (Grand Rapids: Brazos, 2001), 86.

20. I discuss the university as "hotel" more fully in my essay "Hotel or Home? Hospitality and Higher Education," in *Conflicting Allegiances: The Church-Based University in a Liberal Democratic Society*, ed. John Wright and Michael Budde (Grand Rapids: Brazos, 2004).

21. Alasdair MacIntyre, *Whose Justice? Which Rationality?* (Notre Dame, IN: University of Notre Dame Press, 1988), 350.

22. Michael Polanyi, *The Tacit Dimension* (Gloucester, MA: Peter Smith, 1983), 23.

23. Michael Polanyi, *Personal Knowledge: Towards a Post-critical Philosophy* (Chicago: University of Chicago Press, 1962), 54–55.

24. William H. Poteat, *Recovering the Ground: Critical Exercises in Recollection* (New York: State University of New York Press, 1994), 193.

25. Ibid., 210.

26. Nicholas Lash, "Contemplation, Metaphor, and Real Knowledge," paper presented at the Knowing God, Christ, and Nature in the Post-Positivistic Era symposium, University of Notre Dame, South Bend, IN, April 14–17, 1993, 4.

27. From this perspective, even the Enlightenment (its condescension of myth to the contrary) feeds off myth and relies upon a liturgical reenactment. See especially Poteat, *Philosophical Daybook*, 89.

28. At this point, we can note that hospitality is practiced well, though differently, in a variety of traditions and cultures. Christians certainly could learn from other kinds of hospitality. Reinhard Hütter notes that hospitality and honoring the truth "are practices held in high regard by many people. Indeed, one might claim that they are—if not universally practiced—at least widely acknowledged as central to human life." He locates this observation theologically in "the distinction (*not* dichotomy) between God's economy of creation and God's economy of salvation." See his "Hospitality and Truth: The Disclosure of Practices in Worship and Doctrine," in *Practicing Theology: Beliefs and Practices in Christian Life*, ed. Miroslav Volf and Dorothy C. Bass (Grand Rapids: Eerdmans, 2002), 206.

29. In the first midrash, only when God threatens to drop Mount Sinai on the Israelites if they refuse the Torah do they respond, "All that the Lord has spoken we will do and we will hear." In the second interpretation, God offers the Torah to many other nations, but they all refuse. Recounted in Stephen J. Einstein and Lydia Kukoff, *Every Person's Guide to Judaism* (New York: UAHC, 1989), 10.

30. Emphasis mine. The fuller context is as follows:

I do attribute to Hitler the insight that killing Jews drives God out of the world. Hitler's hatred of the Jews was not rooted in the "normal" criminal's desire to obtain the land, property, or personal service of his victim. History is full of conflicts over property and territory and of the enslavement of one people by another. In all such conflicts, surrender yields peace. Slaves were exploited and not murdered as long as they were useful. Nazi murder of Jews was not driven by any interpretation of self-interest—however distorted—but by the desire to achieve a world without Jews, who were seen as the embodiment of evil. Nazi antisemitism therefore had a theological

207

dimension. (Michael Wyschogrod, *The Body of Faith* [Northvale, NJ: Jason Aronson, 1996], xxix)

31. Thomas Aquinas explores the incarnation in light of the goodness of God: "But the very nature of God is goodness. . . . Hence, what belongs to the essence of goodness befits God. But it belongs to the essence of goodness to communicate itself to others, as is plain from Dionysius (*Div. Nom.* iv). Hence it belongs to the essence of the highest good to communicate itself in the highest manner to the creature, and this is brought about chiefly by 'His so joining created nature to Himself that one Person is made up of these three—the Word, a soul and flesh,' as Augustine says (*De Trin.* xiii). Hence it is manifest that it was fitting that God should become incarnate" (*Summa Theologiae*, 3a.1.1).

32. To overaccept frees one to improvise so that accepting and blocking are not the only options. An example from scripture: When the crowds bring the woman caught in adultery to Jesus requesting that she be stoned, he stoops and writes in the sand, and says, "Let him who is without sin cast the first stone." He neither accepts their offer to stone nor blocks their offer by saying, "Don't do that." Instead he overaccepts it by placing it in the more truthful context of our shared sinfulness and of God's forgiveness: "Go and sin no more."

33. Samuel Wells, *Improvisation: The Drama of Christian Ethics* (Grand Rapids: Brazos, 2004), 113.

34. Augustine of Hippo, *Homilies on the Gospels,* sermon 61, quoted in *And You Welcomed Me: A Sourcebook on Hospitality in Early Christianity*, ed. Amy Oden (Nashville: Abingdon), 45.

35. For a fuller discussion of Christians as a diaspora people, see Harvey, *Another City*, especially chap. 5, "Madness, Truth, and Diaspora: The Post-Christendom Form of the Church as *Altera Civitas*," 135–65.

36. Henri Nouwen, "Hospitality," *Monastic Studies* 10 (Easter 1974): 26.

37. I return to this point more fully in chapter 6.

38. Stephen Fowl, *God's Beautiful City: Christian Mission after Christendom* (Eugene, OR: Wifp and Stock, 2001), 7, 13–14.

39. Lohfink states that "they sat down in groups of one-hundreds and fifties" clearly refers to Exodus 18:25, which "describes the order of the camp of the people of God on their way through the wilderness." Gerhard Lohfink, *Does God Need the Church? Toward a Theology of the People of God* (Collegeville, MN: Liturgical, 1999), 147.

40. Ibid., 150.

41. Lohfink makes this statement when analyzing 1 Corinthians 11:20–22, a passage about early Christians failing to celebrate the Lord's Supper truthfully (ibid., 256).

42. MacIntyre, *After Virtue*, 263.

43. Such a university, MacIntyre maintains, will support systematic debate about standards of rational justification among rival traditions, such as the Thomistic and genealogical. The "winner" of such debate will be the tradition that can resolve problems posed by a particular tradition which that tradition is unable to resolve within its own system of thought.

44. Alasdair MacIntyre, *Three Rival Versions of Moral Enquiry: Encyclopaedia, Genealogy, and Tradition* (Notre Dame, IN: University of Notre Dame Press, 1990), 234–35.

45. MacIntyre, lecture, Culture of Death conference.

46. As indicated in earlier chapters and more fully described in chapter 5, the practice of Christian hospitality is necessarily both public and political.

47. Walter M. Miller, *A Canticle for Leibowitz* (New York: Bantam, 1959), 275.

48. Ibid., 309.
49. Ibid., 311.
50. Ibid., 312.
51. Wood, "Lest the World's Amnesia Be Complete," 97.
52. Wood draws this connection (ibid., 85).
53. Miller, *Canticle*, 312.
54. Ibid., my emphasis.
55. It might well be that the full implications of Christian theology do not appear in MacIntyre's thought because of the kind of distinction he draws between philosophy and theology. MacIntyre argues that the integrative tasks of philosophy, rightly understood,

> can be carried out only by rational enquiry, independently of faith and revealed truths, enabling enquirers to understand how the specialized disciplines contribute to, but cannot themselves supply an understanding of the overall order of things. . . . And there is a second set of tasks that can be carried out only by enquiry into the bearing of revealed truths, truths to be acknowledged only by faith, on the work of the university. These are the tasks of theology, rightly understood. ("Catholic Universities: Dangers, Hopes, Choices," lecture presented at the University of Notre Dame, October 13–14, 1999, 5)

I find it misleading, however, to talk about an intellectual space, or a space of inquiry, that is independent of faith and revealed truths. All philosophy draws, even if not explicitly, from some kind of theology. My concern with MacIntyre at this point is that his philosophy fails to draw as fully as it could from a Christian future or eschatology, a future that is as present to us as is our past, which MacIntyre so hopes to reclaim.

56. Wyschogrod, *Body of Faith*, 231.
57. Discussing C.S. Lewis's *The Great Divorce*, Hütter observes:

> Acknowledging and therefore receiving, the truth of who and whose one is liberates one for genuine hospitality. Yet because the inhabitants of Twilight City lack this truth, they are intensely absorbed in themselves—the self-absorption of a void in search of a substance. They want to grasp and own what can only be received as a gift: the gift of a self transparent to the truth that it owes its existence not to itself, but rather to the Giver of Life. Honoring this truth in its constant reception is what makes the self open to the other, to genuine hospitality. ("Hospitality and Truth," 209)

58. "Other food is digested by Christian believers, but the eucharist as a heavenly food digests its own communicants, making them immortal and giving them a share in resurrection life." David Steinmetz, *Memory and Mission* (Nashville: Abingdon, 1988), 136.

Chapter 5

1. John Rawls, *A Theory of Justice* (Cambridge, MA: Harvard University Press, 1971), 554.
2. Richard Rorty, "Priority of Democracy to Philosophy," in *Objectivity, Relativism, and Truth*, vol. 1 of *Philosophical Papers* (New York: Cambridge University Press, 1991), 187–88. My thanks to Kenneth Craycraft for this quotation in *The American Myth of Religious Freedom* (Dallas: Spence, 1999), 9.
3. Alasdair MacIntyre, *Three Rival Versions of Moral Enquiry: Encyclopaedia, Genealogy, and Tradition* (Notre Dame, IN: University of Notre Dame Press, 1990).

As MacIntyre develops it, the encyclopedic version represents the impersonal, tradition-free conception of rational inquiry, a project that places morality in an autonomous realm. The geneologic account sees the encyclopedic project as a will to power and emphasizes a multiplicity of perspectives and a relativizing of the truth of those perspectives.

4. John Murray Cuddihy, *No Offense: Civil Religion and Protestant Taste* (New York: Seabury, 1978), 13.

5. John B. Bennett, "Civic and Moral Virtues: Teaching by Practicing Hospitality," *Journal of College and Character* 2 (2003), accessed at www.collegevalues.org/articles.cfm?a=1&id=374. My criticism of Bennett's definition of hospitality is not intended to negate other helpful insights and suggestions in his essay. For example, he rightly notes that "hospitality points toward a covenant, rather than simply a social contract, with the other."

6. My thanks to Hartley Wootton for putting the matter this way.

7. Stanley Hauerwas has argued persuasively throughout his writings for recovering the church as *polis*. See especially *In Good Company: The Church as Polis* (Notre Dame, IN: University of Notre Dame Press, 1995) and, with William Willimon, *Resident Aliens* (Nashville: Abingdon, 1989).

8. E. Glenn Hinson, "A Word From . . ." *Review and Expositor* 101, no. 4 (Fall 2004): 580.

9. See Murray Jardine, *The Making and Unmaking of Technological Society: How Christianity Can Save Modernity from Itself* (Grand Rapids: Brazos, 2004). For a fuller discussion of liberalism and capitalist democracy, see especially 29–84.

10. Ibid., 31.

11. John Wright, "How Many Masters? From the Church-Related to an Ecclesially Based University," in *Conflicting Allegiances: The Church-Based University in a Liberal Democratic Society*, ed. Michael L. Budde and John Wright (Grand Rapids: Brazos, 2004), 15–16.

12. Jardine, *Making and Unmaking of Technological Society*, 22.

13. W. David Solomon, "Comment on MacIntyre," *Review of Politics* 52 (Summer 1990): 373. William Cavanaugh states more strongly that Kant's view of the good ultimately rested in the state as peacemaker, a point to which I return later in this chapter:

> The conception of the State as peacemaker was given theoretical form by Immanuel Kant, intellectual forebear to many of today's liberal political theorists. For Kant the State is the condition of possibility of morality in history because it ensures that people do not infringe the freedom of others and are thereby free to develop as rational beings. The modern republic is the agent for bringing about perpetual peace because it will allow people to transcend their historical particularities, e.g. Lutheran vs. Catholic, and respect one another on the basis of their common rationality. ("'A Fire Strong Enough to Consume the House': The Wars of Religion and the Rise of the State," *Modern Theology* 11, no. 4 [October 1995]: 409)

Cavanaugh notes that such philosophy now makes war more likely, as any state that doesn't govern itself rationally is a potential enemy.

14. Kenneth R. Craycraft Jr., *The Myth of Religious Freedom* (Dallas: Spence, 1999), 36.

15. Emphasis mine. For a summary of possessive individualism and liberal democracy, see C. B. Macpherson, *The Political Theory of Possessive Individualism, Hobbes to Locke* (London: Oxford University Press, 1962), 263–77.

16. In contemporary life, we can compare Locke's point to the current debate over eminent domain: the government or a corporation can take a family's land if it can make better economic use of it.

17. Jardine, *Making and Unmaking of Technological Society*, 33.

18. Rawls, *Theory of Justice*, 447–48, quoted in Alasdair MacIntyre, "The Privatization of the Good," *Review of Politics* 52 (Summer 1990): 347.

19. Stanley Hauerwas, *Dispatches from the Front: Theological Engagements with the Secular* (Durham, NC: Duke University Press, 1994), 13. For a great analysis of so-called religious pluralism, see Stanley Hauerwas, "The End of 'Religious Pluralism': A Tribute to David Burrell, C.S.C." at http://frontrow.bc.edu/program/hauerwas.

20. As Jardine notes (personal correspondence), pluralist cultures are not really pluralist anyway. They have been characterized by the dominance of scientific rationalism in early stages and by watered-down Nietzchean aestheticism more recently, representing the Enlightenment model in both its prime and its decadence.

21. Cavanaugh, "Fire Strong Enough," 409.

22. E. O.Wilson, quoted in Wendell Berry, *Life Is a Miracle: An Essay against Modern Superstition* (Washington, DC: Counterpoint, 2000), 32.

23. Kirby Godsey, "To Whom Are Baptist Colleges and Universities Accountable? Two Views," paper presented at the Future of Baptist Higher Education Conference, Baylor University, Waco, TX, April 18–19, 2005, 4.

24. Daniel Vestal, "To Whom Are Baptist Colleges and Universities Accountable? Two Views," paper presented at the Future of Baptist Higher Education Conference, Baylor University, Waco, TX, April 18–19, 2005, 1. The full statement is "Fundamentalists don't really believe in education, only in indoctrination. They will stifle academic freedom and excellence."

25. Immanuel Kant, "What Is Enlightenment?" in *The Philosophy of Kant*, ed. and trans. Carl J. Friedrich (New York: Random House, 1949), 132.

26. The Enlightenment, as William H. Poteat notes, has given us a modern suspicion of ritual and myth as "meaningless residues of a tradition that we wish to abandon," but this idea is itself formed by an alternative myth. "Of course, the Enlightenment has intimidated us with its impeachment of myths, all the while preserving and fashioning myths of its own." *A Philosophical Daybook: Post-critical Investigations* (Columbia: University of Missouri Press, 1990), 17, 71. The same can be said about "orthodoxy" and "dogma."

27. Stanley Hauerwas, *Dispatches from the Front*, 13.

28. Godsey, "To Whom Are Baptist Colleges," 9.

29. Ibid., 10.

30. Bill J. Leonard, "Hegemony or Dissent: Signs of Baptist Identity amid the Loss of Baptist Culture in the South," paper presented at the Future of Baptist Higher Education Conference, Baylor University, Waco, TX, April 18–19, 2005. Leonard says that Baptist-related schools ought to "own up to a heritage in which pluralism was not simply tolerated but demanded" (12): his position thus displays the irony of pluralism in its *demand* that all Baptist schools embrace pluralism.

31. Philippe Beneton, *Equality by Default: An Essay on Modernity as Confinement*, trans. Ralph Hancock (Wilmington, DE: ISI, 2004), 7. Beneton adds that this is true of modern political thought more generally: "The work of modern political thought, initiated by Machiavelli and then by Hobbes, and further developed by Locke, issues in a liberal or procedural solution: the duties of man give way to his rights."

32. We see this in pluralist theologian John Hick, who posits a Kantian noumenal "Real" above and behind what is experienced phenomenally and "specifically as the God of Israel, or as the Holy Trinity, or as Shiva, or as Allah, or as Vishnu." Quoted in Kenneth Surin, "A 'Politics of Speech': Religious Pluralism in the Age of the McDonald's Hamburger," in *Christian Uniqueness Reconsidered: The Myth of Religious Pluralism*, ed. Gavin D'Costa (Maryknoll, NY: Orbis, 1990), 199.

33. William L. Portier, "Here Come the Evangelical Catholics," *Communion* 31 (Spring 2004): 41.

34. Livio Melina, *Sharing in Christ's Virtues: For a Renewal of Moral Theology in Light of "Veritatis Splendor"* (Washington, DC: Catholic University of America, 2001), 61. This is a metaphysics in which the human will has ontological priority over creation.

35. John Milbank, *Theology and Social Theory: Beyond Secular Reason* (Oxford: Blackwell, 1990).

36. In one example of the "integrated" approach, traceable to Calvinist theologian Abraham Kuyper, all disciplines seek to be integrated into a Christian "worldview." Baptist scholar William E. Hull has argued against this approach since, according to him, there is not a worldview set forth in scripture. He recommends that we allow Christian belief to interrogate the disciplines. See "A Baptist Vision of Higher Education," keynote address in the Future of Baptist Higher Education Conference, Baylor University, Waco, TX, April 18, 2005. "Delineated" and "confined" refer to the two-spheres approach to education, where religion resides in one sphere (typically campus ministry and the extracurricular realm) and the academic disciplines in another.

37. Wright, "How Many Masters?" 15.

38. Ibid., 25, my emphasis.

39. Claude Polin, "Tocqueville's America and America Today," *Chronicles: A Magazine of American Culture*, October 2004, 20.

40. John Locke, "A Letter concerning Toleration," in *Locke, Berkeley, Hume*, Great Books of the Western World 33 (Chicago: Encyclopaedia Britannica, 1996), 1.

41. Craycraft, *Myth of Religious Freedom*, 45.

42. Ibid., 40. This is because he relied upon a deformed (my word) Protestant theology to underwrite his understanding of politics and the state. For example, Craycraft, following Walter Berns, shows that the state of nature as set forth by Locke is incompatible with Christianity. "In the state of nature . . . man is not obliged to love anyone, but merely to preserve himself and, what is more to the point, 'to preserve the rest of mankind [only] when his own preservation comes not in competition'" (cited in Craycraft, *Myth*, 37). Berns is quoting Locke from the *Second Treatise on Government*, 6.

43. Philip E. Thompson, "Sacraments and Religious Liberty: From Critical Practice to Rejected Infringement," in *Baptist Sacramentalism*, ed. Anthony R. Cross and Philip E. Thompson (Carlisle, UK: Paternoster, 2003), 49–50. In contrast to anthropocentric freedom, Thompson argues that, in the seventeenth century, Baptist practice and theology "revealed a guiding conviction that God must be free to exercise divine prerogative in salvation." The full logic of this divine freedom required a principle of mediation in that "God is free to work in and through the things of earth," a mediation seen primarily in the church and sacraments," 45-46.

44. A position attributed to Hugo Grotius by Melina, *Sharing in Christ's Virtues*, 142.

45. Immanuel Kant, *Perpetual Peace* (Indianapolis: Bobbs-Merrill, 1957). Kant argues against having standing armies or paying men to kill and instead supports voluntary armies. More philosophically, Kant argues that "the state of peace among men living side by side is not the natural state . . . the nature state is one of war. This does not always mean open hostilities, but at least an unceasing threat of war. A state of peace, therefore, must be *established*" (11).

46. For example, Christine Pohl's *Making Room: Recovering Hospitality as a Christian Tradition* (Grand Rapids: Eerdmans, 1999) is a wonderful book on Christian hospitality; even so, there are places where Pohl imagines that politics resides in a "sphere" and that this political sphere must in the final analysis police religious identity. Thus she writes, for example, that "protection of basic human rights, a protection located in the political/civic sphere, must always transcend religious and ethnic identity" (82). At this point, Pohl relies upon classic political liberalism in assuming that the politics of the nation-state is the true public where religious differences are both minimized and overcome.

47. William Cavanaugh, *Theopolitical Imagination: Discovering the Liturgy as a Political Act in an Age of Global Consumerism* (New York: T & T Clark, 2002), 22.

48. Ibid., 31.

49. Talal Asad, quoted in Philip D. Kenneson, *Beyond Sectarianism: Re-imagining Church and World* (Harrisburg, PA: Trinity Press International, 1999), 54–55, my emphasis.

50. William Cavanaugh, "God Is Not Religious," in *God Is Not . . .* , ed. D. Brent Laytham (Grand Rapids: Brazos, 2004), 100.

51. Cavanaugh, "Fire Strong Enough," 404.

52. Ibid., 403. See also Cavanaugh's account of the invention of religion in "God Is Not Religious," 97–115.

53. Locke, "A Letter Concerning Toleration," 4.

54. Friedrich Schleiermacher, *On Religion: Speeches to Its Cultured Despisers*, trans. John Oman (Louisville, KY: Westminster John Knox, 1994), 31.

55. Ibid., 36.

56. Ibid., 8.

57. Ibid., 178.

58. Ibid., 175.

59. Ibid., 148.

60. All quotations in this paragraph are taken from James M. Brandt, "Schleiermacher's Social Witness," *Currents in Theology and Mission*, April 2003. The article can be found at www.findarticles.com/p/articles/mi_m0 MDO/is_2_30/ai_99699732/pg_5.

61. *The Dying of the Light* is the title of James Burtchaell's book. These critics usually suggest that the way things are now is better in many ways than they were. Bill Leonard, for example, as earlier discussed, embraces pluralism as the best (only?) expression of Baptist theology in higher education, yet his position is enmeshed in the kind of liberal democratic politics discussed in this chapter.

62. Wright, "How Many Masters?" 15.

63. *Oxford English Dictionary*, 2nd ed., prepared by J. A. Simpson and E. S. C. Weiner (Oxford: Clarendon, 1989), 12:31.

64. Ibid.

65. Eugene Peterson, *Earth and Altar: The Community of Prayer in a Selfbound Society* (Downers Grove, IL: InterVarsity Press), 18, my emphasis.

66. Barry Harvey, *Another City: An Ecclesiological Primer for a Post-Christian World* (Harrisburg, PA: Trinity Press International, 1999), 17.

67. Michael Baxter, "God Is Not American," in *God Is Not . . .* , ed. D. Brent Laytham (Grand Rapids: Brazos, 2004), 74–75.

68. Stanley Hauerwas and Samuel Wells, "How the Church Managed Before There Was Ethics," in *The Blackwell Companion to Christian Ethics*, ed. Stanley Hauerwas and Samuel Wells (Oxford: Blackwell, 2004), 41.

69. Rowan Williams, "Politics and the Soul: A Reading of the City of God," *Milltown Studies* 19/20 (1987): 58.

70. Alasdair MacIntyre writes, "Marx was fundamentally right in seeing conflict and not consensus at the heart of modern social structures. It is not just that we live too much by a variety and multiplicity of fragmented concepts; it is that these are used at one and the same time to express rival and incompatible social ideals and policies and to furnish us with a pluralist political rhetoric whose function is to conceal the depth of our conflicts" (*After Virtue* [Notre Dame, IN: University of Notre Dame Press, 1984], 253).

71. Stanley Hauerwas, *A Better Hope: Resources for a Church Confronting Capitalism, Democracy, and Postmodernity* (Grand Rapids: Brazos, 2000), 9. Hauerwas adds, "My problem has never been with secular political liberals but rather with the widespread assumption shared by many Christians that political liberalism ought to shape the agenda, if not the very life, of the church."

72. Augustine of Hippo, quoted in Josef Pieper, *Faith, Hope, Love* (San Francisco: Ignatius, 1997), 167.

73. Pieper, *Faith, Hope, Love*, 227.

74. Jeffrey's story and the Robert Bartlett quote are both from Naomi Riley, "God on the Quad," *American Enterprise*, March 2005, 22–23.

75. David Bentley Hart, *The Beauty of the Infinite: The Aesthetics of Christian Truth* (Grand Rapids: Eerdmans, 2003), 20. Hart attributes the idea that divine beauty inflames desire to Gregory of Nyssa.

76. Ibid., 253.

77. My thanks to Hartley Wootton for this way of putting the matter.

78. Robert Louis Wilken, *The Spirit of Early Christian Thought* (New Haven, CT: Yale University Press, 2003), 312–13. We can add to Wilken's analysis that all knowing is a kind of loving: all knowing trains us toward some end.

79. Simone Weil, "Reflections on the Right Use of School Studies with a View to the Love of God," in *Waiting on God* (London: Routledge and Kegan Paul, 1950). Weil also says that "the intelligence can only be led by desire. For there to be desire, there must be pleasure and joy in work. . . .The joy of learning is as indispensable in study as breathing is in running" (55). Joy is a byproduct of love and desire (*eros*) and draws one to the thing loved. She also writes, "We do not obtain the most precious gifts by going in search of them but by waiting for them. . . . In every school exercise there is a special way of waiting upon truth, setting our hearts upon it, yet not allowing ourselves to go out in search of it" (57).

80. Both John Milbank and William Cavanaugh argue that the mythos that determines such polity is a state of nature consisting of discrete individuals subject to a sovereign authority that will protect them from one another. This "story" in turn is informed by a "bare divine unity" that "starkly confronts the other distinct unities which he has ordained," a mythos that differs from a more accurate understanding of creation as communion with the triune God. See Milbank, *Theology and Social Theory*, 14. See also Cavanaugh, *Theopolitical Imagination*, 9–20.

81. I get this term from John Milbank, "Can a Gift Be Given? Prolegomena to a Future Trinitarian Metaphysic," *Modern Theology*, 1995, 151.

82. Wes Avram, *Where the Light Shines Through: Discerning God in Everyday Life* (Grand Rapids: Brazos, 2005), 116.

83. Thomas Aquinas, *Summa Theologica* 1–2.65.5.

84. James W. McClendon, *Ethics*, vol. 1 of *Systematic Theology* (Nashville: Abingdon, 2002), 41.

85. Robert L. Wilken, "Alexandria: A School for Training in Virtue," in *Schools of Thought in the Christian Tradition*, ed. Patrick Henry (Philadelphia: Fortress, 1984), 19.

86. For a very insightful analysis of this point, see Scott H. Moore, "Hospitality as an Alternative to Tolerance," *Communio* 27 (Fall 2000): 600–608. Moore states that it is not his objective to denigrate tolerance. He sees it as a necessity to sustain participatory democracy, avoid violent confrontation, and overcome xenophonic prejudice. At the same time, however, "tolerance is ill-suited to address deep political controversy because of its tendency to trivialize the deepest disagreements of our contemporary political landscape" (600). My thanks to Barry Harvey for helping me see that "tolerance" is the form of hospitality of liberal democracy.

87. Ibid., 603, my emphasis.

88. Jardine, *Making and Unmaking of Technological Society*, 41.

89. Moore, "Hospitality as an Alternative to Tolerance," 602.

90. Discussing the ninth commandment ("You shall not bear false witness"), Walter Brueggemann states that "God" may be "completely enmeshed in social-political-economic realities. In order to maintain social advantage, it is often necessary to tell the truth about God in false ways, because the 'really real,' that is, the gospel truth about God, is revolutionary, subversive and disruptive" ("Truth-Telling as Subversive Obedience," *Journal for Preachers*, Lent 1997, 5).

91. Augustine, *The Confessions*, 13.9.

Part 3

1. Gerhard Lohfink speaks profoundly to this point by reminding us that Christians cannot rest content with the disunity of the church: "The condition of Christianity at the present time is nothing like a colorful field in which wheat is growing and posies and cornflowers are blooming; it is rather like a broken mirror that distorts the image of Christ. In light of the New Testament the splintering of the people of God cannot be regarded in any other way." *Does God Need the Church? Toward a Theology of the People of God* (Collegeville, MN: Liturgical, 1999), 298.

2. Stanley Hauerwas rightly notes the important distinction between inclusivity and unity, concepts that are often used interchangeably. "The unity of which Paul speaks, that between Jews and Greeks, is made possible through the common confession that Jesus is Lord, who has saved us by being raised from the dead. That unity is not based on the acceptance of everyone as they are because we want to be inclusive, but rather comes from the fire of Christ's cross, through which we are transformed by being given distinctive service in God's kingdom." *In Good Company: The Church as Polis* (Notre Dame, IN: University of Notre Dame Press, 1995), 40.

3. Benedict, quoted in Brian E. Daley, "Building the Structure of Love," in *The Ecumenical Future*, ed. Carl E. Braaten and Robert W. Jenson (Grand Rapids: Eerdmans, 2004), 75.

Chapter 6

1. Teresa of Ávila, *Interior Castle*, trans. E. Allison Peter (New York: Doubleday, 1989), 31.

2. "Our true home is the church itself, where we find those who, like us, have been formed by a Savior who was necessarily always on the move." Stanley Hauerwas, *The Peaceable Kingdom* (Notre Dame, IN: University of Notre Dame Press, 1983), 102.

3. *Lumen Gentium* 8, quoted in Avery Dulles, "True and False Reform," *First Things*, no. 135 (August/September 2003): 15.

4. As was emphasized in chapter 2, and as John Milbank reminds us via Augustine, without the virtue of worship there can be no other virtue (*The Word Made Strange: Theology, Language, Culture* [Cambridge, MA: Blackwell, 1997], 230). This is not to say that pagans cannot do good deeds; it is, however, to highlight that Christian virtue is always a participation in the love of God. Without worship, our virtues would be merely our own and would cease to be grace-filled participation in what God is doing in the world.

5. For discussion of baptism as a place of hospitality, see William Willimon, "The Ministry of Hospitality," in *The Church and Abortion*, ed. Paul T. Stallsworth (Nashville: Abingdon, 1993): "The church is the place where, through baptism, we are made to stand and to welcome people whom we [may] not even know. Thereby, in that act of hospitality, our own covenant with Christ is renewed as we are reminded of the astounding hospitality that Christ has shown toward us. From this perspective, the Christian life is simply long, often painful, forever surprising training in the art of hospitality, welcoming the stranger as we strangers have been welcomed by God in Christ" (19). In a similar vein, Samuel Wells writes, "The principal way in which the church welcomes the stranger is through catechesis, baptism, and discipleship" (*Improvisation: The Drama of Christian Ethics* [Grand Rapids: Brazos, 2004], 198).

6. The term *secular parables* is most often associated with Karl Barth, who claimed that the "more seriously and joyfully we believe in Him, the more we shall see such signs in the worldly sphere, and the more we shall be able to receive true words from it" (*Church Dogmatics* 4/3, ed. G. W. Bromiley and T. F. Torrance [Edinburgh: T & T Clark, 1961], 122).

7. Henri de Lubac, *Corpus Mysticum* (Paris: Aubier, 1949). That is, the church receives itself through the reception of Christ's body in the Eucharist, with this reception made possible by "the simultaneous offering of Christ's body by the Church" (Milbank, *Word Made Strange*, 163).

8. De Lubac, *Corpus Mysticum*, 103–4, quoted in Paul McPartlan, *The Eucharist Makes the Church: Henri de Lubac and John Zizioulas in Dialogue* (Edinburgh: T & T Clark, 1993), 79.

9. McPartlan, *Eucharist Makes the Church*, 79. In good Protestant fashion, I would also emphasize the Word (in addition to the Table) as a defining source of the church. That is, the Word, faithfully proclaimed, creates the church. We cannot be church without the word. Here I find Karl Barth's three-fold form of God's word helpful. Jesus Christ is the first form. The Bible as witness to Jesus is the second form, and the third form is the witness of the church. In each of these aspects, which are ultimately united, the Word is creative. See Karl Barth, *Church Dogmatics*, 1/1, trans. G.W. Bromiley (Edinburgh: T & T Clark, 1975), 88–124.

10. Joel James Shuman, "Eating Together: Friendship and Homosexuality," in *The Blackwell Companion to Christian Ethics*, ed. Stanley Hauerwas and Samuel Wells (Oxford: Blackwell, 2004), 407.

11. A nonhierarchical polity has led some Baptists to interpret the priesthood of the believer in terms of "soul competency," the belief that each individual is competent to interpret the Word of God for himself or herself. Such an emphasis is thought necessary to prevent an authoritarian imposition of belief and to allow for genuine freedom. The theological mistake with this position, however, is that it makes the decontextualized individual the final source of truth, rather than the story of God with a people, as embodied in Israel and the church.

12. See, for example, Philip E. Thompson, "Re-envisoning Baptist Identity: Historical, Theological, and Liturgical Analysis," *Perspectives in Religious Studies* 27, no. 3 (Fall 2000): 287–302. Thompson argues that for earlier Baptists, the Lord's Supper was not a symbol of a prior experience but a key place where their faith was nourished. Along with baptism, therefore, this rite "was interpreted as instrumental to salvation" (292). Despite the more recent anemic reception of the Lord's Supper, Baptist life continues to be sustained by preaching and hymn singing, both of which at their best are deeply formative communal practices.

13. The *New York Times* reported this result of a poll in 1994. Peter Casarella, however, objects to the premise that one must choose between a symbolic manifestation (which could be real) and a crude physical presence: "Eucharist: Presence of Gift," in *Rediscovering the Eucharist: Ecumenical Conversations*, ed. Roch A. Kereszty (New York: Paulist, 2003), 200. In any case, if my Saint Mary's students are representative, a large number of younger Catholics speak of the Eucharist as "symbolic" rather than "real."

14. Gregory Dix, *The Shape of the Liturgy* (Glasgow: University Press, 1945), 599. Quoted in Barry Harvey, "Re-membering the Body," in *Baptist Sacramentalism*, ed. Anthony R. Cross and Philip E. Thompson (Carlisle, UK: Paternoster, 2003), 106.

15. William H. Poteat, *A Philosophical Daybook: Post-critical Investigations* (Columbia: University of Missouri Press, 1990), 17.

16. Oliver Sacks, quoted in Gilbert Meilaender, "Why Remember?" *First Things*, no. 135 (August/September 2003): 23.

17. Meilaender, "Why Remember?" 24.

18. James F. White, *The Sacraments in Protestant Practice and Faith* (Nashville: Abingdon, 1999), 104. As Avery Dulles states, the Eucharist is not a crude recalling: "Memorial in the rich biblical sense meant a liturgical feast commemorating some foundational event in such a way that the people could participate by faith in is saving effects" ("The Eucharist as Sacrifice," in *Rediscovering the Eucharist: Ecumenical Conversations*, ed. Roch A. Kereszty [New York: Paulist, 2003], 178).

19. Quoted by Lohfink, *Does God Need the Church?* 67. Lohfink notes that Israel's credo is Deuteronomy 26:5–10, a text where "the past of the people of God is drawn into the speaker's presence."

20. Jean-Luc Marion, "They Recognized Him, and He Became Invisible to Them," *Modern Theology* 18, no. 2 (April 2002): 172.

21. Ibid.

22. This is not to deny the many wanderings and acts of unfaithfulness on the part of God's elected people; rather, their failures provide all the more reason that we can see God's faithfulness present in time.

23. My thanks to Barry Harvey for bringing this point to my attention.

24. Joachim Jeremias, *The Eucharistic Words of Jesus* (New York: Charles Scribner's Sons, 1966), 251.

25. Among other reasons, Jeremias states that we find parallel constructions to "do this in remembrance of me" in Mark 14:9 (where in all probability "in memory of her" relates to the merciful remembrance of God) and Acts 10:4 (where Cornelius's

prayers are extended "as a memorial before God"). Such constructions agree with the Old Testament memorial formulas, in which it is almost always God who remembers. See ibid., 251–52, for a fuller rationale. Geoffrey Wainwright presents a number of criticisms of Jeremias's argument but concludes that "Jeremias's interpretation can be considered thoroughly credible when it is seen against the background of the Old Testament notion of remembrance." *Eucharist and Eschatology* (London: Epworth, 1971), 65.

26. Jeremias, *Eucharistic Words of Jesus*, 255.

27. Marion, "They Recognized Him," 173.

28. Wainwright, *Eucharist and Eschatology*, 151–54.

29. The hymn "The Church's One Foundation" rightly states, "The Church's one foundation is Jesus Christ her Lord. / She is His new creation by water and the Word." In addition to the baptismal water and the Word, the Table is a means through which Christ in the power of the Spirit creates the church.

30. Poteat, *Philosophical Daybook*, 11.

31. Ibid.

32. Anabaptist West Friesland, quoted in Timothy George, "The Spirituality of the Radical Reformation," in *Christian Spirituality: High Middle Ages and Reformation*, ed. Jill Raitt (New York: Crossroad, 1989), 348.

33. Durwood Foster asks, "How can we make the Christian witness intelligible to informed and honest persons of the modern world? . . . We do not live in the second or the sixteenth century, but in a world where, for an awful lot of people, for all kinds of reasons, it has seemed to become both impossible and unnecessary to believe that the words of consecration literally transmute bread and wine into supernatural corporeality" ("A Response to Cardinal Avery Dulles," in *Rediscovering the Eucharist: Ecumenical Conversations*, ed. Roch A. Kereszty [New York: Paulist, 2003], 196). Also, such an approach continues the modern project of the Enlightenment philosophers who, as Poteat notes, "busily set about beginning history *de novo* by uprooting mythos and exposing the emptiness of ritual" all the while "fashioning a new mythos, *necessarily* attended by its emerging new ritual" (*Philosophical Daybook*, 33).

34. Poteat, *Philosophical Daybook*, 10.

35. This is similar to the idea that interpreting an act depends upon the narrative context. See Alasdair MacIntyre, *After Virtue* (Notre Dame, IN: University of Notre Dame Press, 1984).

36. Poteat, *Philosophical Daybook*, 26. Poteat examines the impact of literacy on this way of conceptualizing time and space. Walter Ong draws similar conclusions in his comparison of orality and literacy. See, for example, *Orality and Literacy: The Technologizing of the Word* (New York: Methuen, 1982).

37. Poteat, *Philosophical Daybook*, 30. Ben Quash, quoting Stephen Toulmin, states that at its most epic, modernity presides over a shift "'from the oral to the written'; 'from the local to the general' and from the time-specific to the time-independent" ("Drama and the Ends of Modernity," in *Balthasar at the End of Modernity*, ed. Lucy Gardner et al. [Edinburgh: T & T Clark, 1999], 148).

38. Thinking is like speaking in the sense that it is "as inextricably incarnate and local as everything else we do": Poteat, *Philosophical Daybook*, 24.

39. Harvey, "Re-membering the Body," 112.

40. Lohfink, *Does God Need the Church?* 29.

41. Wainwright, *Eucharist and Eschatology*, 67.

42. Quash, "Drama and the Ends of Modernity," 149.

43. Barry Harvey uses a hyphen in "re-member" to emphasize that the liturgical *re*membering of the body of Christ provides a radical contrast to the modern political "dismembering" that privatizes Christianity or leads Christians to live in accommodation to the current political/economic order. See Harvey, "Remembering the Body," 96–116. My use of the passive "re-membered" also reminds us that the reformation of our bodies as the body of Christ is ultimately the work of God.

44. As is well known, the participation of children varies across Christian traditions. Usually, baptism is required. The Orthodox allow babies to participate in the Eucharist immediately after baptism; Catholics have children wait till after confirmation; Protestant practice, of course, varies widely. Typically, however, baptized children are allowed to come (eventually) to the Communion table. Historically, the newly baptized had to wait (up to two years) while they received further instruction in the Christian faith.

45. John Milbank, *The Word Made Strange: Theology, Language, Culture* (Cambridge, MA: Blackwell, 1997), 154. Milbank is considering here how and why the church differs from a *polis*.

46. Romano Guardini, *The Spirit of the Liturgy* (London: Sheed and Ward, 1930), quoted in Geoffrey Wainwright, *Worship with One Accord* (New York: Oxford University Press, 1997), 213. Milbank refers to such conviviality as a social celebration, but one that in order "to be genuine and secure [because needing a supernatural end], must take the form of worship" (*Word Made Strange*, 155). He emphasizes that the requirement for "transcendence" does not leave behind the material, since "for the Christian understanding of 'creation,' there is no 'spiritual'aspect of the world that in any way transcends our created (material, social and linguistic) condition" (ibid.).

47. M. Therese Lysaught, "Eucharist as Basic Training," in *Theology and Lived Christianity*, ed. David Hammond (Mystic, CT: Twenty-third, 2000), 259. Harvey's articles, previously noted, also powerfully describe such eucharistic reconfiguration. See also Rodney Clapp, "At the Intersection of Eucharist and Capital," in *Border Crossings: Christian Trespasses on Popular Culture and Public Affairs* (Grand Rapids: Brazos, 2000).

48. Quash, "Drama and the Ends of Modernity," 170.

49. Harvey, "Re-membering the Body," 110.

50. The title of a lecture given by George Lindbeck, published in Yale Divinity School's *Spectrum* (no date available).

51. Ephraim Radner, *The End of the Church: A Pneumatology of Christian Division in the West* (Grand Rapids: Eerdmans, 1998), 199–275.

52. Ibid., 265–66.

53. Michael J. Baxter, "Blowing the Dynamite of the Church," in *The Church as Counterculture*, ed. Michael L. Budde and Robert W. Brimlow (New York: State University of New York Press, 2000), 201.

54. P. J. Fitzpatrick, *In Breaking of Bread: The Eucharist and Ritual* (New York: Cambridge University Press, 1993), 178.

55. Hans Urs von Balthasar, *The von Balthasar Reader*, ed. Medard Kehl and Werner Loser (New York: Crossroad, 1997), 287.

56. Ibid., 288.

57. John Murray Cuddihy, *No Offense: Civil Religion and Protestant Taste* (New York: Seabury, 1978), 2. On John Courtney Murray's theology as a theology of "manners" and "containment," see William Portier, "Theology of Manners as Theology of Containment, John Courtney Murray (1904–1967) Forty Years Later," paper pre-

sented at the College Theology Society, National Association of Baptist Professors of Religion, Spring Hill College, Mobile, AL, June 4, 2005.

58. White, *Sacraments in Protestant Practice and Faith*, 109.

59. John Paul II, quoted in Susan K. Wood, "*Ecclesia de Eucharistia*: A Roman Catholic Response," Symposium on the Encyclical Letter *Ecclesia de Eucharistia* of Pope John Paul II, *Pro Ecclesia* 12, no. 4 (Fall 2003): 397. Catholic theologian Wood laments, "Unfortunately the Roman Catholic Church is not yet in full communion with either the Eastern churches or the ecclesial communities dating from the Reformation" (ibid.).

60. See Wainwright, *Worship with One Accord*, 141–43.

61. Benedict XVI, quoted in George Lindbeck, Augsburg and the *Ecclesia de Eucharistia*, *Pro Ecclesia* 12, no. 4 (Fall, 2003): 410.

62. Bruce D. Marshall, "The Disunity of the Church and the Credibility of the Gospel," *Theology Today*, April 1993, 79.

63. Ibid., 81.

64. Ibid., 80.

65. Ibid., 84.

66. Wood states that it seems ecclesiologically possible to admit of varying degrees of relationship which can be described as full or imperfect communion, "rather than the all-or-nothing juridical judgment of valid or invalid" ("*Ecclesia de Eucharistia*: A Roman Catholic Response," 398).

67. Radner, *End of the Church*, 273.

68. Wainwright also places the unitive over the expressive if forced to choose. "When a state of Christian disunity obliges us to choose between the eucharist's value as expressive of existing unity and its value as creative of deeper unity, eschatology then impels us to choose the eucharist's *creative value*, and that means intercommunion" (*Worship with One Accord*, 143).

69. William Cavanaugh, *Torture and Eucharist* (Malden, MA: Blackwell, 1998), 236. Cavanaugh powerfully narrates how the Pinochet regime in Chile sought to "disappear" the church through torture and murder. While we might be horrified by such brutality, we might also be tempted to see it as very distant from where we are. Cavanaugh, however, notes that "while it is problematic to make generalizations about all modern states, it would be equally unhelpful" to confine his analysis to Chile alone. "Amnesty International estimates that half of the world's countries torture today, and—as Pentagon admissions of its use of torture manuals at the Army School of the Americas attest—the practice is not limited" to the Third World (14). Even more, the dominant North American belief that the church is political only when involved in the politics of the nation-state also has the effect of making the church invisible.

70. Alasdair MacIntyre calls wanting to be liked one of the great American vices. "Americans tend under the influence of this vice to turn into parodies of themselves—smiling, earnest, very kind, generous, nice people, who do terrible things quite inexplicably." Quoted in Stanley Hauerwas, *A Better Hope: Resources for a Church Confronting Capitalism, Democracy, and Postmodernity* (Grand Rapids: Brazos, 2000), 30.

71. Cavanaugh, *Torture and Eucharist*, 241.

72. Ibid., 243.

73. Raymond Brown, quoted in ibid., 248.

74. Cavanaugh, *Torture and Eucharist*, 249.

75. Cavanaugh cites the Code of Canon Law, which lists excommunicable offences under four headings: "Offenses against Religion and the Unity of the Church,"

"Offenses against Church Authorities and the Freedom of the Church," "Usurpation of Ecclesiastical Offices and Offenses Committed in their Exercise," and "Offenses against Human Life and Liberty." Cavanaugh notes that a difficulty is that *church* is often defined too narrowly as meaning those who hold ecclesiastical office (ibid., 248). It must be added, however, that "offenses against the unity of the church" has enabled the Catholic Church to maintain a kind of excommunication (at the Table) of all Protestants. In light of what I have been arguing, such a position fails to take account of the unitive and creative possibilities of shared eucharistic practice, even when explicit "beliefs" about the nature of the body and blood are not fully aligned. This is a case where the discipline of excommunication inhibits the work of the Spirit in gathering those who desire to come together around the Lord's Table.

76. Ibid., 249.

77. Christopher J. Ellis, *Gathering: A Theology and Spirituality of Worship in Free Church Tradition* (London: SCM Press, 2004), 196.

78. Ibid., 197. The passage from Matthew reads, "If another member of the church sins against you, go and point out the fault when the two of you are alone. . . . If you are not listened to, take one or two others along with you. . . . If the member refuses to listen to them, tell it to the church; and if the offender refuses to listen even to the church, let such a one be to you as a Gentile and a tax collector" (18:15–17).

79. Ernst Käsemann, quoted in Wainwright, *Worship with One Accord*, 82.

80. Wainwright, *Worship with One Accord*, 106.

81. "The confusion of imagery serves in fact as a salutary reminder that it is a divine mystery how God can give Himself to his creature and yet remain 'outside' as the giver. . . . If this will remain a mystery in the final kingdom, then so must the meal which the Lord has given us as a sign of the kingdom also be characterized by the same mystery" (ibid., 107).

82. Lohfink, *Does God Need the Church?* 259.

83. David F. Ford, *Self and Salvation: Being Transformed* (Cambridge: Cambridge University Press, 1999), 151.

84. Catherine Pickstock continues, "And so we can only receive such gifts in the very act of passing them on. . . . In a sense, according to a theological reading of the gift, to give is already to receive the return, which is the gift *to be able* to give. . . . [The return] is something one is already receiving in giving." "Necrophilia: The Middle of Modernity: A Study of Death, Signs and the Eucharist," *Modern Theology* 12, no. 4 (October 1996): 416.

85. Martin Luther emphasizes that good works are not good as long as they remain our possessions through which we negotiate or bargain with God. However, when we do works out of God's grace (when we receive them as gift), they are truly "good." *Christian Liberty*, trans. W. A. Lambert (Philadelphia: Fortress, 2003).

86. Milbank, *Word Made Strange*, 230.

87. Ibid., 230–31.

88.. These temptations are dissected by Radner, *End of the Church*.

89. Lohfink, *Does God Need the Church?* 298.

90. In a provocative and erudite argument, Ephraim Radner reads the often self-justifying divisions in the Western church as reflecting the abandonment of the Holy Spirit, and suggests that a penitential spirit is now called for. As Radner states, "the possibility that the celebrated Eucharist itself engenders some new flow of blood is not raised." In this sense, we could say that our divisions and brokenness are continuing to wound the body of Christ just as the Roman sol-

diers and others did. Radner's erudite argument is beyond the analysis of this chapter (203).

Chapter 7

1. Daniel Bell makes this claim about how Works of Mercy are misunderstood in "A Response to Volf," *Modern Theology* 19, no. 2 (April 2003): 274.

2. On this point, see especially Gerhard Lohfink, "Why God Needs a Special People," in *Does God Need the Church? Toward a Theology of the People of God* (Collegeville, MN: Liturgical, 1999), 1–49.

3. Philip Kenneson, *Beyond Sectarianism: Re-imagining Church and World* (Harrisburg, PA: Trinity Press International, 1999), 55.

4. Jean Vanier, *The Scandal of Service: Jesus Washes Our Feet* (London: Darton, Longman, and Todd, 1997), 1.

5. Most of the L'Arche communities are Catholic or ecumenically Christian. Some, however, are Hindu or Muslim.

6. Jean Vanier, *Our Journey Home* (Maryknoll, NY: Orbis, 1997), x.

7. Nicholas Peter Harvey, "Normality and Conversion," in *Encounter with Mystery: Reflections on L'Arche and Living with Disability*, ed. Frances M. Young (London: Darton, Longman, and Todd, 1997), 99. Going on to tell a story about a fellow contributor on a religious broadcast who believed that God is antihomosexual, Harvey wonders how he would have reconciled this attitude with the belief from Genesis that all are created in God's image. I think in both of these situations—having to do with eucharistic practice and sexuality—the invocation of "transcending notions of normality" is not helpful because it abstracts us from the concrete story of God's hospitality that we are called to embody. Rather, Vanier's concern with holiness points us in the right direction. How are we as church to be faithful, hopeful, and loving in these particular contexts?

8. Ibid.

9. Jean Vanier, *An Ark for the Poor: The Story of L'Arche* (Toronto: Novalis, 1995), 59–60.

10. Ibid., 60.

11. Stanley Hauerwas and Michael Budde remind us that such friendship is different from a superficial friendship based on having to "like" one another. Neither does such friendship entail sharing common experiences. Rather, friendships of charity, sustained by the Holy Spirit in the Word and sacrament, enable us to share common judgments. See Stanley Hauerwas and Michael L. Budde, *The Ekklesia Project: A School for Subversive Friendships* (Eugene, OR: Wipf and Stock, 2000).

12. Vanier, *Ark for the Poor*, 32.

13. Jean Vanier, "Signs of Hope for the New Millennium," acceptance speech for the Dignitas Humana Award, Saint John University, Collegeville, MN, October 25, 2000. The story is also told in Vanier, *Our Journey Home*, 4–5.

14. Vanier, *Our Journey Home*, 33.

15. Ibid., 35.

16. Hans S. Reinders, "Being Thankful: Parenting the Mentally Disabled," in *The Blackwell Companion to Christian Ethics*, ed. Stanley Hauerwas and Samuel Wells (Oxford: Blackwell, 2004), 434.

17. Ibid., 435.

18. Odile Ceyrac, quoted in ibid., 436.

19. Vanier, *Our Journey Home*, 76.

20. Ibid., 78.

21. Reinders, "Being Thankful," 436.

22. Ibid.

23. Vanier, *Ark for the Poor*, 57.

24. For a development of worship as wasting time, see Marva J. Dawn, *A Royal "Waste" of Time: The Splendor of Worshiping God and Being Church for the World* (Grand Rapids: Eerdmans, 1999). In reference to the Potter's House mission (a coffeehouse sponsored by the Church of the Saviour), Elizabeth O'Connor tells how in the beginning the members felt the effectiveness of the "coffee-house mission was somehow dependent upon someone's saying the wise thing at the appropriate moment. It had never occurred to us with any force that we could just relax and '*be*.' We have given lip service to the doctrine that God is the evangelist and that the Spirit is at work in the coffee house, but the fact is that most of us never really believed it until the world came back again and again to bear witness to that Spirit" (*Journey Inward, Journey Outward* [New York: Harper and Row, 1968], 65).

25. I use the word *bearer* to highlight what I take to be a key point of the parable: that the stranger, the weak, the vulnerable are in the image of God. They (and we) are created by God and thus are in relation to God, even if that relation is not acknowledged.

26. Teresa of Ávila, *Interior Castle*, ed. E. Allison Peers (New York: Doubleday, 1989), 231. She adds, "His food consists in our bringing Him souls, in every possible way, so that they may be saved and may praise Him for ever."

27. Ibid., 233.

28. One of O'Connor's books on the Church of the Saviour is titled *Journey Inward, Journey Outward*.

29. Mary Cosby, "Nature and Work of the Church of the Saviour," audiotape, 1958, William Smith Morton Library, Richmond, VA.

30. Elizabeth O'Connor, *The Call to Commitment* (New York: Harper and Row, 1963), 23, my emphasis.

31. Ibid., 34.

32. Ibid., 89.

33. Gordon and Mary Cosby, "The Church of the Saviour: Lawrence Hoover Lectures," audiotape, pt. 3 of 3, March 3, 1999, William Smith Morton Library, Richmond, VA. On a visit with Gordon Cosby, I asked him about this story. Gordon had actually been the businessman's sponsor for four years before they had this conversation. While the man declined full membership, he nonetheless has given significant financial support to the work of the Church of the Saviour.

34. Ibid.

35. Elizabeth O'Connor, *Servant Leaders, Servant Structures* (Washington, DC: Servant Leadership School, 1991), 34.

36. Ibid., 36.

37. Gerhard Lohfink, *Does God Need the Church? Toward a Theology of the People of God* (Collegeville, MN: Liturgical, 1999), 211.

38. O'Connor, *Servant Leaders, Servant Structures*, 25.

39. Samuel Wells, *Improvisation: The Drama of Christian Ethics* (Grand Rapids: Brazos, 2004), 43.

40. Ibid.

41. Ibid., 45. Wells draws two other contrasts between heroes and saints: (1) the hero's story celebrates valor whereas the saint's celebrates faith, and (2) heroes fear failure and mistakes whereas saints know repentance and are aware that "light only comes through cracks" (43–44).

42. In her writing O'Connor does not hide the many conflicts and struggles that have been a part of the life of the Church of the Saviour. "We who had wanted

to be in the market place so that the world might observe 'how they love one another,' found ourselves giving thanks that the world was not always looking" (*Journey Inward, Journey Outward*, 66).

43. Vanier, *Our Journey Home*, 39.

44. Cosby, quoted in O'Connor, *Servant Leaders, Servant Structures*, 31.

45. O'Connor, *Servant Leaders, Servant Structures*, 85.

46. Jean Vanier, *The Scandal of Service: Jesus Washes Feet* (London: Darton, Longman, and Todd, 1996), 20.

47. O'Connor, *Call to Commitment*, 181.

48. Ibid., 165, my emphasis.

49. Vanier, *Scandal of Service*, 25.

50. Ibid., 9.

51. Ibid., 35.

52. St. Bernard, quoted in ibid., 40.

53. Gordon Cosby, "Spirituality in Action: The Call," audiotape, William Smith Morton Library, Richmond, VA, April 23, 1987.

Index

Also in The Christian Practice of Everyday Life series

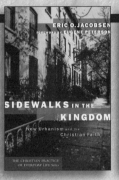

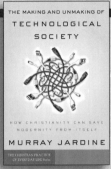

Good Eating
Stephen H. Webb

**Sidewalks
in the Kingdom**
NEW URBANISM
AND THE
CHRISTIAN FAITH
Eric O. Jacobsen

**The Making
and Unmaking
of Technological
Society**
HOW CHRISTIANITY
CAN SAVE MODERNITY
FROM ITSELF
Murray Jardine

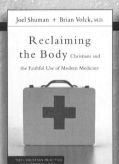

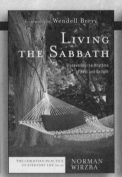

FOLLOWING
JESUS IN A
CULTURE OF
FEAR
Scott Bader-Saye

**Reclaiming
the Body**
CHRISTIANS AND
THE FAITHFUL USE OF
MODERN MEDICINE
*Joel Shuman
and Brian Volck, M.D.*

What about Hitler?
WRESTLING WITH
JESUS'S CALL TO
NONVIOLENCE
IN AN EVIL WORLD
Robert W. Brimlow

Living the Sabbath
DISCOVERING THE
RHYTHMS OF REST
AND DELIGHT
Norman Wirzba

**Following Jesus in
a Culture of Fear**
Scott Bader-Saye
Available June 2007

Brazos Press
The Tradition Alive